Shakespeare's Family

"I do but set a candle in the sun
And add one drop of water to the sea."

Emilia Lanier, from her poem
"To the Countess of Dorset"

Shakespeare's Family

Kate Emery Pogue

PRAEGER

**Westport, Connecticut
London**

Library of Congress Cataloging-in-Publication Data

Pogue, Kate.
Shakespeare's family / Kate Emery Pouge.
    p. cm.
  Includes bibliographical references and index.
  ISBN 978–0–275–99510–2 (alk. paper)
  1. Shakespeare, William, 1564–1616—Family. 2. Dramatists, English—Early modern,
1500–1700—Family relationships. 3. Shakespeare family. 4. Shakespeare, William,
  1564–1616—Homes and haunts—England—Stratford-upon-Avon. 5. Family in literature.   6.
Family—England—History—16th century. 7. Family—England—History—17th century.
  I. Title.
  PR2901.P65   2008
  822.3′3—dc22   2008009951
  [B]

British Library Cataloguing in Publication Data is available.

Library of Congress Catalog Card Number: 2008009951
ISBN: 978–0–275–99510–2

First published in 2008

Praeger Publishers, 88 Post Road West, Westport, CT 06881
An imprint of Greenwood Publishing Group, Inc.
www.praeger.com

Printed in the United States of America

The paper used in this book complies with the
Permanent Paper Standard issued by the National
Information Standards Organization (Z39.48–1984).

10 9 8 7 6 5 4 3 2 1

To my family

Contents

Preface

Even a cursory comparison of William Shakespeare's works with other Elizabethan and Jacobean plays shows him to be the era's preeminent writer of family life. As Peter Ackroyd says in *Shakespeare, The Biography*, "The family is at the centre of Shakespeare's dramaturgy; more than any other contemporary dramatist he is concerned with familial conflict."[1] Indeed, the theme is repeated in almost every Shakespeare play; and it is thus a natural leap for the aficionado to muse about Shakespeare's own family, his domestic life, and his relationship with his various relatives. But whereas nearly every existing biography of Shakespeare necessarily includes references to his home life, none offers us a complete or comprehensive picture of the entire family.

To help fill this gap, my goal has been to gather into a single resource as much information as possible about Shakespeare's family. The result is not a biography of Shakespeare, or even of his family. It is rather a series of essays, each devoted to a family member or group. The text starts with a look at Shakespeare's grandfathers and ends with a focus on Shakespeare's only relative (a nephew) whose descendants live to this day.

In this book, if one longs to know more than is readily available about specific members of Shakespeare's immediate family—his mother, for example, or his father or his children or his wife—one can turn to the needed chapter and read in detail about that particular relationship. Furthermore, as extended family relationships were important in Elizabethan times, this book includes aunts and uncles, cousins, nieces and nephews, all of whom were part of the large family surrounding William Shakespeare from his birth to his death.

The Introduction gives a context for Shakespeare's family life that is to follow, noting to what extent his own family experiences were typical or atypical of the times, while the Conclusion summarizes the impact of his family on his life and work. Although *Shakespeare's Family* is not intended as a traditional biography, reading the chapters in order does much to reveal the developmental pattern of his life.

In order to connect his personal life with his work, a final chapter (necessarily of some length) discusses scenes from Shakespeare's plays that present familial relationships. While these scenes undoubtedly sprang primarily from his imagination, it is nonetheless illuminating to compare these with what we come to know, through this book, of his own family experience. This knowledge impresses us once again not just with Shakespeare's skill at holding the mirror up to nature, but with the imagination that lay at the heart of his dramatic genius.

Shakespeare's Family would have no purpose if the man who was born William Shakespeare in Stratford-upon-Avon was not the London actor, theatre manager, and playwright of the same name. The insistent claims of anti-Stratfordians (those who wish to believe the man from Stratford did not write the plays) that the authorship is in question ignore or devalue the overwhelming evidence that links the playwright to his hometown in Warwickshire. Shakespeare had access to a stringent grammar school education focusing on Latin and classic literature; he was well known to his contemporaries, as the encomiums to his memory in the First Folio demonstrate; the plays contain overwhelming amounts of imagery reflecting his country background; he, a man from Stratford, left bequests in his will to London actors Richard Burbage, John Heminges, and Henry Condell; and there was no question about his authorship during his lifetime or for more than one hundred years after his death.

The two present-day anti-Stratfordian favorites, each touted as the real author of Shakespeare's plays, are Christopher Marlowe and Edward de Vere, the Earl of Oxford. But Marlowe died a well-documented death in 1593 and de Vere met his demise in 1604, while Shakespeare was still writing plays alluding to current events as late as 1613. Though each of these men wrote poems and plays, their writing styles are not at all the same as that found in Shakespeare's work. Faced with these counterindicative realities (among many more) one wonders at the enthusiasm of Marlovians and Oxfordians. But for anyone piqued by their challenge and eager to pursue the controversy, let me recommend *The Case for Shakespeare, the End of the Authorship Question* by Scott McCrea (Praeger, 2003). Having spent many years researching Shakespeare's life and work, I find no reason whatever to doubt, and much evidence to confirm, that William Shakespeare of Stratford-upon-Avon was the author of the plays and poems that bear his name.

Acknowledgments

Among the many friends and colleagues who have helped, supported, and encouraged me, I am especially grateful to Dr. Robert Bearman. He and the staff of the Shakespeare Birthplace Trust Records Office in Stratford-upon-Avon gave me unfailingly gracious assistance and invaluable feedback. Any deep scholarship that might be reflected in these pages is largely due to their help in using their unparalleled resources, and I am most appreciative. I also thank the librarians and staff at the Folger Shakespeare Library, Washington, DC, and express my gratitude as well to Rice University, Houston, Texas, for keeping Fondren Library open to the public. The collection there was helpful to me on a daily basis. Among individuals, I am grateful to my husband, Bill, for saving me from many a syntactical and orthographic embarrassment; Kathie VanderMeer, for her keen editorial eye, structural insights, and unfailing moral support; and Ann Christensen, for the loan of many helpful books. Margaret Roth Brown has been most generous in housing me in Washington, DC, while Pat Laing, David Yarham, Jill and Robin Lunn, Tiffany Stern, and Maire Steadman have made me feel that the England of Gloucestershire and Warwickshire is my second home. Thanks also are due to Dr. Sidney Berger, Charles Krohn, Seymour Wexler, and my colleagues at the University of Houston, Downtown: Drs. Merrilee Cunningham and Michael Dressman. I especially want to thank Dr. Jean DeWitt, whose editing of the book helped to make its presentation respectable, and to Dr. Thomas J. Lyttle, whose generosity in asking me to direct Shakespeare plays for his theatre department has given me enormous pleasure while keeping me close to the real heart of Shakespeare studies: the texts in performance.

Introduction: Family Life in the Age of Shakespeare

William Shakespeare was born in Stratford-upon-Avon, a busy, elm-shaded market town in Warwickshire ninety miles from London. For a time his father was one of the most active and distinguished of its thousand citizens, and his oldest son, William Shakespeare, lived there from the day he was born in April 1564 until he was about twenty-five years old. He then went to London to pursue a career in the theatre, coming back to Stratford as often as was practical, and settling there in his late forties to live out the end of his life (he died at fifty-two).

Stratford was a diverse town, numbering among its inhabitants shepherds and farm laborers, a variety of artisans and tradesmen, as well as some men of leisure aspiring to become members of the minor gentry. In their beliefs, citizens spanned the religious groupings of the time, and thus included zealous Puritans, Roman Catholics, and Anglican Protestants. The town supported residents of almshouses and cared for orphans; while doing so, its burgesses and aldermen also dealt with occasional vagrants and felons, and kept up town properties such as the streets, the Guild hall and chapel, and the handsome Clopton bridge crossing the Avon. Stratford lies in the heart of England and at the time the Shakespeares lived there it was representative of towns and villages scattered throughout the English countryside.[2] From William Shakespeare's surroundings came much of the imagery that fills the language of his plays and poetry; from the people, a wide variety of personality traits to incorporate into characters; and from the activities of daily life, the truth of situation that infuses his plays. Just as Shakespeare's hometown was in so many ways a microcosm of his country at that time, his plays became a microcosm of the age in which he lived.

The English renaissance was an era of change and the evolving careers of the Shakespeares over the years exhibit the thrust for upward mobility that altered the balance of society during this time. Shakespeare's paternal grandfather, Richard, a tenant farmer, sowed and reaped land he leased from others. His son, John, determined to rise in the world, moved into town, became a skilled artisan, a landowner, a member of the town Corporation council, and, at the epitome of his career, high bailiff. John's son, William Shakespeare, bought land, helped his father gain a coat of arms, and gave his daughter in marriage to the finest physician in the area. His granddaughter in turn married a man who became a baron. Thus in a period of 150 years the Shakespeares of the English midlands moved from tenant farmers to a solid position in the gentry of the time.

During these generations, the Shakespeares' home life paralleled the typical life known to us of a rising middle-class Elizabethan family. We have information regarding the clothes they wore, the food they ate, the work and leisure activities that kept them busy; we can plausibly reconstruct their daily routines, legal and judicial experiences, and their religious ceremonies; we know of the education and apprenticeship systems that formed their children's growing-up years, and of their courtship, marriage, birth, and death customs. By examining this information in detail, we can envision with tolerable accuracy William Shakespeare's daily life.

In the middle ages Shakespeare's ancestors, like most families, lived, ate, and slept in a single room with an earthen floor, a hearth for the fire in the middle of the room, and beds squeezed up against the wall. The houses were small, dark, and crowded, with no place for privacy (a concept unknown among lower classes at the time, and undesired in fact by the upper classes, for as Chartier points out, "In the past it had been thought improper for a man of quality to be alone.... Loneliness was the worst form of poverty"[3]).

But as time passed, to own a home and to move into ever larger and more commodious houses was a sign a family was growing and prospering. John Shakespeare bought his first house on Henley Street as a young man in 1556, living first in the western part of the dwelling, then purchasing the eastern half to double the size of his home. His son William ultimately bought the second largest house in Stratford to mark his rise in status.

Within these newer houses, the earthen floors were pounded down into clay, and strewn with rushes, leaves, and branches.[4] Thomas Tusser, in *Points of Good Husbandry*, published in 1557, lists twenty-one herbs suitable for "strewing..." They are: "Basil, baulm, camomile, costmary, cowslip and paggles, daisies of all sorts, sweet fennell, germander, hyssop, lavender, lavender spike, lavender cotten, marjoram, mandeline, pennyroyal, roses of all sorts, red mints, sage, tansy, violets and winter savory."[5] The scents must have been charming in a well-kept house; however, the opposite could also be true. In 1539, Erasmus had complained in a letter to his friend Frances (Cardinal Wolsey's physician): "The floors are commonly of clay, strewed with rushes," he wrote, "under which lies unmolested an ancient collection of beer, grease, fragments, bones, spittle, excrements of dogs and cats, and everything that is nasty."[6]

Human refuse was of course a nasty problem as well. Newly invented water closets were a luxury of the aristocracy. The Shakespeares would have used outdoor privies at the back of the garden, or close stools and/or chamber pots in the house, the emptying of which into nearby muckheaps must have often been the job of an unenviable servant.

Status, season, and region determined the kind of food one ate and the clothes one wore. Whether bread was made from the best wheat or barley flour marked the difference between the gentry and the poor. Lavish meat dishes tempted the wealthy; lower classes ate mutton occasionally and rabbit, but grain was the real staple for ordinary people. Sugar was rare and tea and coffee were not known until the middle of the seventeenth century. Shakespeare's granddaughter, Lady Barnard, might have tasted tea or coffee before she died in 1670, but the rest of the family not. The Shakespeares, like their neighbors, drank ale even for breakfast as the water was dangerously polluted, and for the most part, they brewed ale out of the stores of malt they kept at home.

Wool was the ubiquitous fabric in England, and the dress for the middle classes largely sober and modest. But John Shakespeare, as an alderman, an elected representative of the town, was allowed a fine robe and furs distinguishing his high status, and wearing his red, fur-lined robe as high bailiff was an important symbol of his achievements.

Large numbers of children were common in the families of the time. John Shakespeare's family was about average, with eight births total, two infant deaths, and one daughter dying at the age of seven. (Among William Shakespeare's colleagues in London, John Heminges had fourteen children; Henry Condell, nine; and Richard Burbage, eight.) When William, the oldest Shakespeare son, married early at age eighteen, he quite likely brought his wife home to live on Henley Street, and when William's three children were born, they added to the household. As he left for London in the late 1580s, waving good-bye to him from the Henley Street residence were his parents: John, nearing sixty, and Mary, close to fifty; their twenty-two-year-old son Gilbert; nineteen-year-old daughter Joan; fourteen-year-old son, Richard; and eight-year-old-son Edmund; plus thirty-one-year-old Anne Hathaway and her three children, five-year-old Susanna, and the four-year-old twins, Hamnet and Judith.

Yet according to Abbot, "households which contained three generations were rare" (117). The Shakespeares were in that minority. As we will observe, households of Shakespeare siblings, children, and grandchildren gravitated to large houses (the birthplace on Henley Street and New Place), where, at least for periods of time, mixed generations lived together.

In addition to housing all ages of adults and children, one's dwelling often doubled as workplace and shop. John Shakespeare, for example, made and sold gloves and leatherwork from his home and it is more than likely his wife and or children helped him with his work.

Whereas certain responsibilities tended to be sex-specific, husbands and wives, if not whole families, often acted in partnership, combining household and wage-earning duties. Gervase Markham was a chronicler of the time and the introduction to a modern edition of his book observes: "Markham's tidy mind dictates that the duties of husband and wife should be divided by giving to the man the external activities and to the woman those 'within the house.'" The division, though traditional, is neater than the facts suggest, for even Markham himself allows the housewife to work outside in the growing of hemp and flax. In addition, there were several outdoor activities that Markham does not mention: the housewife would have spent some time in the yard looking after the poultry and the pigs, and further time (if she were married to a farmer) assisting in the fields, particularly during harvest. The housewife would also have been responsible for selling produce from the fields at market, and often she would have been the one who purchased any items the estate could not provide.[7]

Servants and apprentices often lived with the families to whom they were contracted, filling the households and extending the more literal family membership beyond blood relations. For all, work was a dawn-to-dusk affair six days a week and on the seventh, compulsory church attendance brought the family to services at least once or perhaps twice in the day. William Shakespeare was born six years into the reign of Queen Elizabeth I, who insisted all her subjects worship in a protestant-oriented Anglican church where services were codified in the Book of Common Prayer. Roman Catholics or rebellious Puritans could pay a substantial fine in order not to attend services. But the Shakespeares were conforming Anglicans, baptizing, marrying, and burying family members within the established church. However, they had many friends in Stratford among the recusants (the name for those, particularly Catholics, who refused to attend Anglican services or recognize the authority of the Anglican church); and William's son-in-law, John Hall, though a very active member of Holy Trinity Church in Stratford had Puritanical leanings. Religion was a contentious issue throughout William Shakespeare's life and Stratford claimed families of all the major persuasions, but religion was a subject on which Shakespeare himself took no stand.

Sundays, after church-going, were days of recreation. In a small town like Stratford leisure time was filled with visiting one's neighbors, meeting for a drink at one of the numerous inns or taverns in the town, practicing archery, bowling, trapping birds or animals in the nearby woods, or gathering to sing, dance, and play music.

Then, early Monday morning, the household rose, the servants lit the fires, the children were awakened to prepare for school and the workweek began again. Prayers needed to be said, faces to be washed, breakfast of bread and cheese and ale consumed, and the children sent off before the work of the day began. Children of both sexes went to petty school to learn to read, write, and perhaps learn figures. Thereafter, boys of William Shakespeare's generation most often went to the local school while the girls learned housewifely arts from their mothers. There were schools for girls past petty school, but they were not as numerous as those for boys and more often than not a girl's learning centered around needlework, gardening, and food preparation.

Young people were specifically prepared for marriage. Boys were educated until the age of fifteen or so in the local school. A very few went on to university to study for a profession like the law or the church, but most entered into an apprenticeship at home or in another town to prepare for a trade. Unless he were a settled farmer, a young man in village, town, or city, above all needed to avoid becoming a "masterless man." Through education and apprenticeships, his goal was affiliation with a master and ultimately membership in a trade guild. To be a masterless man left one without work, trudging the open road hoping to find day labor, prey to accusations of vagrancy. Such men turned so often to thievery that communities exiled or imprisoned them as rogues or vagabonds. The strict laws of the time affected Shakespeare and his future colleagues. Whether as members of a small touring company or a large London group, it became imperative for actors to join in companies and gain the sponsorship of an aristocratic patron to avoid such a fate. Shakespeare's known affiliations came to be with the Lord Chamberlain's Men later the King's Men, the most prestigious London companies of the time. However, William Shakespeare was not the only Stratford lad to become a successful Londoner: his school friend Richard Field had led the way several years before. Following the traditional path, after his Stratford schooling Field was apprenticed as a teenager to the printer Vetrollier in London, and ultimately became one of the finest printers of his generation.

Once a young man had completed his apprenticeship, he established himself in his field and bought a house. Then, in his late twenties, he was ready to find a wife. Women in the meantime were perfecting their skills at managing the home, and in their mid-twenties were considered the right age to marry. Early parentally arranged marriages existed primarily among members of the aristocracy whose concern was less with the feelings of their children than with the stabilizing of their estates and pedigree. Within the middle class, marriages were for the most part arranged between the man and woman themselves, and affection was important.

It was not unheard of for a woman to find herself pregnant before she was married. In fact, this was the circumstance that prompted William Shakespeare's marriage to Anne Hathaway. It was vital for a pregnant woman to marry. As Abbot points out, "Bastard bearing, and indeed extramarital sex, was an offence. So strong was the presumption that an unmarried mother would resort to infanticide 'to avoid shame and to escape punishment' that an Act passed in 1624 determined that, if her child was found dead, she should be executed for its murder unless she could produce proof that it was stillborn." And further: "The plight of the small minority of women who gave birth outside marriage was bleak. Unless she had a powerful protector, the single mother was at the mercy of parish officers anxious to avoid responsibility for maintaining her and her child. Her supporters risked prosecution in the Church courts: in 1608 John Philips of Stratford-upon-Avon found himself in trouble when he took his pregnant daughter in."[8]

But children, feared and unwanted before marriage, became the desire and the focus of family life afterward, and large families were most common. Childbirth was woman's work—women in childbirth were attended by other women in the family and perhaps by an experienced midwife, while doctors were called only for troublesome births. William Shakespeare was a toddler of two when his brother Gilbert was born, a boy of five at the birth of his sister Joan, ten at the arrival of

Richard, and sixteen when his youngest brother Edmund came into the world. He would gradually have come to know the family routine when a child was being born.

With little in the way of anesthesia and no effective way to counteract infection, childbirth was painful, brutal, and dangerous. Many women died, as did many children. Upper-class women stayed indoors for a month after the birth of a child, spending up to four days in bed, while middle- and lower-class mothers returned to their household duties as soon as possible. New mothers received visitors no matter the sex of the child, but the most joyful celebrations occurred for a male child. Even if a child died, visitors still brought presents, celebrating the survival of the mother and comforting her for her loss.

Immediately after birth, the child was wrapped tightly in swaddling, and within a very short time (one to three days usually) the baby was taken by the father and the godparents, plus other family members, to the church to be baptized. William Shakespeare, his brothers and sisters, and his own three children were all baptized in Holy Trinity Church, Stratford. The mother would not normally attend the christening; she would stay in bed recovering and not return to normal life until her "churching," the religious service that welcomed a woman back into the world.

Mothers faced the same choice then that they do today after bearing a child—to nurse it oneself or find an alternative. But men and women knew the value of nursing as a means of contraception, so the choice of a mother to feed her own baby could relate to family planning as well as convenience. Alternatively, it was not at all unusual to send an infant away from home to a wet nurse for as much as the first year or two of life. Sometimes these women were chosen because they lived in the safety of the country, far from the dangers of a disease-ridden city. This separation was painful for some parents. In the mid-seventeenth century Henry Newcome, a clergyman, wrote:

> My first child, a daughter . . . was inconsiderately nursed out . . . where it pleased God to bless her that she prospered well; though after we were sensible of the neglect of duty in not having her nursed at home, which made her mother resolved to endeavor to nurse, if the Lord gave her any more children.[9]

The Newcomes found a compromise when Mrs. Newcome did not have enough milk for her fifth child: a wet nurse came to live with them. Wet nurses were paid and fed well, so economics played a part in the choice of how to nourish an infant. Care was taken in choosing the nurse as it was believed by some that character traits could be passed down through a mother's milk. Furthermore, wet nursing could tie the nurse very closely to the family and the child, as witness the Nurse in *Romeo and Juliet*, who often seems closer to Juliet than her own mother.

Most families experienced the death of at least one child. The John Shakespeares lost their first two little girls shortly after each was born, so the birth of their third child, William, must have been greeted with as much apprehension as joy. Their daughter Anne died when she was seven, a loss felt by her siblings (William was turning fifteen) as well as by her parents. And the whole family must have been struck with grief when later William's only son Hamnet died at age eleven.

These deaths might well have been caused by illness. Infections came recurrently to small towns—from vermin, from polluted water, from the sewage that ran in open streams along the center of the street, or from unknown sources. When infections became particularly deadly, regulations went into effect. In London these regulations affected Shakespeare directly, as whenever the death rate from disease (usually the plague) in the city reached thirty people a day the theaters were closed. Often the companies of players went on tour during these closings, which also, however, may have given William Shakespeare the opportunity to come home to Stratford.

Death was familial, and a more frequently and universally experienced occurrence than most deaths today. And death could even be a public event. Particularly in the larger cities, executions, like other punishments for wrong-doing, were to be witnessed by all and taken as examples of just retribution for bad behavior. In and out of London, the stroke of the ax, the jerk of the hangman's noose, the disemboweling of bodies, heads stuck on pikes, even the horror of burnings at the stake, were seen repeatedly by crowds of ordinary people. David Riggs notes that forty-nine Protestants were burned at the stake in Wincheap near Canterbury, an event Christopher Marlowe's father could have witnessed in 1556.[10] Shakespeare and his family likely might have seen a thief, a vagrant, or an immoral woman whipped publicly, or confined to the stocks. But the citizens of Stratford only heard of the public executions in London and elsewhere; for the most part, they were spared the grisly experience itself. Natural deaths took place at home, in bed, surrounded by family and/or friends.[11]

Writings of the time indicate how people struggled with the meaning of death, and the reasons for untimely death. In his diary in 1648, for instance, Ralph Jossellin, a parson, sought in his own sinfulness the reason for the death of his son: "Whereas I have given my mind to unseasonable playing at chess. . . . Whereas I have walked with much vanity in my thoughts . . . have served divers lusts too much in thoughts and in actions, whereas both body and soul should be the Lord's who hath called me to holiness, God hath taken away a son."[12] And in a similar vein, Ben Jonson struggled with the death of his son and blamed himself: "My sin was too much hope of thee, loved boy" he wrote in a poem of 1603 called simply "On My First Son."

Love and marriage, birth and death: William Shakespeare's family experienced this recurring cycle from the late years of the fifteenth century to 1670, the year William's granddaughter died. As with every family in every culture, the Shakespeares were both typical and unique, but without question they were part of the great changes Chartier speaks of when he writes of English families changing between 1500 and 1800. The family gradually became a social structure involving conversation, reading aloud, singing, and playing music.

He goes on to point out: "No longer was it merely an economic unit for the sake of whose reproduction everything had to be sacrificed. No longer was it a restraint on individual freedom, a place in which power was wielded by women. It became something it had never been: a refuge, to which people fled in order to escape the scrutiny of outsiders; an emotional center, and a place where, for better or for worse, children were the focus of attention."

In developing these new functions, the family became a haven, a defense against outsiders. It separated itself more sharply from the public realm. It extended its influence at the expense of the anonymous sociability of street and square. The family head became a figure of morality, a prominent fixture on the local scene."[13]

With these changes in mind, changes that the Shakespeares experienced first hand, let us get to know the members of Shakespeare's family.

Part I
Shakespeare's Family
of Origin

1

Shakespeare's Grandfathers

But you must know your father lost a father
That father lost, lost his, and the survivor bound
In filial obligation for some term
To do obsequious sorrow.

Hamlet, act 1, scene 2

Robert Arden (d. 1556)
Richard Shakespeare (d. 1561)

William Shakespeare's father, John, was the first of the poet's family to settle in Stratford-upon-Avon. He moved there from Snitterfield as an apprentice glover in the 1540s. But hardworking, yeoman-class Shakespeares date back as far as the fourteenth century in the nearby small villages and market towns of Balsall, Baddesley Clinton, Wroxall, Rowington, and Coventry.

William Shakespeare's mother, Mary, was an Arden, a family from Wilmcote boasting the same name as the Ardens of Park Hall, a village some twenty miles north of Stratford. A connection between the two Arden branches cannot be proved but is often sought and claimed on Shakespeare's behalf, as the Park Hall Ardens were one of the most distinguished families in the area. Not only had they been lords of Warwick, the surrounding shire, but they could trace their ancestry to before the Norman Conquest in 1066 and were one of the very few families who could claim a male line of descent to the days of Alfred the Great.[1]

Ardens and Shakespeares (with each name spelled in a variety of ways) proliferated throughout the area, and William Shakespeare's heritage from the two families combined to give him deep and ineradicable roots in Warwickshire. His grandfathers knew each other well. The Wilmcote Ardens had owned land in nearby Snitterfield for generation[2] and Robert Arden, William's mother's father, owned the house Richard Shakespeare, his father's father, leased and farmed for over thirty years. As we study the lives of these two grandfathers a vivid picture emerges of William Shakespeare's rural origins.[3]

ROBERT ARDEN

On May 10, 1501, Thomas Arden (Shakespeare's great-grandfather) bought property in Snitterfield described as eighty acres of land including a house "between the tenement of William Palmer and 'Maryes lane.'" It was a complicated transaction involving five trustees for his son, Robert. But the early lesson in land acquisition stuck: after he came of age, Robert continued to acquire property in the neighborhood.[4]

Robert Arden joined the Stratford Guild of the Holy Cross as a brother in 1517–1518.[5] The Guild was a semi-religious organization with members including both men and women, prominent merchants, artisans, and farmers of the area. The Guild of the Holy Cross had, over the generations, amassed a good deal of property in Stratford: tenements and other rental properties, plus the Guild Hall and the Guild Chapel that they had built and where meetings, religious services, and schooling for local boys took place. The Guild owned and controlled so much property that it was the town's de facto government until its final dissolution in the reign of Edward VI. Shortly afterwards, in 1553, the town petitioned Edward for a new charter, which was granted just before the young king's death. From then on, the town was governed by a secular corporation made up of burgesses and aldermen, of which Shakespeare's father was one.[6]

Robert Arden became a new member of the Guild of Knowle the same year. While enjoying membership in these guilds, he shows up on tax records that establish him as residing in Wilmcote, for he was assessed in Aston Cantlow, the home parish for Wilmcote, in 1523 (on £8 for goods) and in 1546 (on £10 a year in land). And, just as we will observe with his future tenant, Richard Shakespeare, Robert Arden's name comes up in local court records: once when he was fined for not attending a court session, and again when he was ordered to mend his hedges.

Robert married a woman whose name is unknown and by her (undoubtedly to his discouragement) had eight daughters: Agnes, Joan, Katherine, Margaret, Elizabeth, Joyce, Alice, and the youngest, Mary, who would become Mary Shakespeare, mother of the poet.

Robert's first wife had died by the spring of 1548; as on April 21 of that year Agnes Hill, the widow of John Hill of Bearly, obtained a license from the steward of Balsall manor to marry Robert Ardern,[7] and one assumes the wedding followed soon after. Agnes brought with her four children by John Hill: two sons, John and Thomas, and two daughters, Eleanor and Mary; she and Robert Arden were to have none together.

Their marriage, her children, his advancing age, and realizations that unhappy relations between Agnes and his daughters might threaten his own daughters' inheritance all contributed to Robert's decision in 1550 to make settlements of his Snitterfield property "for the benefit of himself and his wife for life, afterwards of his daughters, Agnes, Joan, Katherine, Margaret, Joyce and Alice."[8] The disposal of this Snitterfield property when inheritances changed hands gives us much of our information concerning Robert Arden's daughters. Why Elizabeth was left out of this settlement is unknown. Mary, who was only about twelve at the time, would receive a separate legacy in her father's will six years later.

Robert and Agnes had been married nearly eight years when Robert became ill and called in the lawyer to make his will. His married daughters undoubtedly lived in their own homes, but still in Wilmcote were Joyce (possibly), Alice (certainly), and his youngest and favorite, Mary.

Robert had been over fifty when he married Agnes, and was past sixty when he died in 1556, a respectable if not an old age for the time.[9] His will was granted probate in Worcester, December 16, 1556, "in the thirde and forthe yeare of the raygne of our soveragne lorde and ladye Phylipe and Marye." According to the Catholic form of wills, reinstituted by Mary Tudor when she became queen, Robert bequeathed his soul to Almighty God and to the blessed lady Saint Mary, and asked that his body be buried in the church yard of Saint John the Baptist in Aston (his parish church in nearby Aston Cantlow).

The form of the will chosen describes Robert as "secke in bodye and good and perfett of rememberence." His inventory reveals a life of ease, for it lists tables, chairs, a cupboard, two cushions, three benches, and one little table with shelves separately valued at eight shillings. More indicative of his lifestyle are the two painted cloths described as decorating his hall and the five painted cloths decorating his chamber with four more hanging in the upper rooms. Sheets, towels, clothes, a feather bed with two mattresses, a coverlet, bolster, and pillow all point to a certain level of comfort. His kitchen was filled with utilitarian items, and outdoors his farm equipment was meticulously listed as including an ax, two hatchets, a mattock, an iron crow (crowbar, reminding us of Friar Lawrence frantically sending Balthasar for a crow to break in on the Capulet's tomb in *Romeo and Juliet*), a kneading trough and a quern (hand mill). His animals included eight oxen, two bulls, four horses, and three colts. His barn was filled with the crops he grew: wheat, barley, hay, pease, oats, and straw.[10]

Robert's will further tells us how much he favored his youngest daughter: he left her £6 xiii*s* iv*d* in cash and his chief property in Wilmcote, Asbies, which consisted of about sixty acres of land. It is thought that he gave her other Wilmcote property as well, and she later came to have a small share from her sisters in the reversion of the Snitterfield lands.[11] Furthermore Mary was named with her sister Alice as a full executor of the will—this when she had barely come of age.

Moreover, Robert's will reveals that there had been trouble in his paradise. He leaves his wife Agnes, like Mary, £6 xiii*s* 4*d* "upon this condition that she shall suffer my daughter Alice quietly to enjoy half my copyhold in Wilmcote during the time of her widowhood, and if she will not suffer my daughter Alice quietly to occupy half with her then I will that my wife shall have but £3 vi*s* iv*d* and her jointure in Snitterfield."[12] So Robert's will indicates that Agnes, her children, and his younger daughters had never blended into the happy family he perhaps envisioned when he courted and married her. A wealthy man, owning his farmhouse and land in Wilmcote, as well as two additional farmhouses and about a hundred acres in Snitterfield, he presented himself simply as a husbandman and working farmer rather than as a gentleman. We can imagine that his roaming his pastures, tending his stock, and cultivating his fields may have been a happy escape from quarrels inside the house and his testy new wife, for Robert seems to place responsibility for the trouble with Alice squarely on Agnes's shoulders. Within a year after Robert Arden's death, his daughter Mary married John Shakespeare and left the quarrelsome household in Wilmcote. Seven years later, in Mary and John's own home on Henley Street, William Shakespeare was born.

Edgar Fripp indicates that Agnes and Alice worked out their troubles, as it seems Agnes never had to move to Snitterfield. He adds: "There is no evidence of disagreement between Mary and her stepmother, who lived at Wilmcote until 1580. On the contrary, she and her husband, John Shakespeare, seem to have been on cordial terms with her family—with her brother Alexander Webbe, and his children, with her son, John Hill of Bearly, and with her daughter, Mary Hill, who married a gentleman-farmer of Little Alne, named John Fulwood. This is not without significance when we consider the number of country houses where William Shakespeare in his youth would be welcome."[13] Indeed, William grew up near enough to have visited often his step-grandmother Agnes and his aunt Alice in his mother's girlhood home. There he would no doubt have heard tell of Robert Arden and could have seen in his mind's eye the old man, his grandfather, striding across the fields of Wilmcote—fields that one day were intended to be his.

RICHARD SHAKESPEARE

William Shakespeare's other grandfather, Richard Shakespeare, spent all his adult life as a tenant farmer in Snitterfield. He seems to have asked no more than to be one of the husbandmen who, with the yeomen who owned the thousands of small farms dotting the English countryside, were the muscle and the heart of early renaissance English society.

Richard was born around the turn of the sixteenth century. As a young man in his mid to late twenties (1528), he took a lease of property in Snitterfield from Robert Arden, a man perhaps some five years his senior, including a house that "doth abut on the High Street" and land that ran down to a brook that still runs through the village.[14] He must have been optimistic and successful, for he soon leased additional property, this time from two local manors: one owned first by the collegiate church of St. Mary in Warwick and afterwards by the crown; the second owned by the earls of Warwick as part of the chief manor of Snitterfield and eventually by Bartholomew and Mary Hales.[15] Richard farmed the land he leased from Robert Arden in 1528 for thirty-two years, and also appears to have held land, probably as a leaseholder, from St. Mary's College, Warwick, and from the

Earls of Warwick (later belonging to the Hales) for nearly as long.[16] He kept cattle and pigs, and he plowed, sowed, and harvested all these properties until 1560, just before his death. As late as that year, Richard was mentioned in a directive to other tenants to make their ditches and hedges "betwixt the end of the lane of Richard Shakespere, and the hedge called Dawkins hedge."[17] F.E. Halliday notes that there was a field nearby on the north lane toward Warwick called Dawkins Close that may help envision Shakespeare's holding.

The first record of Richard Shakespeare in Snitterfield occurs on April 14, 1529, when his name, spelled Richard Shakkespere, appears among the list of those tenants who failed to attend the manor court at Warwick. A deputy steward presided over this court twice a year, at Easter in the spring and Michaelmas in the fall. Tenant farmers were required to attend these court sessions, or, if not attending, to pay a fine of two pence, or to send in a good excuse. Accounts show that Richard was fined in 1529, but availed himself of the latter option in 1532, 1538, and 1550.[18] Various records report on events in Richard Shakespeare's life, though as noted earlier his name is not always spelled the same: in the records of 1533, for instance, his name was copied as "Shakstaff."[19] In 1535, he was cited for having too many cattle grazing on the common pasture. Three years later, in 1538, he was ordered to mend his hedges between his land and his neighbor Thomas Palmer's. In 1543 he was left four oxen then in his keeping, in the will of Thomas Atwood, alias Taylor, who was a well-to-do alderman of Stratford.

Unfortunately, neither the birth date, nor the death date, nor the marriage, nor even the name of Richard Shakespeare's wife is recorded; but he had two sons about whom a good deal is known. Their names were John (William Shakespeare's father) and Henry, and they would have been born in the late 1520s or early 1530s. Indeed, one wonders if the birth of one of his sons was the reason for Richard's failure to make the six-mile trip to Warwick to attend the court in 1529. Though Henry died first (in 1596), John, throughout his life, presented the more mature, responsible character, so the instinct is to think of him as the older son, and the scapegrace Henry as the younger.

Richard was by all evidence a successful farmer, and it may have startled him when, in the early 1540s, his son John expressed a desire to leave Snitterfield and the farm to become an artisan in Stratford. One of Stratford's glovers, an alderman of the town named Dickson, had a wife whose family (the Townsends) lived in the Wold near Snitterfield, so it's likely that when John announced he did not want only to be a farmer his father arranged an apprenticeship for him with master Dickson.[20] John's brother Henry had no such ambitions and like his father would be a tenant farmer in the Snitterfield area for the rest of his life. Oddly, as we shall see, the ambitious brother turned out to be the more conservative personality, while the stay-at-home farming lad was hard-pressed to contain his rebellious spirit.

In those days as men reached their fifties and sixties they were often called upon to appraise the goods of friends who had died (the statute required "persons two at the least, to whom the person dying was indebted").[21] Without banks or financial institutions, people who needed to lend, borrow, or have money held for them most often turned to friends or relatives. Not surprisingly, these transactions often wound up in courts of law. Richard Shakespeare's respectable position in the community can be assessed by the number of times he was called on to appraise the properties of friends to whom he had lent money, as opposed to the few times he was listed as indebted. While on November 26, 1557, for instance, he was recorded as indebted to the late Hugh Porter of Snitterfield, earlier that year, on May 15, he had helped appraise the inventory of the vicar, Sir Thomas Hargreave. On September 13, he had appraised the goods of Richard Maydes, and the following year, witnessed the will of Henry Walker (August 31, 1558). In 1559, he was called on to value the estate of Roger Lyncecombe. Lyncecombe claimed addresses in both Snitterfield and on Henley Street in Stratford—the same street on which Richard Shakespeare's son John had recently set up housekeeping with his young wife Mary Arden. On May 7, 1559, Richard was again called on to inventory the goods of John Sanbridge, and on January 3, 1560, those of Thomas Palmer.[22]

Richard Shakespeare was last summoned on June 1, 1560, this time to appraise the goods of Henry Cole of Snitterfield.[23] According to Edgar Fripp, Cole was a blacksmith known throughout the area for his skill at tuning church bells. Cole's son Edward had died in September 1558 and his wife soon after. Cole's will was made shortly after his son died and before the death of then reigning Queen Mary. Therefore, although he actually died after Queen Elizabeth returned the country to Protestantism, Cole's will was written, like Robert Arden's, in the old Catholic form. And we are reminded that individuals of Richard Shakespeare's generation, and those of the two to follow, had to navigate a treacherous course through England's violent religious upheavals if they were to survive and prosper. The Coles were Catholic; the major branch of the Ardens in Park Hall were Catholic; but the Shakespeares, ever moderate, seem to have aligned themselves with the conservative center, thus allowing them to be Catholic or Protestant, as demanded by the ruler in power at the time.

In 1560 Richard was required to pay a fine for failing to yoke or ring his pigs, and for allowing his livestock to run loose on the meadows. Perhaps it was just such a lack of control of animals that led the court that same year to direct each farmer to repair his hedges and ditches.

A number of tenants were also fined for "making frays," but Richard Shakespeare was not one of them.[24] Of course he was an older man by then, but those "frays" were not always insignificant—the records show Richard Quiney of Stratford, a close friend to both John Shakespeare and his son William, as being killed in 1602 while trying to put down a fray in which a crowd of Stratfordians took part.[25] Violence may have often erupted near him, but overall, John Shakespeare seems to have been a remarkably peaceable man for the time. A generation later, William Shakespeare was notable among Elizabethan playwrights for his "gentle" and unusually calm disposition. In an era of high emotion, drama, and violence, if the lack of legal record to the contrary may stand as evidence, William Shakespeare's grandfather, his father, and he himself all seem to have possessed remarkably restrained temperaments.

One wonders if Richard had become ill by the time of the 1560 court hearing or was too frail to keep up his farm as he had before, for soon after the fine for failing to control his swine, he died. Now his own goods needed to be assessed; they were valued at £38 xvii*s*, more at that time than those of the local vicar, whose estate Richard himself had appraised not long before.[26]

The administration of Richard Shakespeare's estate was granted in Worcester, February 10, 1600/01, to his son, John (thus constituting yet another argument for John being the elder of Richard Shakespeare's two boys). In addition to his trade as a glover, John must have farmed on the side, for this document identifies him as "Johannes Shakespere de Snytterfyld agricola (farmer)" the son of "Richard Shakespere deceased late while he lyved of the parishe of Snytterfyld."[27]

William Shakespeare was born four years after the death of his grandfather Richard. His knowledge of Snitterfield and the Shakespeare family history there thus would come from visits made to, and stories told by, his father's high-spirited, hot-blooded, rebellious brother: William Shakespeare's uncle Henry.

2

Shakespeare's Father

Hamlet: My father, methinks I see my father.
Horatio: Where, my lord?
Hamlet: In my mind's eye, Horatio.
                                    Hamlet, act 1, scene 2

JOHN SHAKESPEARE (c. 1528–1602)

William Shakespeare shared his father's ambition, drive, and courage to change the life into which he was born. William went further afield and achieved eminence following a trade far different from his father's. But John would have understood his son's need to strike out on his own, for he had done the same in his youth.

The son of a tenant farmer, John Shakespeare was not content to stay at home to work the land. He left the country to settle in nearby Stratford to take up work as an artisan and a town-dweller. There we discover in the court records of April 1552 a young John Shakespeare fined for making an unauthorized dunghill (*sterquinarium*) in front of the house of his Stratford neighbor, the wheelwright William Chambers. Human refuse was supposed to be taken to the communal muck hill at the end of the street, but John Shakespeare along with his friend Adrian Quiney and fellow citizen Humphrey Reynolds evidently had not done so. John Shakespeare was in his early twenties and not yet a property owner, and so was seemingly as careless of his surroundings as many another young man first starting out on his own.

John Shakespeare had set himself up as a glover. To have done so by 1552 he must have left the Snitterfield farm about 1544. He would have been apprenticed for seven years to one of the seven or eight master glovers in Stratford,[1] and since the usual age to start such an apprenticeship was around fifteen we can calculate that John Shakespeare was born in the late 1520s.[2]

Shakespeare's father might have chosen another trade: wheelwright, apothecary, blacksmith, beer-maker, weaver, dyer, rope-maker, butcher, baker, joiner, carpenter, fuller, saddler, shoemaker, chandler, cooper, plowright, carter, mercer, draper, haberdasher—all these trades and more were practiced then in the busy market town of Stratford.[3] But between 1556 and 1592 when three different John Shakespeares were mentioned in legal documents concerning such matters as unpaid debts and bail sureties, Shakespeare's father is identified as a glover most often, though and twice as a whittawer.

A whittawer was a man who boiled and scraped animal skins, particularly fine, white ones, to make them ready for cutting and sewing into gloves. This skill was part of the glover's trade. When John Aubrey, in his gossipy *Brief Lives*, claimed William Shakespeare was the son of a butcher ("When he killed a calf, he would do it in high style, and make a speech"),[4] he may have been telling us that killing the oxen, horses, deer, calves, sheep, goats, and dogs needed for their skins was also sometimes part of the glover's trade. But there is no indication John Shakespeare ever processed or sold meat as a profession; there were butchers in Stratford who did that and Michael Wood goes so far as to assume John Shakespeare "got his skins from the Taylor's slaughterhouse near by."[5]

Skins of different properties were needed since glovers made and sold all kinds of leather goods: hose, jerkins, aprons, belts, purses, bags—anything worn between the head (the province of the hatter or haberdasher) and the feet (which belonged to the shoemaker). Gloves were especially important, more so than today. Clearly they were needed to protect the hands; but more, they were crucial accessories to an elegant outfit. Gloves for self-adornment and for gifts were often highly detailed, trimmed with elaborate embroidery and jewels. And they could be very expensive. Gloves were an appropriate gift for the queen, were a traditional gift from the bridegroom to the bride, and often became the present from a bride or groom to members of the wedding party.

As a young glove-maker John Shakespeare first lived on Henley Street, a location that must have gone well for his new business: four years later the first building he bought in Stratford (October 1556) was the east end of the Henley Street house now called the Birthplace—a small building formerly owned by Edward West and called the Woolhouse.[6] The name is indicative, for in addition to being a whittawer and a glover John Shakespeare was to become a dealer in wool (a speculative activity that would cause him a great deal of grief as time went by) and a middle man for "grain, malt, and other farm products."[7] (His son carried on this tradition, according to A. L. Rowse, who states that next to being a market center, "the principal business of the town was malting . . . One-third of the more substantial householders were invested in malt, Shakespeare among them: at one time he held ten quarters at New Place."[8])

John Shakespeare's industry shows that he had ambitions to better his station. As a tenant farmer, his father was a yeoman in the clearly stratified society of Elizabethan England; but, as his subsequent actions show, John Shakespeare wanted to be a gentleman. Property ownership in the town made him a burgess. The next step was to become a working member of the town government.

Timing was on his side. In 1553, just three years before John Shakespeare bought the Henley Street Woolhouse, the young King Edward VI, responding to a petition from the leaders of Stratford, dissolved the Guild of the Holy Cross, a religious/social organization with origins in the Middle Ages that owned so many of the buildings in the town that it had come to administer much of its business. The young king granted the town's request for a Charter of Incorporation and turned the rental revenues (and upkeep) of the Guild properties over to the new secular corporation, which from that time forward would control and administer the town's business. According to the new Charter, the citizens would select fourteen aldermen yearly from "the better and more discreet inhabitants" of the town. These would choose fourteen others, to be called "Capital Burgesses." Together they constituted the Common Council.[9]

In 1556, John Shakespeare, who by that time had added another house in Greenhill Street to his ownership of the Woolhouse in Henley Street, was named ale-taster, one of the offices of the corporation determined annually at the Michaelmas Leet (semi-annual Law Day). In 1557 he was named burgess and the same year, when he was close to thirty, he wooed and married Mary Arden.

Since John's father, Richard, had leased his Snitterfield farm from Mary's father, Robert, Richard Shakespeare's two sons and Robert Arden's eight daughters must have been aware of each other their entire lives. But traveling the three miles to Wilmcote to court Mary Arden, John Shakespeare could tell himself he came not as just the son of her father's tenant farmer but as a craftsman with a prosperous business, an owner of two different properties in town, a burgess, and a member of the Stratford corporation council with the important job, as ale-taster, of monitoring the quality of the work of all the brewers and bakers in town.

However he was still a yeoman wooing the landlord's daughter, and he knew that if Mary Arden married him she would make a sacrifice: she would take a step down in class and give up her right to display the Arden coat of arms.[10]

On the other hand, if she were to accept his proposal she would give a lift to his ambitions. A gentleman had to own land and Mary Arden's inheritance of Asbies, a farm of sixty acres, would become her husband's property on her marriage. But more important than owning land, Mary, the youngest of Robert Arden's eight daughters, had been named co-executor of his will, an indication of her intelligence and reliability.

She accepted him. Mary Arden and John Shakespeare likely were married in the charming little village of Aston Cantlow whose church was the parish church for Wilmcote where Mary lived. The church records from the time have been lost; the evidence that they had married comes with the baptismal record in September 1558 of their first child, a little girl Joan, christened at Trinity Church in Stratford. Happy at first, Mary and John needed to support each other with all the mutual affection they could muster in the next few years. Joan died shortly after her birth. In 1561 Richard Shakespeare, John's father, died and John was named to administer his father's estate. Another little girl, Margaret, was born to John and Mary in December 1562. She died the following April.

Despite the great sorrow of losing his two baby daughters and his father, John Shakespeare became an increasingly successful businessman and active member of the Stratford corporation. After his stint as ale-taster he was named, successively, constable (1558, reelected 1559), affeeror (one who assessed fines, 1559), and chamberlain, an office we would call city treasurer (1561, 1562). There were in fact two chamberlains elected each year to keep the city accounts. They recorded each item of revenue and expenditure and reported to the first council of the year the last year's revenues and disbursements. As John Shakespeare was twice elected to this office, it becomes a powerful evidence for his intelligence and perhaps his literacy.

John Shakespeare's education is likely to have been minimal. There was no school in Snitterfield. But in his book *The World of Christopher Marlowe*, David Riggs writes, "In his watershed Injunction of 1536, Henry VIII ordered all parents and masters to teach their children and servants the Lord's Prayer, the Apostle's Creed, and the Ten Commandments. He further instructed them to furnish these texts 'in writing, or show where printed books containing the same be to be sold, to them that can read or will desire the same.'"[11] John Shakespeare would have been about eight years old at the time of this directive and the Snitterfield parish priest most likely would have been his teacher.

But we have no sample of John Shakespeare's handwriting; his preferred signature was either a plain cross or an elegantly drawn "mark" representing a measuring compass or divider—an instrument used in his work. From this, arguments are made that he was illiterate. And it must be noted that Christopher Marlowe's father, a Canterbury shoemaker who never rose as high in public services as John Shakespeare, left his signature on thirteen documents.[12] He was proud to show off his ability to read and write. And yet when it came time to sign his will he, like John Shakespeare, used a mark.[13] His long years of managing his own business, his serving high offices in the corporation, and the fact that many literate people of the time (such as his close friend Adrian Quiney) chose to sign with a mark rather than a signature argue for John Shakespeare's literacy. As Marchette Chute points out: "There is no record of a chamberlain in Stratford who did not know how to write, and an illiterate man would be a curious choice for an office that consisted of so much careful bookkeeping."[14] Other scholars, however, suggest that John Shakespeare might well have been able to read, but not to write. Writing required sharpening pens from quill feathers, carrying ink around that stained one's fingers; better to leave writing chores to an underling, a clerk, in much the way that in recent times, before computers, many executives did not type.[15] Such menial work was left to a secretary as John Shakespeare might have left his to a servant or hired scribe—and whether he could write or not, John Shakespeare was a very able and dedicated public servant.

Mary and John Shakespeare's sorrowful luck with their children changed at last when William, their first son, was born in April 1564. Soon they had to fear for his life, for in July a virulent outbreak of plague devastated Stratford. John Shakespeare and the other council members met outdoors that season to avoid contagion[16] and quite possibly John encouraged Mary to take the little boy to her property at Wilmcote away from the contagion in Stratford until the plague had run its course.

By the time of William's birth John had leased the attached west end of the building housing the woolshop that he already owned on Henley Street, making the family living quarters out of the west end while keeping the east end for his shop. This is the building that still stands and is known worldwide as Shakespeare's birthplace.

When his son was a year old, in 1565, John Shakespeare was elected alderman, replacing Mr. William Bott, the resident of New Place (the large house William Shakespeare would buy thirty some years later), when Bott was expelled from the council for indulging in "too many opprobrious words."[17] To be alderman gave him the right to a special seat in church, to wear a black robe faced with fur, to hang a lantern in front of his house during Christmas, and to call himself Master John Shakespeare.[18] Furthermore he was privileged to wear a large ring that William would remember when he has Mercutio describe Queen Mab in *Romeo and Juliet*:

> She is the fairies' midwife, and she comes
> In shape no bigger than an agate stone
> On the forefinger of an alderman.
>   *Romeo and Juliet*, act 1, scene 4

And the image returns in *Henry IV Part I* when Falstaff tries to convince young Prince Hal that in his youth he was thin:

> When I was about thy years, Hal, I was not an eagle's talon in
> the waist; I could have crept into any alderman's thumb ring.
>   *Henry IV Part I*, act 2, scene 4

In 1566 a second son, Gilbert, was born, followed by Joan (1569), Anne (1571), Richard (1574), and Edmund (1580). As Shakespeare and his brothers and sisters grew up in the Henley Street house, they witnessed their father practicing his craft. It would be surprising if, as the oldest son, William had not often helped him with one or another aspect of his work.

Normally when John Shakespeare was ready to sell the gloves and leather goods he made, he simply opened the window of his shop facing the street, displayed the goods he had for sale on an extended window ledge, and greeted his customers from the building that was both his shop and his home. But every Thursday was market day in Stratford. Then John Shakespeare and his family packed up his shop and moved all his salable goods to a place near the High Cross where the glovers had their stalls.

In 1569, John Shakespeare was elected bailiff of Stratford, an office equivalent to being mayor and the highest office the corporation had to offer. Being bailiff gave him the right to wear an elaborate red robe, to have reserved for him the first pew on the north side in Trinity Church, and to have carried before him the symbols of his office when the aldermen paraded through the town to church, public events, or meetings. At five, William must have been aware of his father's importance, importance so great that having obtained this "office of dignity" he could now, according to the Office of Heralds, apply for a coat of arms for his family.[19]

As bailiff John Shakespeare did something no Stratford bailiff before him had ever done—he approved the payment for two companies of actors to perform in Stratford: 9s to pay the Queen's men and later 12d to pay Lord Worcester's men. Stratford was not a regular stop on the touring schedule of traveling acting companies, but these two may have come through the town on their way between London and one of the larger towns in the area to which they toured regularly: Coventry, Leicester, Bath, or Gloucester. This is the first documented connection between Shakespeare, his family, and the theatre.

Though it describes a performance in Gloucester, not Stratford, a document by R. Willis (Mount Tabor. Or Private Exercises of a Penitent Sinner . . . Published in the year of his age 75, Anno Dom. 1639)[20] gives a clear image of the circumstances when the players came to Stratford and played for John Shakespeare and the families of the corporation:

> In the city of Gloucester the manner is, as I think it is in other like corporations, that when players of interludes come to town, they first attend the Mayor to inform him what nobleman's servants they are, and so to get license for their public playing. And if the Mayor like the actors, or would show respect to their lord and master, he appoints them to play their first play before himself and the Aldermen and Common Council of the city; and that is called the Mayor's play, where every one that will comes in without money, the Mayor giving the players a reward as he thinks fit to show respect unto them. At such a play my father took me with him and made me stand between his legs as he sat upon one of the benches, where we saw and heard very well.[21]

After his time as bailiff, John Shakespeare was elected chief alderman and justice of the peace (1571); the following year (1572) his fellow citizens appointed him (along with his friend Adrian Quiney—also a former bailiff—and the same young man fined for the muckhill with John Shakespeare twenty years before) to assist the high bailiff in settling some affairs concerning "the commonwealth of the borough."[22] Though the affairs cited are not made clear, in order to help settle them John Shakespeare and Adrian Quiney gave a dinner in Stratford for Sir Thomas Lucy.[23] Sir Thomas, the resident of Charlecote, a manor house nearby, was a major local figure and the dinner must have been much talked about in the Shakespeare household. Eight-year-old William and his younger brother and sister would have been well aware of the excitement caused in the planning of such an event.

Three calm years followed. In 1574 William (ten), Gilbert (eight), Joan (five), and Anne (three) helped welcome a new baby, Richard. In 1575 John Shakespeare bought two more houses—one probably the west end of the Birthplace that he had been leasing for so long, the other perhaps an adjoining house to the west, destroyed in the fire of 1594.[24]

William's days of running around the house and observing his father at work had ended when he began school (about 1571). The King Edward's School in Stratford, inheriting its building and traditions from the Guild of the Holy Cross, was one of the finest grammar schools in the area. The council paid the school master twenty pounds a year, twice the amount paid to the school master at Eton,[25] and the succession of school masters who taught the Shakespeare boys possessed degrees from Oxford. The school was open, free to sons of all the burgesses in town, and, though all the records from the time have been lost, it is hard to believe that John Shakespeare with his ambitions for advancement would not have sent his sons to school.

William, followed as the years passed by Gilbert, Richard, and Edmund, set off for school at six in the morning, came home for dinner, then returned for a long afternoon of hard classical study. Whatever minimal education his parents might have received from the local priests paled beside the intense curriculum of the Stratford grammar school. To prepare for a university education, to become a lawyer, a high-level civil servant, a schoolmaster, or a priest, a Renaissance English child needed to be fluent in reading, writing, and speaking Latin and have some knowledge of Greek. Rhetoric, logic, Bible study, mathematics, astronomy, music all were part of William Shakespeare's education.[26] Memorization was the method and recitation the test. The prodigious memory of English actors was formed in the grammar schools of the time where reams of Latin and English facts, phrases, literature, and even plays were learned and recited (standing straight and speaking loudly and clearly, according to a directive from the bishop)[27] by the boys. John Shakespeare must have derived pleasure, astonishment, and pride as his sons practiced their lessons and demonstrated their learning.

Every Sunday the family went to church; attendance was compulsory. When Queen Elizabeth came onto the throne in 1558, the year after John and Mary Shakespeare were married, she, with her advisor Burghley, crafted the Elizabethan compromise on the question of religion. She returned the English state religion to Protestantism, reversing the Roman Catholicism imposed by her older sister Mary. By the Act of Uniformity she insisted that everyone attend a church using the Book of Common Prayer of the Anglican church. As long as people abided by that regulation, what they chose to believe privately was their own business. What the Shakespeares really believed tantalizes scholars. But it is an unanswerable question. When he became bailiff, John Shakespeare took the loyalty oath of the time: the oath of supremacy. He led his family, the leading family of the community, as they processed to their reserved pew in Trinity Church to follow the service in the Church of England Book of Common Prayer. Furthermore, during those years as bailiff and chief alderman, John Shakespeare (seemingly without complaint) supervised the whitewashing of the Catholic frescos in the Guild Hall, the selling off of Catholic vestments, and the removal of the stained glass windows from the Guild Hall Chapel. There is no evidence any of the Shakespeares resisted these religious edicts. After all, as Riggs notes: "The English state religion changed three times between 1547 and 1558: from the Anglo-Catholicism of the ageing Henry VIII to radical Protestantism under his short-lived son Edward VI; then to the reactionary Roman Catholicism of his elder daughter Mary I, and again to moderate Protestantism under his younger daughter Elizabeth I. . . .These upheavals demoralized parish life; for the clergy who contrived to continue their ministry throughout all the changes, conformity was a means of survival."[28] For individuals, too, conformity meant survival, and despite their baptism as Catholics (as was everyone of that generation), and despite Mary Arden's distant connection with the Arden family of Park Hall who were recusant Catholics, the Shakespeares of Stratford were a conforming family.[29]

Family life for the young Shakespeares was not all work, religion, and no play; and John Shakespeare was not a man to be confined to the limits of his town. He had walked four miles to move into Stratford from the family farm; he had traveled three miles to woo his wife in Wilmcote; he had been sent at least twice to London on business on orders from the Stratford corporation, stopping at Oxford or another one of the intermediate cities along the way; he had entertained Sir Thomas Lucy from Charlecote four miles away; he had an instinct to connect with the world beyond his doorstep—why would he not take his family to see the exciting events of the time?

Coventry, the nearest city to Stratford, was famous for producing every year a cycle of medieval mystery plays that dated back to the Middle Ages. Retelling the biblical stories from Adam and Eve to the resurrection, these locally produced amateur theatre plays were presented with humor, imagination, and a primitive theatrical vigor. Such emotionalism and amateur overdoing of passion was not lost on young William Shakespeare who later had Hamlet warn the players:

> O, it offends me to the soul, to hear a robustious, periwig-pated
> fellow tear a passion to tatters, to very rags, to split the ears of the
> groundlings. . . I would have such a fellow whipped for o'erdoing
> Termagant, it out-Herods Herod, pray you avoid it.
>
> *Hamlet*, act 3, scene 2

Then in 1575 Queen Elizabeth I made one of her famous processions, this time to Kenilworth to visit the Earl of Leicester. Her carriage may well have come right across the Clopton Bridge, with John and William Shakespeare and all the citizens of Stratford lining the way to throw their hats in the air and cheer their queen. Leicester welcomed her with celebrations open to the local people and talked of for counties round. One part of the spectacle, the pageant of the Lady of the Lake (taking advantage of the lakes at Kenilworth), showed a dolphin rising from the water, Arion on its back, with Triton riding on a mermaid and speaking verses to the queen. Evidence that John Shakespeare might have brought his eleven-year-old son to see the spectacle crops up in *A Midsummer Night's Dream* when Oberon says to Puck:

> Thou remembrest
> Since once I sat upon a promontory
> And heard a mermaid on a dolphin's back
> Uttering such dulcet and harmonious breath
> That the rude sea grew civil at her song
> And certain stars shot madly from their spheres
> To hear the sea maid's music.
> *Midsummer Night's Dream*, act 2, scene 1

William Shakespeare's boyhood in Stratford seems idyllic. But John Shakespeare's happy years ended abruptly in 1576, and for the next twenty years the Shakespeare family struggled.

Joseph Quincy Adams suggests that the crowning blow came when the lease on the west end of the Henley Street house ran out in 1575 and John Shakespeare, just as he was facing other financial problems, was forced to pay £40 to buy the house he had lived in so long.[30] In 1576 John Shakespeare, having applied for a coat of arms to confirm his rise in status to gentleman, never followed through on his application. The fee charged for a coat of arms (as quoted by Sogliardo in Ben Jonson's *Every Man Out of His Humour*) was not less than £30. John Shakespeare could not afford to pay it.[31]

What caused this sudden, yet long-lasting financial crisis? Michael Wood in his television program (and subsequent book) *Shakespeare* comes down heavily on the illegality of John Shakespeare's "brogging" or black market wool-dealing. John Shakespeare's reputation as a wool-dealer rests on a seventeenth-century story, on the wool wastes that were discovered under the Woolhouse in the nineteenth century, and on a court case that documents John Shakespeare's 1569 sale of wool to an alderman in Marlborough, Wiltshire. This man bought the wool from John Shakespeare and then Shakespeare sued him for non-payment—he was desperate to get his money.

The troubles that reached a head in 1576 had their roots more than six years earlier. In addition to the suit above, in 1570 John Shakespeare had been brought to court by a shepherd called John Mussem, from a village near Stratford (Walton). Mussem charged Shakespeare with usury. John Shakespeare had lent him money twice: once £80 and once £100 and Shakespeare had charged £20 interest for each loan—a rate far higher than the 10 percent the law allowed.

In 1572 John Shakespeare was brought before the courts twice on charges of illegally dealing in wool. The wool industry was hugely important to England's prosperity; it gave the country a major export as well as a crucial industry at home, and it was severely regulated. John Shakespeare was not licensed to trade in wool. He was charged and fined for purchasing "a couple of tons"[32] of wool for £210, an enormous amount of money when one remembers that the two houses he recently bought cost him £40. He scrambled to find money to pay the fines.

Wood presents the high-risk activities of wool-dealing and money-lending as constants in John Shakespeare's adult life from an early date. The suit of John Shakespeare against John Luther (a glover from Banbury) to recover a debt of £50 in 1572, and the suit by Henry Higford against John Shakespeare for a debt of £30 (a suit brought in 1572 and renewed in 1578 as it still had not been paid) could have been linked to wool-dealing.

By 1577 the pattern of John Shakespeare's life changed completely. His situation had become so dire that he stopped going to corporation meetings. After two decades of the most dedicated public service, his name starts to show up as absent in the corporation's monthly role.

In 1578 a request is recorded for funds to be contributed by corporation members for the purchase of military equipment: "At this hall it is agreed that every Alderman, except such under-written excepted, shall pay towards the furniture of three pikemen, two billmen, and one archer, vi*s*. viii*d*." John Shakespeare was one of those excused. Later in the year there was another resolution: "Item, it is ordered that every Alderman shall pay weekly towards the relief of the poor iv*d*., saving Mr. John Shakespeare and Mr. Robert Bratt, who shall not be taxed to pay anything."[33] It is evident that the aldermen knew of John Shakespeare's monetary troubles and were understanding of them. But it must have been hard for a proud man to see his pecuniary difficulties made so public.

By 1578, when William Shakespeare turned fourteen, his father still was not going to council meetings, even on election day, though the council decided not to fine him and in fact excused him from the aldermen's payments for the relief of the poor. A nadir was marked in that year. On November 12, John and Mary Shakespeare had to raise money by mortgaging their inherited land, the Arden land that had come to John Shakespeare with his marriage, the land that would help establish him as a gentleman, the land that was to be the inheritance for his children, the land that rightly belonged to his wife. Together they conveyed eighty-six acres of her Wilmcote property to Thomas Webbe and Henry Hooper, who in turn leased the land to George Gibbes for twenty-one years. After the lease expired the Shakespeares undoubtedly hoped to reclaim the land. In fact it never came back to them.

Two days later, on November 14, John Shakespeare in his desperation borrowed forty pounds by mortgaging a house and fifty-six more acres in Wilmcote to Edmund Lambert. Lambert was married to Mary's sister Joan, so they could feel that the land had not totally been lost to the family. But once again, though they tried to retrieve it later, it was gone never to return. The same day, Roger Sadler's will mentions a debt of five pounds owed him by John Shakespeare that Edmund Lambert and Edward Cornwell were supposed to cover.

Then came April 4, 1579, one of the saddest days in the Shakespeare family's life. The misery of their financial worries dimmed in comparison to the grief they faced on the death of their seven-year-old daughter Anne. There is no indication of what caused her death, but her funeral is listed in the Trinity Church records with the note that a special fee was paid for the "bell & paulle [black cloth]."[34] That John Shakespeare at a time of severe financial difficulty would pay this extra fee for the funeral of a child reveals a stubborn emotionalism, a depth of feeling, a refusal to be practical in the face of the important things in life that reveals much about his character. The family would have gathered around her grave: Mary and John, fifteen-year-old William, thirteen-year-old Gilbert, ten-year-old Joan, now without her only sister, and five-year-old Richard trying to understand the meaning of death. "Troubles come not single spies but in battalions," says Claudius in *Hamlet*. Not yet expressed, the vestige of that thought must flitted in and out of William Shakespeare's mind as he and his family dealt with their Job-like trials.

It cost the Shakespeares nothing to have their boys in school, so William likely stayed at his studies until the end of term that year (1579) when he turned fifteen, the usual age for an Elizabethan boy to leave school. The economic difficulties, however, made it difficult if not impossible to consider sending William to university. What he did when he left school has given the delight of speculation to generations of scholars. These would be the years he went off as a schoolmaster (as reported by Aubrey) either to the Hoghtons in Lancastershire (the choice of those pursuing Shakespearean Catholic theory), or perhaps, as Anne-Marie Edwards suggests in her charming *Walking with William Shakespeare,* to nearby Dursley in the Cotswolds.[35] Or, if his family expected him to be a gentleman farmer, he could have been working the land with his Uncle Henry.

Whatever he did, the pressure was on him to contribute to the family income. Witnessing his parents struggle with finances and especially the sale of family property, his own rightful inheritance, could not help but affect him. The legal terms that rise up so spontaneously throughout his plays suggest to some that William worked for one of the lawyers in Stratford at this time. E. I. Fripp is convinced William Shakespeare worked in the office of Henry Rogers, Town Clerk and Steward of Stratford from 1571 to 1586.[36] But no papers exist that show his signature, no documents with initials W.S. that would identify him as a clerk or assistant. And the language of bonds and leases and sales and terminations and signatures and agreements and courtrooms and witnesses and loss of inheritance must have echoed repeatedly through the Henley Street house during these difficult years.

More than once John Shakespeare's oldest son brought trouble home himself. One hard day at the end of November in 1582 William told his parents that he was marrying Anne Hathaway. At twenty-six she was eight years his senior and pregnant.

In the sixteenth and seventeenth centuries the average age for a middle-class man to marry was his late twenties; for women, mid-twenties.[37] As noted in the introduction to this book, it was expected that the young man would finish school, take on a seven-year apprenticeship in a trade, set himself up in business, and earn enough money to buy a house and support a wife before marrying. This was exactly the pattern followed by John Shakespeare.

His son was eighteen and had no occupation. Without a house of his own, William most likely brought his wife home to his parents who had no money to spare, and within three years added three children to the family burden. In 1585 the Shakespeare family consisted of John and Mary; William and Anne and their three children Susannah, Judith, and Hamnet; Gilbert, Joan, Richard, and Edmund, who at five years old was just two years older than his niece Susannah. In an age when three-generation families were rare, somehow John and Mary Shakespeare accommodated their daughter-in-law and three grandchildren, adding them to their own large family, and keeping them under their roof for sixteen years.

Then about 1587 or 1588, the first the year of the death of Mary Queen of Scots, the second the year of the Spanish Armada, their oldest son once again gave the family cause for apprehension. He left them and went to London. It is possible he went in a general pursuit of some kind of career, one not available in Stratford. It is also possible he knew he wanted to join a theatre company—and possible again that he might already have done so.

After the first appearance of players in Stratford in 1569 there had been no more performances until 1575/76 when two companies (Warwick's and Worcester's) performed. In 1577/78 Leicester's and Worcester's Men (again) came through. At age eleven, again at thirteen, again at fifteen (Lord Strange's and the Earl of Essex's Men) Shakespeare saw actors perform. At seventeen he saw Worcester's Men again and, for the first time, Berkeley's troupe; and when he was eighteen in 1582 (the year he married Anne Hathaway and must have felt tied down indeed) Worcester's Men came through Stratford again, this time with the incandescent young Edward Alleyn in the company. The next year (1583/84), Davy Jones (who was married to a cousin of Anne Hathaway) produced a Whitsuntide "pastime" in Stratford itself, the only time payment was made by the corporation for a locally produced theatre event. Did Shakespeare take part? Did he write some scenes? Did he help out? Or did he stand by and watch? Whatever his connection we can only surmise that his hunger grew, and his realization, as Oxford's Men and Worcester's Men came through the next year, that there was a great distance between what a small town could produce on a amateur level and what the professional theatre had to offer.

Then, in 1587–1588, William Shakespeare must have felt his destiny call with an irresistible insistence. That year five theatre companies played in Stratford: one unnamed company; Lord Stafford's company; Essex's Men; and, of greater significance, Leicester's Men, and the Queen's Men. Among Leicester's Men were James Burbage, Will Kempe, George Bryan, and Thomas Pope, all of whom were to become Shakespeare's close friends and colleagues in the following decade. Furthermore, Leicester's Men were playing with a diminished company since several of their members were touring abroad, and they could well have needed a strong, young, eager new actor. For that matter, the Queen's Men had lost an actor, William Knell, who died in a fight a few months before. Did either of these companies tempt William Shakespeare to come with them as they left Stratford? Did they encourage him by telling him to look them up if he ever came to London?

Did he feel Stratford unbearable as they left? He knew that their life was the life he wanted, for very soon afterwards he was on his way, leaving his family, leaving Stratford, leaving the countryside he loved for the great city of London and a life in the theatre.

And somewhere deep in his heart as he turned his back on Stratford grew William Shakespeare's iron determination to replace his father's lost fortune and redeem his family's reputation. It didn't happen quickly. For four years John Shakespeare and his family in Stratford waited for him to establish himself, to become successful. Fairly soon after leaving he started to act in and to write plays: *Henry VI* was a great popular success and was played by at least two different professional companies (Lord Strange's men and the Earl of Pembroke's men[38]). Perhaps William Shakespeare and his father took hope from this success and were proud of it, but this would not be a reassuring activity to the conservative small town artisans of Stratford. And Shakespeare must have discovered that offering a play to a company meant he was paid once, perhaps not very much, and that was it. And in 1592, three or four years after arriving in London, William Shakespeare was not praised but rather excoriated by the playwright Robert Greene for being an "upstart crow, beautified with our feathers" (that is the feathers of the university-educated playwrights of the time), who had a "player's heart wrapped in a Tyger's hide"—disparagement of his actor's craft expressed by distorting a line of Queen Margaret in his *Henry VI Part III*. Was this his destiny? Was this why he had left Stratford? To become a hack playwright, subject to the derision of educated men, supplementing his chancy writer's income by making a spectacle of himself on the stage ("Alas! 'tis true I have gone here and there, and made myself a motley to the view" *Sonnet 110*) while his father had to support his wife and children? John Shakespeare would have had a hard time defending his oldest son's choice to his friends, to his family; perhaps to himself.

But in 1593 at long last John Shakespeare had news of real success from his son. William's work—the *Henry VI* trilogy, *Richard III*, *Titus Andronicus*, and the comedies *Taming of the Shrew* and *A Comedy of Errors*—had caught the interest not only of theatre professionals, but of members of the aristocracy. To impress them, when the theatres closed down in 1592 because of plague, William had set himself to write a poem. Not a play for the general rabble, but a literary poem on a proper classical theme: *Venus and Adonis*. And it had been offered to the Earl of Southampton, one of the glittering jewels of Elizabeth's court, who was willing to accept the dedication as the poem's patron. This meant Shakespeare would receive a hefty fee as a reward. And the poem was to be published— published by William Shakespeare's old school friend from Stratford, Richard Field, now one of London's distinguished printers and the son of the same Henry Field whose goods John Shakespeare had been asked to appraise when Henry had died just the year before. And, since the plague was slow to lift, William Shakespeare was going to write another poem, *The Rape of Lucrece*, again for his aristocratic patron, again to be published by Richard Field. His years of success had begun.

When the plague lifted, the money he earned for his poems enabled him to join with the Burbage family in 1594 to found a new theatre company to be sponsored by Lord Hunsdon (Henry Carey), Elizabeth's Lord Chamberlain. They would be called the Lord Chamberlain's Men, and the arrangement was that Shakespeare, with the other shareholders, would earn money not just for his acting and his playwriting, but also from a percentage of the admission fees for every play presented. He had made the first brilliant investment of his life.

Now he could start to redeem his father, John Shakespeare's, reputation. In 1596 William Shakespeare (we assume) applied for a coat of arms, not in his own name but in his father's. He chose a design, on record in the Herald's Office: "Gold, on a Bend Sable, a spear of the first steeled argent. And for his crest or cognizance a falcon his wings displaying argent standing on a wreath of his colours: supporting a spear gold steeled as aforesaid set upon a helmet with mantles and tassels."[39] He chose a motto—*Non Sanz Droict*, Not Without Right. This time he had the fee to pay, this time the coat of arms was granted. John Shakespeare was a gentleman, and his son, the actor, inherited the title and status.

For eight years John Shakespeare had acted as a father to William's children—they had been born and had grown up in his, their grandfather's, house, and for much of the time their father was absent in London or on tour. So the summer of 1596 brought a grief to John Shakespeare and his family as powerful as that from Anne's death in 1579. On August 11 William Shakespeare's only son Hamnet was buried. He was eleven and a half. No one knows what happened, whether it was accident or illness that took him, or whether his father, whose company was on tour in Kent at the time, even knew of his illness and death before he was buried. His gravesite somewhere in the Trinity Church churchyard is unmarked and unknown. But wherever it was, William Shakespeare's dream of establishing a family to whom to leave his properties, his name, and his coat of arms, lay buried in the coffin with the body of his son. Hamnet's sisters would marry and have children, but none of them carried the name and all Shakespeare's grandchildren died without descendents. Six months later John's only sibling, his colorful, volatile, brother Henry, Henry who had been in and out of scrapes with the law, Henry, who had continued to farm in Snitterfield, died at Christmastime, to be followed soon after by his wife Margaret. They left a daughter, Lettice, born the same year William Shakespeare married (1582). She was fourteen, close in age to William's Susanna, and one wonders if she came to join John Shakespeare's household.

Any doubts John Shakespeare might have had about William Shakespeare's commitment to Stratford were put to rest in 1597 when the historic Clopton house called New Place came up for sale. William Shakespeare bought it and from then on continued to buy properties and in and around Stratford.

Thanks to the genius and industry of John Shakespeare's son, at the end of the century the Shakespeare family had come out of the years of indebtedness. They were once again prosperous landowners in the area. They had a proper coat of arms and a motto filled with pride: Not Without Right. Master John Shakespeare, son of the tenant farmer, was a gentleman with a gentleman for a son.

Facts abound but glimpses of personality are rare in Shakespeare's family. Joseph Quincy Adams in his 1925 biography comments that John Shakespeare's "merry disposition, combined with recognized success in business and a genuine interest in the welfare of the borough, would naturally make him popular with the townsmen. We may suppose too, that he was kindly of heart; his frequent and generous contributions to those in distress indicate as much, and the following incident may be cited as further evidence. On February 1, 1558, he sued one Mathew Bramley for debt; but when the case came up again on February 15, he incurred the usual penalty of 2*d.* for not following his suit. 'Apparently,': says Fripp, 'he declined to prosecute in consequence of the illness of Bramley's wife, who was buried on the 22nd.'"[40] Furthermore, John Shakespeare contributed generously to the sufferers of the plague in 1564.[41] When he was chamberlain, along with his friend and colleague John Taylor, he collected the town revenues, administered them, and turned in an annual report. "The expenditures were miscellaneous, apart from standard ones to the schoolmaster and the vicar, and ranged from seventeen shillings for mending the vicar's chimney to twelve pence for repairs of the much-repaired town clock. When the revenues fell short of the expenses, John Shakespeare made up the difference out of his own pocket. In the end the borough owned him a substantial sum of more than four pounds, but Shakespeare asked no interest and was willing to wait some time for repayment."[42] Rowse agrees: "One gets the impression of his being easy-going about money matters, and there is no doubt that he neglected his own business for the town's . . . . It was not until ten years of non-attendance (at meetings) had passed that at last they elected another alderman in his place. This forbearance and special treatment show their sense that he had sacrificed himself for the town."[43]

But our knowledge of the merry disposition Adams notes above comes from one extraordinary remembrance we have of John Shakespeare. Half a century after Shakespeare's father's death Thomas Plume collected a number of papers about William Shakespeare, among which was the following record: "He was a glover's son. Sir John Mennis saw once his old father in his shop—a merry-cheeked old man that said Will was a good honest fellow, but he durst have cracked a jest with him at any time."

A merry-cheeked man, working in his shop and looking up to crack a jest with his quick-witted, talented son. What a lovely, revealing description is this, the only one we have, of Shakespeare and his father.

3
Shakespeare's Uncle

Bolingbroke: My gracious uncle!
York: Tut, tut!
Grace me no grace, nor uncle me no uncle.
                       Richard II, act 2, scene 3

HENRY SHAKESPEARE (c. 1529–1596)

Richard Shakespeare undoubtedly had two sons, John and Henry. Some attribute to him a third son, Thomas, but evidence of the relationship is too inconclusive to number him as one of the family here. John was most likely the elder son, but Henry was close to him in age, and they must have grown up together, rising early in the morning to do chores, trudging off first to Vicar Donne, then to his successor Sir Thomas Hargreave, at Snitterfield church to learn to read and figure, then returning to help their father in his long days working the fields, plowing, sowing, and harvesting as the seasons rolled by.

As a young man, John left the farm to lead an ambitious life in town where his risk-taking was matched by hard work and dedicated public service. Henry chose the traditional life of a tenant farmer. But his hard work and ultimate success were matched by irresponsibility, indebtedness, and rebellion. This made him a difficult brother for John, but an exceptionally interesting uncle for William.

Our knowledge of Henry begins in 1569 when a Henry Shaxper appraised the goods of John Pardie of Snitterfield.[1] The next year, 1570, when Henry was about forty years old, his brother John Shakespeare was reported as the tenant of a fourteen-acre property called Ingon Meadow (according to Lewis the property of John Combe and according to Schoenbaum and Eccles the property of William Clopton). Ingon was two miles northeast of Stratford, two miles from Hampton

Lucy, and a mile from Snitterfield. The rent of eight pounds was high for an empty field, so some speculate there was a house on the property, and, as Henry Shakespeare's two children were baptized in nearby Hampton Lucy in 1582 and 1585, one supposes Henry lived there and farmed the property that later came to be called Shakespeare's Close.

The next bit of information comes three years later, in 1573, when Henry was a witness and his brother John was an overseer to the will of Alexander Webbe. Webbe was part of the family as he had married Margaret Arden, sister to John Shakespeare's wife, Mary. Webbe was both Margaret's husband and her and Mary's step-uncle as he was the brother of Robert Arden's second wife, Agnes. In 1560, Webbe had leased from his sister, the widowed Agnes Arden, the Snitterfield property that was occupied and farmed by Richard Shakespeare and his son Henry. Thus Alexander Webbe became the Shakespeares' landlord and John and Henry's place in Alexander's will is an evidence of how often financial and legal dealings were kept within families at the time. Further it seems to affirm a long-term and positive relationship between the Ardens and the Shakespeares.

Henry was an industrious man: in addition to Ingon Meadow and the property leased from Alexander Webbe, from 1574 until his death in 1596 Henry was a tenant on another property in Snitterfield owned by the Hales.[2] But in 1574, when Henry was in his mid-forties, and his nephew William was a boy of ten, we begin to have reports of his bellicose nature.

The first and most violent incident concerned an Edward Cornwell (Cornwaile) who at that time was courting Margaret, his brother John's sister-in-law and the widow of Alexander Webbe. The Court Leet (law day) records for October 12, 1574, state that Henry Shakespeare "drew blood to the injury of Edward Cornwaile," for which he was fined £3 3*d*. Fault was found on both sides: the wounded Edward was fined 2*s* as well for actions against the Queen's peace. Careless or rebellious, Henry Shakespeare was then fined an additional 2*d* for not showing up at the court hearing.[3] But in spite of this discord Cornwell became Margaret Arden's second husband.[4]

Henry embroiled himself in a longer and more extended struggle in the years 1580–1582 when he refused to pay tithes to a Mr. Sheldon and a Mr. Bewfoe, who were trying to collect what they claimed Henry owed the Snitterfield church. The extent of Henry's wealth is made specific in the crops cited as taxable in this suit: wheat, muslin, rye, barley, oats, and pease.[5] Henry claimed he was not refusing to pay his tithes, he was simply paying them to a Richard Brooke of Warwick who, Henry believed, owned the rights to them. The selling of tithes, the right to collect the proportion of a farmer's goods owed to the church, was a way for a church to raise ready money, and an investment for the purchaser: later one of William Shakespeare's largest personal investments would be buying up tithes in Stratford. But Mr. Richard Brooke of Warwick was a questionable character (images can't help but come to mind of the jealous Mr. Ford in *Merry Wives of Windsor* disguising himself as one "Mr. Brooke" to spy on his wife).

Mr. Richard Brooke, according to Roland Lewis, was a well-to-do tenant of farms near Warwick: Temple Farm, Castle Mills, and others. He was also one of the aldermen of Warwick who resisted the growing power of a fellow city councilman named John Fisher. In this age of religious conflict Brooke was "in favor with the Puritan lordships of Warwick and Kenelworth[6] But more, Brooke was greedy to possess Church property with its tithes. Five years earlier he had claimed tithes from Myton, and his enemy, Fisher, openly resisted him. "At the tithe barn, on November 27, 1576, there was a short but lively siege—Brooke's men defending the barn with bows and arrows and calivers [early musket]. Fisher's attacking servants routed them, some of them escaping to Brooke's house, where his malicious and contriving wife Mary gave them protection."[7] Not surprisingly, Fisher accused Brooke of "encouraging his followers to make frays and bloodshed in the fields of Snitterfield."[8] In due time Brooke claimed ownership of the Snitterfield tithes, and when Sheldon, for the Church, pressed for the payment of his tithes, Henry Shakespeare declined to pay. The details of any agreement concerning the tithes between Richard Brooke and Henry Shakespeare are not on record. Lewis calls Henry Shakespeare an "accomplice" of Brooke, and notes that Brooke was soon expelled from the Warwick council by vote of the principal burgesses. As a result of the tithe suits, one on November 21, 1581 and another May 22, 1582, Henry was declared to be contumacious ("contumax") and was excommunicated by the ecclesiastical court at Snitterfield until he should pay the tithes.[9]

On a still litigious but more peaceable note, in that same year (1582), a Hary Shakspere (common spelling variant) appeared in a list of witnesses for a lawsuit concerning the farm owned by Warwick College Manor and once occupied by Richard Shakespeare.[10] At this same time, Henry was expecting the birth of his first child. The date of his marriage to a woman named Margaret is unknown; she must have been very much younger than he, for their daughter Lettice was baptized in Hampton Lucy in 1582, when Henry was well past fifty.

Henry was not the only Shakespeare who had a busy 1582; this was the year his nephew William married Anne Hathaway. William's daughter Susanna was baptized soon after Henry's daughter Lettice, and the overlapping of the generations continued when Henry's son, James, was baptized in Hampton Lucy in 1585, the same year William Shakespeare's twins Hamnet and Judith were baptized in Stratford.

Before those christenings, however, was Henry's wool cap protest.

In 1571, in a effort to help the cappers guild, stimulate the wool industry, and encourage the raising of sheep, Parliament passed an act ordering all men to wear woolen caps instead of hats to church on Sundays and holidays. Farmers objected, for the act would lead to enclosing pasturage for more sheep, land that had been open for them to farm. Henry was not alone in protesting the act. Records show towns and villages paying fines out of public funds in support of the farmers:

twice in 1577, again in 1578, and again ten years later, church records report the following:

> Stratford: paid 10s 8p for fine re caps
> Item paid at Stratford for the statue of caps 14s
> Item at Stratford for Caps 7s 5d.
> Item paid for the Statute of Caps 3s, 7d.[11]

Eleven years after the passing of the act, the Court Leet entry of October 25, 1583 notes a fine: "Of Henry Shakesper, viijd, for not havinge and wearinge cappes on Sondays and hollydayes to the Churche, according to the forme of the statute; of Henry Shakesper ijd for not doinge there sute at the courts." He was fined for not obeying the statute, and, so like contumacious Henry, fined again for not showing up to pay.

In 1586 the will of Christopher Smith claimed a debt of five pounds, nine shillings against Henry Shakespeare of Snitterfield, but Henry's economic vagaries seem not to have totally discredited him as that same year he stood as pledge, or godparent, along with William Meades (of whom we will hear more later), for Henry Townsend, son of his friend John Townsend, at Snitterfield.[12] In 1587, Nicholas Lane, through his lawyer Thomas Trussell, sued John Shakespeare for ten pounds. This was the remainder of a twenty-two pound debt of Henry's that John had guaranteed on June 4, 1586, and that Henry had not paid. John denied responsibility for the debt and Nicholas (who had a history of violent behavior and a notoriously bad temper) pressed the suit. When the decision went against John, he appealed to a higher court.[13] The ultimate outcome is unknown, but John himself was in the midst of financial troubles at the time and one can assume he was not best pleased that Henry's feckless behavior had left him liable for the debt.

Henry and Margaret suffered the death of a child, as did almost every family at the time: their little boy James died in 1589 at the age of four. But suffering did not bring wisdom, and age did not improve Henry Shakespeare's financial situation. In 1591, when he was over sixty, the Court of Record of September 22 shows that Henry was imprisoned in the jail of High Street in Stratford for an unpaid debt to Richard Ange (Ainge), a baker and a burgess in Stratford, who made a further plea of trespass on October 20.[14]

The last citations against Henry were in 1596: on September 29 he was attached for debt to John Tomlins, who continued the suit on October 13; and finally on October 22, 1596, the Court Leet in Snitterfield fined Henry two shillings six pence for "having a diche betweene Redd Hill and Burman in decaye for want of repayringe."[15] He was further cited for refusing to join a team of workers assigned to repair the Queen's highway. To be charitable, he was an elderly man and this was just two months before he died, so perhaps he was in no condition to repair either his own property or the Queen's road. But some creditors were not to be denied: as Samuel Schoenbaum reports, "When he was in jail in the High

Street for debt, his surety William Rounde marched over to Henry's house and appropriated two oxen which the latter had bought but characteristically not paid for."[16]

Mrs. Stopes, the indefatigable Shakespearean researcher of the early twentieth century, has a most interesting chapter called "Henry Shakespeare's Death," in her book *Shakespeare's Environment*. As her information has not to my knowledge been reprinted elsewhere I will cite it at length here. She says of Henry's end (pp. 68–71):

"My new papers come to darken the circumstances into tragic intensity (Uncal. Court of Requests, Elizabeth B. III). There are two complaints both by John Blythe of Allesley, co., Warwick, against William Meades, who, it may be remembered, stood sponsor with Henry Shakespeare for John Townsend's child. The first complaint, presented 30 June 40 Eliz., 1598, narrates that about three years previously John Blythe had become, along with William Meades of Coleshall, surety for a debt of John Cowper of Coleshall to an unnamed creditor. Cowper did not pay, neither did Meades, and the creditor recovered from John Blythe alone, and he appealed for protection. This complaint is scratched out, though it is pinned together with the other papers.

"The second complaint is to the effect that, about three years before, John Blythe of Allesley had sold and 'delivered to Henry Shakespeare of Snitfield,' two oxen for the sum of £6 13s. 4d. and the purchaser became bound in a bill obligatory to pay at a date specified, now past, and had not paid. The reason was that

> Shakespeare falling extremely sicke, about such time as the money was due, died about the time whereon the money ought to have been paid, having it provided in his house against the day of payment. . . . Now soe it is . . . that [Henry] Shakespeare living alone, without any companie in his house, and dying without either friends or neighbours with him or about him, one William Meades, dwelling near unto him, having understanding of his death, presently entered into the house of the said Shakespeare after that he was dead, and, pretending that the said Shakespeare was indebted to him, ransacked his house, broke open his coffers, and took away divers sums of money and other things; went into the stable, and led away a mare; carried away the corn and hay out of the barn, amounting to a great value, being all the proper goods and chattels of the said Shakespeare while he lived; and not contented therewith, in the night time, no one being present but his servants and such as he sent for that purpose, he caused to be conveyed away all the goods and household stuff belonging to the said Shakespeare, which money and goods were of a great value . . . and converted them to his own proper use.

"John Blythe cannot speak with certainty upon the subject, as no witnesses were present but those brought by Meades, and it was worked in secret, so that he cannot proceed by the course of the Common Law. He had frequently asked Meades to pay the £6 13s. 4d. due to him for Henry Shakespeare's oxen, from the goods he had taken. Blythe did not think it fair that Meades should satisfy himself without considering the other creditors, and thought that if there was not enough to pay all, they should share it in proportion, and prayed that William Meades be summoned before the Court to make personal answer.

"A Privy Seal for a Commission to inquire into the truth was granted, dated 30th October 40 Eliz., 1598, on which is written 'The execution in another schedule attached' (now lost).

"The answer of William Meades, dated 13th January 41 Eliz., 1598–9 lightens the horror a little. He does not acknowledge anything in Blythe's complaint to be true, but is willing to declare all he knows. Henry Shakespeare, late of Snitterfield, having a wife living in the house with him named Margaret, died at Snitterfield about two years ago. He, William Meades, understanding of his death, went to the house about two hours after his decease, being accompanied by Thomas Baxter, Christopher Horn, Richard Taylor, and others, neighbours, hoping that Shakespeare had taken order with his wife to satisfy him of the sum of £4 5s. 8d. due by Shakespeare to him, William Meades. But the said Margaret said there was no order taken by her late husband for the payment of any debt to him or any other creditor, and he departed quietly, without any ransacking of the house or taking away any money or goods which were Henry Shakespeare's while he lived, as most untruly and slanderously hath been alleged against him. But he hath been credibly informed, and verily believeth, that one William Rownde of Allesley, co. Warr, husbandman, standing bound to John Blythe jointly with Henry Shakespeare in the said sum of £6 13s. 4d. for the said oxen, and understanding that Henry Shakespeare was under arrest at Stratford-upon-Avon, and there detained in pryson for debt, and fearing lest he, the said William Rownde, should be compelled to paie the sum of £6 13s. 4d. to the said John Blythe for the debt of Henry Shakespeare, he, the said Rownde, did fetch the said two oxen from the said Henry Shakespeare and delivered them to the said John Blythe of Allesley in discharge of the same debt.

"Meades denied that he had gone in the night time and taken away Henry Shakespeare's goods, that he had detained anything to his own use, or that John Blythe had asked him to pay the six pounds, thirteen shillings, four pence as surety. This is signed by Bartholomew Hales, William Jeffereys, William Cookes, and Ambrose Cowper, the Commissioners, the first being lord of the manor.

"The replication of John Blythe to William Meades, 23rd June 41 Eliz., 1599, upholds his former complaint, which he is willing to prove. But the name of Henry Shakespeare does not appear in it. There is no trace of further action, or of any decision. But we have the tragic picture of Henry Shakespeare's haunted death-bed. John Shakespeare, only four miles off, must have felt inclined, when he heard of it, to say what Macduff did: 'And I must be from hence!'

"Even more touching is the picture of the widow of two hours being worried about her husband's debts. Bereaved and childless, she was left alone in the dismantled house, where the wheels of life stood still, for a short time (only six weeks), and then in Snitterfield 'Margaret Sakspere, being tymes the syff of Henry Sakspere, was buried, ix Feb., 1596/7.'"

In the summer of 1596 the family of William Shakespeare was devastated when William's son Hamnet died. Four months later, at the cold end of December, just before the year was out, Henry died. In spite of all his debts, the John Blythe mentioned above (admittedly a creditor wanting to collect) reported that "Henry died in his own house with money in his coffers and corn and hay in his barn 'amounting to a great value.'"[17] Henry Shakespeare was buried in Snitterfield, December 29, 1596. His wife Margaret was buried there six weeks later. No one knows what became of their daughter, Lettice. We only know it was a long, sad winter for the Shakespeare family.

The year before his uncle's death, William Shakespeare's writing had exploded with the gritty realism, wild humor, diverse characterizations, and vitality that mark *Henry IV Part 1*. In the two years after losing his uncle and his son, Shakespeare's energies diminished somewhat. Changing from a customary pace of about two plays a year he now wrote three over the course of two years. However, his output shows to what extent he was a consummate professional, for in 1597 and 1598 when he wrote *Much Ado About Nothing,* and turned back to Falstaff with *Henry IV Part 2*, and *The Merry Wives of Windsor*, little in the plays reflect his grief. But transmogrified experience fills all of Shakespeare's work. Acknowledging this, Stephen Greenblatt makes an intriguing case for the London playwright Robert Greene as a progenitor of Falstaff.[18] Maybe so. But somewhere in the background of this extraordinary character, in the scenes between prince Hal and Falstaff where we see the young heir apparent deferring his acceptance of responsibility and the old scoundrel rebelling against rules and regulations, surely here—in the shadows of the Boar's Head Inn and in Shallow's garden in Gloucestershire—here lurks the ghost of William Shakespeare's youth and the chimes he might once have heard at midnight with his scapegrace uncle Henry.

4

Shakespeare's Mother

Mother, mother, mother!
Hamlet, act 3, scene 4

MARY ARDEN (c. 1538–1608)

Mary Arden was the last of Robert Arden's eight daughters, and his fondness for her is reflected in the provisions he made for her in his will (1556):

> I give and bequeath to my youngest daughter Mary all my land in Wilmcote, called Asbies and the crop upon the ground sown and tilled as it is and £6 13s. 4d. of money to be paid before my goods be divided.... Also I ordain and constitute and make my full executors Alice and Mary my daughters of this my last will and testament and they to have no more for their painstaking now as before given them.[1]

Mary was born about 1538; the circumstances of her childhood in Wilmcote are suggested by the house, the barns, pig sty, dovecote, and fields of the Arden farm, one of the Shakespeare properties now so evocatively restored by the Shakespeare Trust. At the time of his death Robert Arden owned eight oxen, two bullocks, seven cows, four horses, three colts, fifty sheep, and nine pigs along with numberless bees and poultry. Inside, though his inventory includes no knives, forks, or crockery (spoons and wooden trenchers sufficed for meals), his home boasted eleven painted cloths, hung on the walls like the tapestries in the great houses of the day.

Mary's mother was Robert Arden's first wife.[2] She died when Mary was under ten, just about the time several of Mary's older sisters were marrying and thus also leaving the family home. On April 21, 1548, Robert married Agnes Hill, the widow of John Hill of Bearley, a man who had died in 1545. Agnes brought her four children into the household: among them two girls, Eleanor and Mary, and—unique for this family—two young boys, John and Thomas.[3] Though Mary had watched four of her sisters take husbands and leave home, she now had the company of four stepsiblings. The adjustment to this new family was not without strain. Robert Arden, in his will, leaves his wife Agnes the right to live in the house plus ten marks only "on condition that she should suffer Alice quietly to enjoy half the copyhold." If not, Agnes would have to be content with five marks and her jointure in Snitterfield, an indication, surely, that his daughter Alice and new wife Agnes had not lived easily together.[4]

Robert Arden owned two houses and land in Snitterfield, a village five and a half miles northeast of Wilmcote. He leased the Snitterfield farmland to Richard Shakespeare, so John Shakespeare, Richard's son, knew of Mary Arden virtually from the time she was born. Just when the son of the tenant farmer decided the landlord's daughter was the wife for him is not known, but John Shakespeare came wooing Mary Arden in 1557, soon after her father's death. At about nineteen, Mary was young; young to inherit so much property, young to be named an executor for her father's will, and young to take a husband. Girls of her status usually reached their mid-twenties before marrying,[5] but her father's will suggests she was unusually mature for her age, and this man who came a courting, John Shakespeare, had many attractive qualities. As a very young man he had turned his back on full-time farming to become apprenticed to a glover in Stratford. He now had a successful business, owned two houses, and had been given a position (ale taster) by the Stratford corporation. He had high aspirations, though as Ian Wilson charmingly points out, his ambition took a back seat to love in the year 1557, for the year he was courting Mary Arden he missed three corporation meetings.[6]

The Wilmcote Ardens were a minor branch of a very distinguished family, the Ardens of Park Hall some twenty miles from Wilmcote. Mary's father owned a considerable amount of land, however (over sixty acres in Wilmcote and a hundred in Snitterfield), and could perhaps have claimed the relationship and asserted himself as a gentleman farmer. But he chose to present himself as a husbandman, a working farmer, and thus he probably raised his daughters to be hard working middle-class women. Some scholars suggest Mary's connection to the Park Hall Ardens was close enough to give her gentility if she chose to claim it, including the right to display the Arden coat of arms and that she would lose this right if she married a man not of the gentry like John Shakespeare.[7] But the glover from Stratford had a lot to offer the young heiress from Wilmcote: in particular, a forward-looking life epitomized by his new-style house on Henley Street. Whereas her farmhouse still had the open fire in the center of the room, with smoke drifting into the thatched roof to discourage insects, birds, and vermin from nesting there, John Shakespeare's house in Stratford had been built with fireplaces set into the wall and proper chimneys to control the smoke. Some might think she had married down, but Mary would be trading an old, traditional farmhouse shared with her stepmother for a modern house, a stimulating life in town, an ambitious husband, and, perhaps soon, children. Furthermore, though John Shakespeare's ancestors had been tenant farmers, he had ambitions to become a gentleman. The land Mary inherited would help him in this quest, and if she had lost caste by marrying him, he would do everything in his power as the years went by to give her a coat of arms and a gentlewoman's status.[8]

Traditionally brides married from their home church, in which case St. John the Baptist's in the charming little town of Aston Cantlow, Mary's parish, was the site of the wedding of John Shakespeare and Mary Arden in 1557. Though the marriage register in Aston Cantlow is missing, the fact of Mary and John's marriage is confirmed by the records of Trinity Church, Stratford, which note the baptism a year later (September 1558) of the Shakespeare's first child, a little girl they named for Mary's sister Joan.

Mary Shakespeare's new life revolved around her family, her house on Henley Street, and the large garden behind. To visualize her daily activities we can turn to *The Book of Husbandry* by Sir Anthony Fitzherbert where he describes "What Works a Wife Should Do." A wife, he suggests, should start the morning with prayers. "And when thou art up and ready, then first sweep thy house, dress up thy dishboard, and set all things in good order within thy house. Milk thy kie [kine or cows], suckle thy calves, sile up [strain] thy milk, take up thy children and array them, and provide for thy husband's breakfast, dinner, supper, and for thy children and servants; and take thy part with them. And . . . ordain [set aside a portion of] corn [grain] and malt to the mill to bake and brew withal when need is . . . Thou must make butter and cheese when thou may. Serve thy swine both morning and evening, and give thy pullen [poultry] meat [food] in the morning. And when the time of year cometh, thou must take heed how thy hens, ducks, and geese do lay, and to gather up their eggs, and when they wax broody to set them there as no beasts, swine nor other vermin hurt them."[9]

Shakespeare's own memory of the kind of work his mother did surely prompted the images in *Sonnet 143*:

> Lo, as a careful housewife runs to catch
> One of her feathered creatures broke away,
> Sets down her babe, and makes all swift dispatch
> In pursuit of the thing she would have stay;
> Whilst her neglected child holds her in chase,
> Cries to catch her whose busy care is bent
> To follow that which flies before her face,
> Not prizing her poor infant's discontent:
> So run'st thou after that which flies from thee,
> Whilst I, thy babe, chase thee afar behind;
> But if thou catch thy hope, turn back to me
> And play the mother's part, kiss me, be kind.
>   So will I pray that thou mayst have thy Will,
>   If thou turn back and my loud crying still.

Mary and John Shakespeare's first baby, Joan, died. Their next child, Margaret, was born in December 1562, but died at the age of five months. In five years of marriage Mary had bourn John two children both of whom died in infancy, a heavy burden for a young couple to bear. But in April of 1564, seven years after her marriage, their first son, William, was born. Three months later the plague came to devastate Stratford. Whole families died within days. In all likelihood an apprehensive Mary took her baby to her sister and stepmother at Wilmcote, three miles outside Stratford, to protect him from contagion. Despite the fears his parents must have felt, and fortunately for the world, this child at last thrived.

Like young mothers of any era Mary was faced with a number of child-rearing decisions. One of the first would have been whether to nurse her baby herself or employ the services of a wet nurse. Hiring one presented difficulties: it was believed moral and ethical influences could enter the baby through the milk he drank, so not only health and cleanliness but the behavior of the wet nurse was important.[10] Finding a woman who would nurse only the one baby was also an issue. Then the decision needed to be made about whether the wet nurse should live with the family, or the baby taken to live with the woman, to be visited occasionally and brought back to the parents only when weaned. Expense was a consideration; wet nurses were costly and therefore common choices for the aristocracy who could easily afford them. The decision was more difficult for middle class couples watching their expenses.[11]

Whatever choice Mary and John made for nursing William they were faced with the same choice five more times: for Gilbert, born in 1566; Joan, 1569; Anne, 1571; Richard, 1574; and Edmund, 1580. William grew up the oldest of six children, with two sisters and three brothers. (All six children were not in the family together, however, for Anne died when she was seven, a year before the youngest, Edmund, was born in 1580). So Mary's family included five children spread out over ten years, and one, undoubtedly a surprise, six years later. Births normally took place at home, thus (after William) each birth required the care and diversion of the older children while the newest was being born. Lacking a mother, Mary was most likely tended at home by her sisters, friends, and perhaps a midwife during her deliveries. Only if there were difficulties with the birth would a doctor be called in. By the time Anne was born William was seven and would have known what was happening; he would have memories of Anne's birth, and Richard's, and Edmund's that he would take into adulthood.

The daily life of Shakespeare's family went from dawn to dark. As noted, Mary Shakespeare started the day at sunrise, getting the children up, presiding over family prayers, making breakfast (bread, cheese, butter, and home-made ale, the common drink as coffee and tea where unheard of and the water was not safe), then sending children off to school. Education for children had changed since John and Mary's childhood. There was a school in Stratford for their sons. Both boys and girls were first taught to read by their parents, or the local clergy, or the school master's assistant in a petty school, for before starting regular school the boys would be expected to know their letters and numbers and have basic skills in arithmetic and in reading and writing English. Girls often had the same petty school education, but not as many proceeded to formal schooling; instead, when boys went off to school, girls learned the arts of housework and needlework from their mothers. Rarely girls had a formal education, taught by tutors or sent to one of the few girls' schools.

After the boys left for school Mary's real work began. To turn once again to *The Book of Husbandry*:

> In the beginning of March, or a little before, is the time for a wife to make her garden and to get as many good seeds and herbs as she can, and specially such as be good for the pot and for to eat. And as oft as need shall require, it must be weeded, for else the weed will overgrow the herbs. And also in March is time to sow flax and hemp . . . But how it should be sown, weeded, pulled, rippled [combed], watered, washed, dried, beaten, braked [crushed], tawed [softened], hackled [hacked], spun, wound, wrapped, and woven, it needed not for me to show, for they be wise enough. And thereof may they make sheets, boardcloths [tablecloths] towels, shirts, smocks, and such other necessaries. And therefore let thy distaff be always ready for a pastime that thou be not idle.
>
> It is a wife's occupation to winnow all manner of corns, to make malt [for brewing beer], wash and wring . . . And also to buy all manner of necessary things belonging to a household, and to make a true reckoning and account to her husband what she hath received and what she hath paid. And if the husband to the market to buy or sell (as they oft do), he then to show his wife in like manner. For if one of them should use [practice] to deceive the other, he deceiveth himself and he is not like to thrive, and therefore they must be true either to other.[12]

In addition to her work at home Mary and the children likely helped her husband set up his wares each Thursday at the Stratford market, and used her time there to buy what she needed, and to chat with the farm wives on their weekly visit to town.

The main meal of the day was at noon when children came home from school for an hour's break to eat with the family. Then, after a long afternoon at school, the boys returned around six; supper was served, and shortly after sunset the family prepared for bed.

On Sundays the family went together to church services. The boys were made to pay close attention to the readings and the sermon as a report on them was part of Monday's school curriculum. In church Mary and her family followed the Church of England service in the Book of Common Prayer as all subjects were directed to do by Queen Elizabeth. There were Catholic recusants in Stratford who paid a fine rather than attend Holy Trinity Church, but the reported instances when members of the Shakespeare family did not go to church were rare. For the majority of their lives there is little evidence to suggest anything other than that they were compliant Protestants, neither excessively Puritan nor declared Catholics. Shakespeare carried many traces of his early religious education into his plays; quotations from the Geneva Bible and references to biblical stories appear constantly in his work, but one searches there in vain for dogma or the preaching of specific religious beliefs.

In 1576, after she and John had been married nineteen years, Mary's husband began a long battle with debt and disgrace. John's ambition had led him to risky speculations in money lending and even more in wool trading; poor business management left him owing more money than he could raise.[13] As lawsuits piled up many conversations about what to do must have filled the Henley Street house. And surely Mary, who as a very young woman had been named an executor for her father's will, and who had brought property into her marriage, had opinions and spoke her mind.

Soon John Shakespeare, for two decades a loyal and enthusiastic public servant, stopped going to corporation meetings. The records of the corporation show understanding on the part of the burgesses and aldermen for the difficulties experienced by their long-time colleague: they did not fine him, they spared him from assessments to aid the poor, they kept him on the rolls as an alderman for ten years in spite of John's continual absence from meetings. Mary and John had the sympathy of their friends and colleagues; but sympathy is difficult to bear for proud, independent, successful people and these years must have been a trial for Mary and for John. A dire moment came late in 1578 when John Shakespeare had to mortgage the land Mary had brought to him with their marriage. William, the eldest son, was fourteen years old; at issue was his future inheritance; Mary's family was party to their trouble as the person to whom they mortgaged her Asbies estate was her brother-in-law Edmund Lambert, married to her older sister Joan.

This year and the next two brought loss after loss to Mary. In 1578 she experienced the first death of a sister when Katherine died. The next year even more intense sorrow came with the death of her seven-year-old Anne. Mary's grieving husband paid extra for his little girl to be buried to the ringing of the bell, on April 4, 1579, with a black pall draping her child's coffin. The fall of that sad year found them conveying land at Snitterfield to Robert Webbe, one of Mary's nephews, a sign of continuing financial trouble. Mary's stepmother Agnes Arden died in 1580 and was buried in Aston Cantlow on December 29; the next year she lost her sister Elizabeth.

In the midst of this grief and trouble Mary discovered she was pregnant for the eighth time—eight pregnancies in the span of twenty-two years—pregnant with her last child, Edmund, who was baptized on May 3, 1580. A new and unexpected trouble came when Edmund was two years old: William, her oldest (though at eighteen still a minor), had to ask his parents for permission to get married. It could not have been an easy moment. His parents were suffering financially and he had no settled career, training, housing, or income. With no way of supporting a family William had been careless enough to impregnate Anne Hathaway, the daughter of an old family friend. A hasty marriage for the two young people was decided upon with the result that Mary found herself having to welcome into the Henley Street house her son's new wife, a twenty-six-year-old pregnant woman. Within six months her first grandchild was born, William and Anne's daughter Susanna.

Financial struggles did not cease and the greater world was about to have an impact on Mary's Stratford life. On December 20, 1583, Edward Arden of Park Hall, the head of the Arden family in Warwickshire and a distant relative of Mary Arden Shakespeare, was executed for treason. Everyone in Stratford would have known about, gossiped about, discussed, and analyzed this horrifying scandal. Arden's young son-in-law John Sommerville had implicated his own sister, plus Mary Shakespeare's distant cousin Edward Arden, Arden's wife Mary, and the Catholic Father Hugh Hall in a crazed threat to assassinate Queen Elizabeth. The accused were indicted in nearby Warwick, tried in London, and on this grim December day Arden was taken from his prison cell, hanged, drawn and quartered, and his head posted on a pike on London bridge. Father Hall disappeared and was perhaps murdered; Sommerville was found strangled in his cell on the day he was to be executed; the lone survivor, Arden's wife Mary, was kept in prison then released several months later. This Park Hall branch of the Arden family was openly Catholic and nothing suggests that the Wilmcote Ardens were anything more than a minor branch on an old family tree. But Mary Shakespeare must have been grateful that her husband and her family (whatever their religion of origin and private beliefs might have been) were conforming Protestants who worshiped regularly in Stratford's Holy Trinity Church, and posed no overt threat to Queen Elizabeth's life or government.

A year and a half later the Henley Street house grew more crowded when Mary Shakespeare's next two grandchildren were born: the twins, Hamnet and Judith. They were named for William's close friends Hamnet and Judith Sadler. Hamnet Sadler and Will Shakespeare had gone to school together, played together, been boyhood friends. Mary would have watched Hamnet grow up with her children and felt he was one of the family.

The year 1586 started badly and the following year was worse: on January 19 and again on February 16, 1586, a writ was authorized for the arrest of John Shakespeare for debt. The action was not pursued by the accuser, a man named John Brown, who had been trying to get payment from John Shakespeare since October, 1585/6. However another suit was brought in January of 1587 by Nicholas Lane. Here it would seem the sergeants-at-mace actually arrested John Shakespeare and he was released only when Richard Hill offered surety for him. This action was extreme, for as Robert Bearman points out: "Arrests for debt rarely happened, either because the creditor decided it was not worth the trouble or because the debtor could evade arrest by not venturing abroad."[14]

Troubles increased. Also in 1587 Edmund Lambert, Mary's brother-in-law died and in November of that year John and Mary sued Edmund's son John to regain title to land in Wilmcote (Mary's inheritance) that they, in their deepest financial distress, had mortgaged to him for forty pounds. Mary and John claimed John Shakespeare had offered to repay Edmund Lambert the total amount. Lambert countered that the money had not been repaid when due, that now the property was worth more, and that he had to counter sue "to wringe from him this defendante some further recompence."[15] In 1588 John Shakespeare sued Lambert again, still trying to reclaim the land, and eleven years later, in 1599, John Shakespeare brought another Chancery bill on the same matter; but the land, so persistently sought, was never recovered. Mary's relationship with her nephew and his family must have been sorely tested.

The dire nature of his family's situation made it imperative Mary's oldest son establish himself in a trade where he could make money. Surely it's more than coincidence that in 1587, his father was arrested for debt, Asbies seemed lost to the family forever, five professional acting companies performed in Stratford, and William Shakespeare made his decision to leave Stratford to attempt a career as an actor in London. What must it have been like for Mary Shakespeare to watch her oldest son leave her and the family? What a combination of hope and fear and sorrow and prayers and weeping and stoicism must have spurred him on his way. Who knew what to expect?

For seven years, a term filled with biblical resonances, Mary and John watched over the family while their oldest son worked to establish himself in the world of the professional London theatre. He had early successes with his first plays: *Henry VI Parts 1, 2,* and *3, The Comedy of Errors, Titus Andronicus,* and in particular *Richard III,* but these were plays sold outright or leased for a modest amount of money by Shakespeare on a freelance basis: payment was immediate but irregular. Then, just as he was experiencing the hope of real success as a writer and an actor, the worst siege of plague in decades forced the closing of all the London theaters for two years (1592–1594).

At the moment William Shakespeare's London career was threatened (1592) news came that John Shakespeare had been named in two lists of recusants (those, mostly Catholics, not attending church services). John gave as his reason "for feare of processe for Debtte."[16] John Shakespeare knew that if he stayed within his house he could not be arrested for debt. At church, however, he would be in public and he had learned from his earlier arrest just how vulnerable that made him. So he stayed inside his own four walls, hiding out from the law. For Mary and the family to go to church without John was an inescapably public event. How to present her family? How to hold their heads up high when their situation was evident for all to see? William was in London; surely his determination to work and to succeed was heightened by this disturbing news from home.

In the fall of 1593, seven months after her son published his first epic poem, *Venus and Adonis,* Mary endured the loss of her favorite sister, Joan. Her first little girl who died was named for this sister. Her daughter Joan whose children would carry on the Shakespeare line was also named for her, and, as one of Robert Arden's older daughters, Joan was a mother figure to Mary after their mother died. Contention over the Asbies property may have complicated Mary's relationship with Joan, her late husband, and their son John, but her sorrow at her sister's death must have been great.

Yet good news was to come from London: for William, the crisis of the plague turned to an advantage. While plays could not be performed in London, poems could be written and aristocratic patronage sought. By 1594 Shakespeare could tell his family that Henry Wriothesley, the young and glamorous Earl of Southampton, had become his patron, welcoming the dedication of two epic poems, *Venus and Adonis* and *The Rape of Lucrece*. These poems were printed and published by Shakespeare's boyhood friend from Stratford, Richard Field, now a successful London printer. Furthermore, in 1594 Shakespeare was invited to be a shareholder in a new company formed by actors returning to the city from the plague-induced tour. Led by James Burbage and his sons Cuthbert and Richard, the actors had found a patron in the Lord Chamberlain. After eighteen years of financial struggle the fortunes of the Shakespeare family were about to turn, and Mary could be proud of her oldest son as the rescuer of her family.

"Will fortune never come with both hands full?" The words of Shakespeare's Henry IV express the paradox of Mary Shakespeare's life. In 1594, the same year as her son's success as a published poet and a new shareholder in a theatre company, one of the two fires that devastated Stratford in the 1590s destroyed part of the Henley Street house.[17] How terrifying to watch fire threaten the family residence of so many years, and what relief to salvage most of it.

But the trauma of the fire was nothing compared to the tragedy of 1596, when Hamnet Shakespeare, William Shakespeare's only son, Mary's only grandson, died at the age of eleven and one-half. This time there was no payment for the pall registered, no payment for the ringing of the bell as there had been for Mary's little Anne seventeen years before, just an end of summer funeral and silent burial in the Trinity Church graveyard, just the resurgence of grief past expression for the loss of a child.

How ironic that in that same year John Shakespeare was at last granted his coat of arms. What satisfaction could the family take, faced with the loss of the young heir, in the granting of gentleman's status to John Shakespeare?

As if a great storm had blown itself out leaving behind sunshine and blue skies, the next five years seem to have been happy ones for Mary Shakespeare. In 1597 her son William, now so highly successful in London that Mary might well have feared the city would keep him for good, bought New Place, the second largest house in Stratford. With what mixed feelings Mary must have watched Anne and her daughters Susannah and Judith move from Henley Street three and a half streets away to their fine new home. Her own house would be emptier, but the move was a good sign that William, too, would one day come back permanently to Stratford.

The end of the century saw the wedding, at thirty years of age, of Mary's daughter Joan to William Hart, a local hatter by trade. There had been little to celebrate in William and Anne's hasty marriage seventeen years earlier, and Joan was her only daughter, so as Mary and John seemed sociable people, Joan's wedding was the chance for the Shakespeares to enjoy their new prosperity and to host a proper ceremony and celebration. Arguing against this is the fact that Joan and William Hart's marriage is not registered in the Holy Trinity records; perhaps Joan, like her mother, preferred to be married in a neighboring small village. As with William and Anne and John and Mary, the first evidence of Joan's marriage is the baptismal record in Stratford of her first child.

Joan's may not have been a brilliant marriage, but it gave her four children. The Harts resided in the Henley Street house, so Joan's children grew to fill the vacant rooms left by the move to New Place of William's family. Mary Shakespeare never had an empty nest, for, although Gilbert it seems lived for a while in London (a Gilbert Shakespeare was known there as a haberdasher at least for a time), in addition to the Hart family her own sons Richard and Edmund were still at home. Mary's grandson William Hart was baptized in August 1600, a happy family event preceding her next, perhaps greatest, loss.

For in 1601, after a marriage of nearly forty-four years, John Shakespeare died. Mary would help prepare his body, shroud it or wrap it in winding cloths, as she had done with her daughters and grandson, and see it taken from the house where they had lived and worked for over four decades.[18] She would follow the body to Trinity Church yard, see it committed to the earth, then live on, widowed but not alone, until 1608.

William, the eldest son, inherited the Henley Street House and leased it for a very modest sum to Joan and her husband. By 1603 or thereabouts the eastern half of the house was converted to an inn called the Maidenhead, which leads to the belief that after her husband's death Mary Shakespeare moved to New Place to live with Anne, William (as often as he was there), Susanna, and Judith.

In 1603 Joan Hart gave birth to a daughter she called Mary, and in 1605 to another son, Thomas. Mary's first grandchild, Susanna Shakespeare, was now a young woman and on June 5, 1607, she married John Hall. But a year that began so happily for Mary Shakespeare ended with sorrow. On the 17th of December little Mary Hart died at the age of four. She was scarcely buried when, two weeks later, William had to send word from London that Mary's youngest son, Edmund, who had followed his older brother to London to be a player, had died at the age of twenty-seven. Edmund was laid to rest, forever far away from his family, in St. Saviour's, Southwark (now Southwark Cathedral), on the south bank of the Thames not far from his brother's Globe Theatre.

Mary herself would die nine months later, but not before seeing and holding her first great-grandchild: for Susanna's daughter Elizabeth, William's first grandchild, was born that May. Joan's son Michael was born the same year and Mary, close to her allotted three score years and ten, died in the early fall. On the ninth of September she was buried near the graves of her children, her husband, and her grandchildren in a now unknown part of the Trinity Church graveyard.

William Shakespeare, who had sustained and supported the family for so long, was now the head of the family indeed.

5

Shakespeare's Brothers

We came into the world like brother and brother...
The Comedy of Errors, act 5, scene 1

Gilbert Shakespeare (1566–1612)
Richard Shakespeare (1574–1613)
Edmund Shakespeare (1580–1607)

GILBERT SHAKESPEARE (1566–1612)

Gilbert Shakespeare, who was just two years younger than his famous brother, was likely the closest to him. Gilbert was baptized in Holy Trinity Church, Stratford, on the 13th of October, 1566. The occasion would have been well-celebrated, this christening of John Shakespeare's second son, for at this time the Shakespeare boys' father was deputy to the bailiff of Stratford and still very active in civic life. E.I. Fripp believes Gilbert was named for a glover colleague of John Shakespeare, Gilbert Bradley, who lived in a home near the Birthplace House (Bradley's home is now the Stratford Public Library), and that Gilbert Bradley was the baby's godfather.[1]

From age seven to about fifteen, Gilbert would have attended the Stratford Grammar School along with his older brother, studying first with schoolmaster Simon Hunt. Hunt had a degree from Oxford (1569) and was named to the Stratford Grammar School by the Earl of Warwick in 1571. The situation of their schoolmasters would impress on the young Shakespeares ramifications of the religious upheaval of the time, for Simon Hunt may have retained a loyalty to the old faith: certainly a man of that name went to Douai, a town in northern France that was a major refuge for English Catholics. This Simon Hunt then went to Rome to become a Jesuit; he remained abroad until his death in 1585. Thomas

Jenkins, M.A. and Fellow of St. John's, Oxford, succeeded Hunt as the Stratford school master in 1575. Jenkins came to Stratford from having been master at the nearby Warwick School. Gilbert would have studied with Jenkins from ages nine to thirteen, and must often have compared notes about him with his older brother. Because of his Welsh name, Jenkins is often suggested as a model for Shakespeare's Welsh characters, particularly the schoolmaster Hugh Evans in *The Merry Wives of Windsor*; however his roots were not in Wales at all but in London and at Oxford.

William likely left school by 1579, but Gilbert would have stayed two more years and experienced the teaching of the man Jenkins himself chose as his successor, John Cottam. Cottam had been at Oxford the same time as Jenkins, graduating from Brasenose College in 1566 when Jenkins was a Fellow of St. John's. It is unknown why Jenkins chose to leave Stratford, but Cottam's history takes us back to Simon Hunt. Cottam resigned in 1581 after just two years at his post. Possibly the town asked for his resignation, for his brother, Thomas, a known Jesuit, had just returned to England from Rheims bringing a letter to John Debdale of nearby Shottery. Thomas Cottam was arrested in 1580, arraigned with Edmund Campion in November, 1581 and executed in 1582. After he left Stratford, John Cottam inherited land in Lancashire from his father and retired there where Catholic recusancy was very strong.[2] In fact when scholars try to decide what William Shakespeare was doing between 1585 and 1590 it is the connection with John Cottam that tempts some to believe Shakespeare went to Lancashire to teach. Cottam was succeeded by Alexander Aspinall, a happy choice at last, as he remained Stratford's schoolmaster for forty-two years. Religious beliefs aside, one of these scholar-teachers succeeded in teaching Gilbert Shakespeare fine penmanship: his signature on a lease in the Records Office in Stratford is clear, tidy, and elegant.

As the brother nearest him in age, Gilbert was not only William's schoolmate but likely his most common playmate as well. Caroline Spurgeon, in *Shakespeare's Imagery*, has traced recurring images in William Shakespeare's plays and poems, many of which suggest Shakespeare's pastimes as a boy, pastimes William would have shared with his closest brother. Mrs. Spurgeon notes in particular how often the river occurs as an image in Shakespeare's plays, and one can imagine William, undoubtedly often accompanied by Gilbert, walking by the river, staring down at it from the same Clopton bridge that spans the river today, and swimming in its currents. Perhaps a memory of swimming with Gilbert triggered the image in *Henry VIII* of "little wanton boys that swim on bladders" (act 3, scene 2),[3] or that in *Macbeth* (act 1, scene 2) of "two spent swimmers, that do cling together."[4] Undoubtedly they fished as well, but Mrs. Spurgeon denies William was an avid fisherman, feeling that his twenty-four fishing images (half the number of those referring to snaring birds or hawking) are simple and obvious, less vivid and particular than pictures of his other pastimes.

Hunting images occur again and again. The Shakespeare boys knew much about hunting, but William didn't love it. With very few exceptions, his sympathy is not with the hunters but with the hunted: the wounded deer, the snared bird, or the fearful hare. Mrs. Spurgeon says: "Of this sympathy with the trapped bird I find not a trace in other Elizabethan writers . . . Shakespeare's intense sympathy with the feelings of animals is illustrated again and again in his similes, and most especially his feeling for and love of birds, and his horror of their sufferings when limed or snared."[5] Other images show he loved watching animals, including dogs on the chase, birds on the wing, and deer, unaware of the threatening hunter, existing peacefully in their natural habitat.

The young Shakespeares had a public shooting range near the river to sharpen their aim and build their strength in the essential skill of archery. How often they must have watched an arrow leave the bow as Oberon describes Cupid's arrow in *A Midsummer Night's Dream*:

> That very time I saw, but thou couldst not,
> Flying between the cold moon and the earth,
> Cupid, all arm'd; a certain aim he took
> At a fair vestal throned by the west,
> And loos'd his love-shaft smartly from his bow,
> As it might pierce a hundred thousand hearts.
> (act 2, scene 1)

or sought out a lost arrow in the way Bassanio describes in *The Merchant of Venice*:

> In my school days, when I had lost one shaft,
> I shot his fellow of the self-same flight
> The self-same way with more advised watch,
> I oft found both.
> (act 1, scene 1)

Shakespeare mentions tennis, football, fencing, tilting, wrestling, and (if numbers of references are indicative) his favorite sport, bowling. Stratford had a bowling green then as it does today, and Shakespeare used it often: no other Elizabethan playwright except Dekker mentions bowling, and Dekker refers to the game only five times, Shakespeare: nineteen.[6]

In addition to going to school and playing together, Gilbert and William helped their mother in the garden. Here the older brother, at least, developed a knowledge of flowers and trees, of weeds and pests, and found a passion for planting, growing, cultivating, grafting, and nurturing plants as revealed later in images in his work. The boys also helped their father in his glove-making business. Edgar Fripp notes: "William Shakespeare refers to the hides of oxen and horses, to calf-skin, sheep-skin, lamb-skin, fox-skin, and dog-skin, deer-skin and cheveril. He knew that 'neat's leather' was used for shoes, sheep's leather for a bridle. 'Is not parchment,' asks Hamlet, 'made of sheep's skins?' Horatio replies, 'Ay, my lord, and calf-skins too.' . . . Shakespeare speaks of 'a wit of cheveril, that stretches from an inch narrow to an ell broad.' This is technical language, borrowed from his father's business. He mentions also a 'soft cheveril conscience,' capable of 'receiving gifts' if the owner will 'please to stretch it,' and a 'cheveril glove' . . . how quickly the wrong side may be turned outward."[7] One wonders if John Shakespeare was disappointed when his oldest son chose not to follow him into his trade, or if he knew how often William alluded to the glover's profession in his plays.

The companionship of Gilbert and William's youth continued into their adult years when, it seems, Gilbert followed William to London to seek his fortune: in 1597 a Gilbert Shakespeare, haberdasher, turns up in St. Brigitte's (St. Bride's) parish, London. He is believed to be William Shakespeare's brother as he is listed as surety in 1597 for the bail of William Sampson, a clock maker from Stratford-upon-Avon[8] who had been called before the Queen's Bench.[9] Five years later (1602) Gilbert was back in Stratford, helping his older brother by accepting the conveyance of William's purchase of 127 acres of Old Stratford land. The conveyance reads: "Sealed and deliuered to Gilbert Shakespere, to the vse of . . . William Shakespere."[10]

The lease deed with Gilbert's tidy, clear signature dates from 1610. Two years later he died and was buried on February 3, 1612. The entry in the Trinity Church records, Stratford, reads "Gilbert Shakspere, adolescens." As Gilbert was forty-six years old this word indicates not a youthful age but his status as an unmarried man.[11] William and Gilbert's mother had died in 1608. At the time of Gilbert's death his brother William had been settled back in Stratford for over a year and was the principal mourner, the one to plan the funeral, the one to lead the grieving procession. Forty six-years of memories accompanied William as he walked by the body of his brother to the churchyard, walking alone this time as he had so often walked with Gilbert when they were boys, to church, to school, down by the river, or out to the woods to play.

RICHARD SHAKESPEARE (1574–1613)

Of William Shakespeare's three younger brothers, we know the least about Richard. He was christened March 11, 1574, the month before William turned ten, and Gilbert, eight. Edgar Fripp suggests his godfather was Richard Hill, a neighbor who had long been active with John Shakespeare in town politics: Hill was listed as a taster in 1556, a principal burgess in 1557, chamberlain from 1558 to 1559, and an arbiter with John Shakespeare in a case settled out of court on November 14, 1559.[12] As an alderman, Hill contributed to the victims of the plague of 1564, the plague that struck in Stratford just three months after William Shakespeare was born.

Other than notices for his christening and his burial, Richard Shakespeare's name occurs only once in the records of the day: on July 1, 1608 he was fined a shilling (for an unspecified offence) to be given to the poor by the Stratford Church Court.[13] It would seem likely he lived his entire early life with his parents, and after their deaths, either with his sister still on Henley Street, or conceivably with William and his family at New Place. Until his father's death in 1601 Richard may have helped his father with his business. The fact that he never married is interesting when we note that two of his brothers also remained single. Single men were not unheard of in this period, but three in one family is remarkable and one speculates on possible causes. Possibly Richard was unsuccessful in setting up the kind of work that would make him an eligible husband. Traditionally a man trained in a profession or apprenticed in a trade, established himself, perhaps bought a house, then found a wife. So a lack of profession or means might be one reason.

There are, however, two other possibilities never mentioned in connection with the Shakespeare family: mental retardation and homosexuality. Is it not possible Richard could have been mentally or physically disabled and therefore not of interest to women, or homosexual and therefore disinclined to pursue them? As there is no evidence for the former, and as a life-span of thirty-nine years argues against a severe disability, let's look at the possibility of the second. In *The World of Christopher Marlowe* David Riggs discusses the "paradoxical status of Renaissance homosexuality." He observes: "The venerable custom of sleeping with a same-sex bedfellow, the exaltation of male friendship, the fear of being emasculated by heterosexual passion . . . and the recovery of Greek and Roman gender systems, all served to legitimate homoerotic affection, especially in the universities. Love between men was intrinsic to the humanist educational programme. Yet the medieval Christian impulse to demonize homosexual acts persisted regardless. The so-called buggers, pathics, ingles, cinaeduses, catamites, Ganymedes and sodomites who performed such acts were still regarded with horror and disgust. The law too was equivocal on this issue. Tudor parliaments made sodomy a crime punishable by death, but the offence was almost never prosecuted, and then only in cases where a man had raped a boy."[14]

Citizens in a market town like Stratford would have been far less likely than those at the universities, the Inns of Court, or worldly aristocratic circles to tolerate actions they would have been taught to consider aberrant, but that does not mean homosexuality or sexual deviance did not exist among them.

Of interest is the freedom with which William Shakespeare expressed homoerotic feeling—or his understanding of homoerotic feeling—both personally in the sonnets and through characters in his plays: for instance, Antonio's feelings for Bassanio in *The Merchant of Venice*, the eagerness of Proteus and Valentine in *Two Gentlemen of Verona* to exalt male friendship above the feelings of men for women; the devotion of Antonio to Sebastian in *Twelfth Night*, the twisted feelings of Iago toward Othello; the ambiguous sexual identities underlying the relationships between Rosaline and Orlando in *As You Like It* and Viola and Orsino (and Viola and Olivia) in *Twelfth Night*. Though Shakespeare lived most of his life as a conservative heterosexual husband and father whose over-riding concerns were for his family, these examples from his work demonstrate Shakespeare's comprehension of male to male attraction. One hesitates to say homosexuality "ran in the family" but the unusual fact will not go away that here was a family where three out of four sons never married, and the one who did had at least one extraordinary emotional infatuation with a man.[15]

Richard however remains a mystery. He died, single, at age thirty-nine in February of 1613, two years after his brother William had returned to Stratford to retire. He was buried on the 4th of February, a year and a day after the burial of his brother, Gilbert.

EDMUND SHAKESPEARE (1580–1607)

The most intriguing of Shakespeare's brothers is Edmund. He was sixteen years younger than William, almost the contemporary of his older brother's children, and was born the year after John and Mary Shakespeare's younger daughter, seven-year-old Anne, had died. Grieving for Anne, the parents were also beset with financial difficulties and had recently mortgaged Mary's land, Asbies, to her sister Joan and her husband Edmund Lambert. The name Edmund could have been given to the child out of gratitude for the Lambert's help in keeping the consequences of John Shakespeare's indebtedness in the family, or in hopes that the land would come back to the namesake child eventually. This never happened. What did occur is that Edmund, alone of the Shakespeare siblings, became a "player" in London like his brother.

There the record is slim, but tantalizing. To this day if you enter Southwark Cathedral not far from the Globe Theatre on London's south bank, and walk the length of the nave, past the transept to the choir stalls, looking down you will see a grey slab of pavement with the name engraved: Edmund Shakespeare. Above him is a similar stone carved with the name of the dramatist Philip Massinger. A little further off lies the playwright who was Shakespeare's collaborator and most popular successor, John Fletcher.

The records of the Cathedral identify Edmund Shakespeare as a player, and give the particulars concerning his funeral: it took place on New Year's Eve day, in the morning (the records cite the ringing of a "forenoon knell") and the funeral was expensive: the cost, 20s. Edmund could have been buried in the churchyard for two or three shillings, but his brother chose to honor him with burial inside the church, with the ringing of the great bell, and with a ceremony held at an unusual hour; most funerals were held in the afternoon, but at that time actors performed and many could not have come to honor the brother of their colleague if the funeral had been held later in the day.

Another church record adds a sad touch to the picture of Edmund's life: St. Giles Church without Cripplegate notes the burial on August 12, 1607, of "Edward, son of Edward Shackspeere, player, base-born." Edward, Edmund, Edmond were all variants of the same name, and all were used to refer to Shakespeare's youngest brother.

It is generally accepted that this is all we know of Edmund Shakespeare's life: his christening date, his name connected with that of his uncle Edmund Lambert, his listing twice, once in the records of his illegitimate son's burial, and once in the record of his own, as a "player" in London, and the slab of pavement bearing his name in Southwark Cathedral.

But James Shapiro in his *A Year in the Life of William Shakespeare* introduces a concern Edmund and his family must have felt, a worry that would have made his older brother doubly eager to assure Edmund was properly connected with a theatre company: impressments. This feared term referred to the military draft that "pressed" men into the army against their will, arbitrarily, and with no warning. At the end of the 1590s, as Edmund was approaching his eighteenth birthday, England was embroiled in a disastrous phase of her continuing war with Ireland. Queen Elizabeth did not keep a large standing army: when she needed soldiers, recruiters were sent out to gather them. The government impressed 2,800 men in 1594, 1,806 in 1595, 8,840 in 1596, 4,835 in 1597, and in 1598, the year Edmund turned eighteen, the number rose to 9,164.[16] It is no mere coincidence that Shakespeare was writing of wars and conscription in these years. The recruiting scene in *Henry IV Part 2* (act 3, scene 2), written in 1597 and introducing Moldy, Wart, Shadow, Feeble, and Bullcalf, the pitiful recruits from Shakespeare's neighboring county of Gloucestershire, shows the practice and all its potential for corruption. The upper classes could buy their way out of service. Those more vulnerable could not. Men, young and old, were hauled out of churches, fairs, inns, and other gathering spots. In 1602 government recruiters raided all the theatres in London in search of 4,000 men. Those viewing the plays were vulnerable, but, according to Shapiro, "Shakespeare and other players, because they performed for the Queen, were exempt from military service."[17]

Conscription fears aside, a mother's letter suggests how difficult it was for young men to find work in country towns and villages. The widow of George Bardell (Bardolf) of Stratford wrote to Shakespeare's friend Richard Quiney in London to ask him for help in finding a position for her twenty-year-old son, Adrian. "If it please you to send me word I will send him up unto you," she said, continuing: "I can get no place for him in the country."[18]

Whether out of concern for safety from impressments, or out of need to find work, or out of pure desire, Edmund Shakespeare became a player in London. He was twenty-seven when he died, old enough to have made his mark had he been a performer of noticeable talent, but his name does not appear in any of the theatrical records we possess. What sort of roles did he play, and for which company did he perform?

An interesting and illuminating scenario is conjectured by T.W. Baldwin in his book *The Organization and Personnel of the Shakespearean Company*. The book has not to my knowledge been reprinted since it first appeared in 1927, yet it is a most careful and comprehensive speculation based on his analysis of how the Elizabethan theatre companies actually worked. Copies are increasingly difficult to find, so I would like here to summarize Baldwin's ideas especially as they affect our picture of William Shakespeare, his youngest brother, and their craft.

Baldwin observes that according to his analysis of the apprenticeship structure within the Lord Chamberlain's Company, two apprentices graduated, or came into the company to play female roles, about 1601. One of these had talent as a serious actor and is thought to have been Samuel Gilburne who had been apprenticed to Augustine Phillips.

"Yet his running mate," says Baldwin,[19] "was probably the only other female actor in that plot (*The Seven Deadly Sins*), one Ned by name, who performed the part of Rhodope. We do not know certainly who that Ned was. Two Edwards appear years later (1624) as servants of the company: Edward Knight, and Edward Ashborn . . .

"But there is a much greater likelihood that this actor was Edmund Shakespeare, younger brother of William, baptized May 3, 1580. It is true that we have no other record that Edmund was ever connected with the Shakespearean company, and yet it is practically certain that he was so connected at his death, since he was buried in St. Saviour's[20] as a 'player' December 31, 1607. This player-brother of Shakespeare, buried at the parish church in which the Globe was situated, must surely have been attached to the Shakespeare company. Further, the age of Edmund was almost exactly that which belonged to this line.[21] Baptized May 3, 1580, he would have entered the company at ten about the summer of 1590, would have been not quite twelve as Rhodope in *The Seven Deadly Sins*, and would have graduated at twenty-one about the summer of 1601. Now one character in the line seems to give fairly definite indication concerning the age of the actor. Francis, the drawer, in *I Henry IV*, summer of 1596, has five years to serve and seemingly as much more as till Michaelmas. He is thus ending his apprenticeship about Michaelmas, 1601, the approximate time when this line ends. Thus Edmund Shakespeare was almost exactly of the age demanded by this line. There is strong probability, then, though no certainty, that Ned was Edmund Shakespeare."

Baldwin makes points earlier to support his view, including the fact that boy apprentices in acting companies often started as young as ten or younger, a pattern different from other guilds who normally started apprentices at an older age. The fact that he can find no Edwards or Neds of the right age associated with other companies also leads one to feel the Ned connected with Shakespeare's company might likely be Shakespeare's brother. The Elizabethan acting world was small and limited enough that Edmund Shakespeare, identified as he was as a player, must be one of the Neds listed. Baldwin's point about the age of the character Francis is substantiated by his observation that the age of characters, particularly for minor roles and female parts in the plays, was often descriptive of the age of the actor at the time the play was written, for which he gives numerous examples.

If we accept Baldwin's conclusions as likely, we can logically construct the following picture. William Shakespeare leaves Stratford-upon-Avon in 1587 and himself takes up training if not a formal apprenticeship, probably with Leicester's men. For three years he works for the company in whatever capacity demanded of him, learning acting, writing, and production skills. His parents are still fighting massive debt. His youngest brother has perhaps become enamored of William's life as a London actor and begs to be taken there with him. William, knowing that he has left his own family in Stratford to be cared for by his parents, in turn, agrees to take Edmund to London. In 1590 Edmund goes with William and becomes an apprentice in his brother's company.[22] In 1592, as William is enjoying the success of his first half dozen plays, Edmund, at age twelve is cast as Rhodope in *The Seven Deadly Sins*. In the mid 1590s, as he reaches his teen years, he starts playing other female roles or young boys, including that of Francis the drawer in his brother's play *Henry IV Part 1*. In 1601 he graduates from his eleven year apprenticeship and, competent but not greatly gifted, he continues to play minor roles as a hired man for the next six years until his death at age twenty-seven.

Whether or not Edmund spent much of his life with his brother's company he would have known his brother's colleague William Sly, one of the Lord Chamberlain's company actor-shareholders. Sly was also in *The Seven Deadly Sins*, where, if Edmund were the Ned who played Rhodope, they would have worked together. Baldwin describes Sly as "a mercurial and temperamental young man," a vigorous swordsman who played such roles as Hotspur, Tybalt, and Laertes.[23] Sly must have been at least twenty-one years of age when he became one of the founding members of the Lord Chamberlain's company in 1594, and was probably a bit older than that. He was born most likely, then, between 1568 and 1573 making him at least seven and more likely a dozen years older than young Edmund Shakespeare. However, circumstances drew them close, for William Sly had and lost an illegitimate son the year before Edmund went through the same experience. In the records, once again of St. Giles, Cripplegate, is written: "Christened: John, sonne of William Sley (player), base-borne on the body of Margaret Chambers, 24 Sept., 1606." The boy was buried nine days later, October 4, 1606, less than a year before Edmund's child was buried there.

We remember, then, that William Shakespeare married Anne Hathaway after she became pregnant. He must fully have understood his young brother's actions. He would also appreciate how their circumstances were different: Anne's father and Shakespeare's father were good friends, and the families, of similar status, had long known each other. We have no idea who the mother of Edmund's child was; she was obviously not someone he wanted to or felt he could marry. But women who bore children out of wedlock suffered stern social opprobrium; this occurrence was not a happy one for William Shakespeare to guide his young brother through, nor a pleasure to report (if indeed he did so) to the family back in Stratford.

With Edmund in the picture, William Shakespeare's domestic life in London is at once less isolated and more complicated than one might heretofore have thought. And in the end, William Shakespeare, who worked all his adult life to support and care for his family, could not protect the life of his brother. Edmund, his youngest sibling had followed him into the theatre, and met with little professional success; had followed him to London, and met with personal sorrow. Death was the final, inexorable foe. William's son, Hamnet, had been left home in Stratford and died.

Edmund, his youngest brother, had come with him to London and died. Edmund is in fact the only member of the immediate Shakespeare family buried outside Stratford. Hollow comfort to William Shakespeare's family the expensive London funeral. Hollow comfort to William the morning's pealing forth of Southwark's great bell.

6

Shakespeare's Sisters

Good sister, let us dine and never fret.
The Comedy of Errors, act 2, scene 1

Laertes: And sister, as the winds give benefit
And convoy is assistant, do not sleep
But let me hear from you. . . .

Ophelia: Do not, as some ungracious pastors do.
Show me the steep and thorny way to heaven,
While like a puffed and reckless libertine
Himself the primrose path of dalliance treads
And recks not his own rede.
Hamlet, act 1, scene 3

Joan Shakespeare I (1558–?)
Margaret Shakespeare (1562–1563)
Joan Shakespeare II (Hart) (1569–1646)
Anne Shakespeare (1571–1579)

JOAN SHAKESPEARE I (1558–?) AND
MARGARET SHAKESPEARE (1562–1563)

Of three of Shakespeare's sisters very little can be said: Joan (the first), Margaret, and Anne were born and died tragically young. The death of the first two, Joan and Margaret, blighted the early years of John and Mary Shakespeare's marriage. The parents suffered the death of these two baby girls before the birth of William Shakespeare, who did not appear until seven years after they were married. One can imagine the care lavished on this new baby boy, and the terror John and Mary felt when the plague devastated Stratford just a few months after his birth. Every day, month, year of his survival was cause for rejoicing.

ANNE SHAKESPEARE (1571–1579)

William Shakespeare had no experience of his two older sisters Joan and Margaret. But Anne was born in 1571 when William was seven. She died seven and a half years later. He was not quite fifteen when she was buried in Trinity churchyard on April 4, 1579. With his parents, he would have walked in deep mourning to the cemetery to watch her committed to the earth, would have seen the black pall his father had paid to cover her coffin, would have witnessed his mother's grief, and heard the mournful ringing of the bell. He was old enough to carry the memory of her death through the rest of his life. This is all we know: Anne was born; she was an only sister for the second Joan; for a time there were two little girls in the family. Then Anne died and there was only one.

JOAN SHAKESPEARE HART (1569–1646)

Born not quite five years after William, the second Joan was baptized on April 15, 1569. She was named after her mother's sister, and surely in memory of the little Joan who had been born and died eleven years before.

Joan had a companion in her sister, Anne, for nearly eight years, but when Anne died (in 1579) Joan was left the only girl in a family of three, soon to be four, boys: William, five years older than she; Gilbert, three years older; Richard, five years younger; and finally Edmund, born the year after Anne died when Joan was eleven.

Two years later, as Joan entered her teens, William brought his wife Anne Hathaway home and suddenly there were women in this household so filled with male figures: even Anne's baby, born within six months, was a little girl—Joan's first niece, Susanna.

Joan herself was the only one of Shakespeare's siblings to marry, and it would seem she married late for the time, at about age thirty. Neither her mother, Mary, nor her brother, William, nor Joan herself were married in Stratford. Why this is so, or where they did marry, has not been discovered. The knowledge of the wedding of each couple comes with the christening record of their first child. So we learn Joan Shakespeare had married William Hart when Wilhelmus filius Wilhelmi Hart is recorded in the Stratford baptismal records on August 28, 1600. Hart was a hatter in town, but not particularly successful; he was sued for debt by three of his neighbors (Richard Collins, Robert Cawdrey, and Arthur Ange) the year his son was born, and again the next year by William Wyatt.[1] The Harts never had a home of their own but lived their entire married life in the Henley Street house of Joan's parents. When their son William was born Joan must have been pleased to give both her brother and her husband a namesake and her aging father, John, a grandson—the first since William Shakespeare's son Hamnet whom they had lost to death in 1596.

John Shakespeare had only a year to enjoy this new little boy; he died in 1601 having lived in the Henley Street house over fifty years. As the oldest son, William Shakespeare inherited his father's property, and changes started to happen to the house, which give a picture of Shakespeare's family life just after the turn of the century. First there was a change in the number of people occupying the house. A few years earlier Anne Shakespeare and her two daughters had moved to New Place, the home William bought in 1597. When John died it is likely that Mary Shakespeare moved to New Place as well, leaving just Joan, Richard, and occasionally Gilbert (who spent time in London) rattling around the large space that included the elder Shakespeare's living quarters at the west side, John Shakespeare's shop on the east side, and the wing called the Back built just after the turn of the century. The biggest change came about 1603 when the eastern half was leased out and became an inn known as the Maidenhead.

While the inn filled the eastern half of the property with activity, Joan's marriage to William Hart brought children again to the western half. Joan's son William (1600) was followed by Mary (1604), who lived just four years (she died in 1607, the same year her uncle Edmund died in London). Thomas came along in 1605 and Michael in 1608, the year Joan's mother Mary died. Except for Thomas, her children brought Joan as much grief as joy. Mary died at age four, Michael at age ten, and William, though he grew to manhood, died before his mother, when he was thirty-nine.

The year 1616 brought Joan Shakespeare Hart a double blow: the death of her husband, April 17; and, just a week later, the death of her brother. In his will William Shakespeare left to "my sister Joan Hart . . . £20 and all my wearing apparel. . . . the house with the appurtenances in Stratford wherein she dwelleth for her natural life under the yearly rent of 12d."[2] She lived in the house with her son Thomas until she died in 1646, just the two of them to remember her older son William who had died in 1639, Michael whom they had lost in 1618, and little Mary who had died so young in 1607.

Joan Shakespeare Hart outlived all other members of her generation. Born in 1569, she lived until 1646, reaching the ripe old age of seventy-seven. She was five years younger than her famous brother, and outlived him by thirty years. She was close to him throughout his life, and hers were the only children whose descendants carried the Shakespeare family line into the twenty-first century.[3]

Part II
Shakespeare's Nuclear Family

7

Shakespeare's Wife

Wedding is great Juno's crown,
O blessed bond of board and bed:
'Tis Hymen peoples every town,
High wedlock then be honored.
                    As You Like It, act 5, scene 4

ANNE HATHAWAY (1555/56–1623)

By far the most valuable piece of furniture was the bed which, in a great house, sometimes cost what we should now consider an altogether disproportionate sum. A really splendid specimen might run into hundreds of pounds, and indeed there was no limit to the amount that could be spent on delicately carved woodwork and magnificent draperies. Even when too great extravagance was eschewed, a bed could be very expensive, and in gentle and simple families alike it was considered sufficiently important to be left as a separate bequest in a will . . . [1]

When William Shakespeare took Anne Hathaway to wife he married into a large family who were longtime residents of nearby Hewland Farm. When he was courting her, a half hour's stroll from Stratford brought the teen-aged Shakespeare to the village of Shottery and on to Hewland farmhouse, the charming thatched structure now known as Anne Hathaway's cottage.

Anne's grandfather, John Hathaway, was a tenant of the house as early as 1543,[2] the same time Shakespeare's grandfathers were in residence at Wilmcote and Snitterfield. Anne's father, Richard, was a friend of Shakespeare's father, John, for in 1566 (when Anne was ten and William Shakespeare a toddler two years old) Richard owed money and John Shakespeare agreed to be his surety and paid some of his debts.[3]

Anne's father married twice.[4] With his first wife, he had three children: Bartholomew, Anne, and Catherine.[5] Anne, who was born in 1555 or 1556,[6] lost her mother when she was about ten years old. Richard, her father, then married a woman named Joan, with whom he had a second family, giving Anne three young stepbrothers and two stepsisters. One of the little girls, six-year-old Joan, died when Anne was in her teens. Though the girl was a stepsister, this family loss was similar to the one William Shakespeare suffered when, at age fifteen, he lost his seven-year-old sister Anne.[7]

The first mention of Anne Hathaway is found in her father's will, made September 1, 1581, just days before he died (he was buried September 7). He left bequests to his wife Joan, his sons Bartholomew (about 26), Thomas (12), John (6), and William (2), and to daughters Agnes (Anne) (25), Catherine (18), and Margaret (9).[8] Fulk Sandells was the will supervisor and John Richardson was one of the witnesses. They were close family friends whose names will become important later in Anne's story.

Richard left his oldest daughter, Anne (Agnes), and her sister Catherine, the traditional ten marks dowry (£6 13s and 4d) to be paid on the day of their marriages, which led Joseph William Gray (author of *Shakespeare's Marriage*, the most detailed study of the subject) to think that a marriage for Catherine was planned and that one between Anne Hathaway and William Shakespeare was already contemplated. Yet there is no subsequent record of a marriage for Catherine, and she was only eighteen at the time, which was young for a woman to marry (the average age being twenty-six). As for Anne's choice, Shakespeare, her intended groom, would only have been seventeen, a youth with no profession and too young to be considered by her father a good choice for a husband. Since Richard was leaving his estate to Joan, Anne's stepmother (shared with and supervised by his adult son Bartholomew), Richard's legacy to his older daughters seems simply his means of making sure they had the traditional dowry whenever they married. The youngest daughter, Margaret, who was only nine, was left a similar legacy to be paid on her seventeenth birthday.

A year later, by November 1582, when Anne Hathaway was twenty-six years old, fatherless, and husbandless, she had found she was pregnant. Her hasty marriage to William Shakespeare and the birth of her first child six months later has disturbed some scholars (particularly the Victorians). Biographers of the nineteenth century expended a great deal of energy arguing that there must have been at least an informal or "handfast" marriage between William Shakespeare and Anne Hathaway before the official ceremony. Such an agreement, suitably witnessed, had some powers of a marriage; for instance children born from such unions were legitimate, and if minds were changed on either side, the aggrieved could sue for a proper marriage on the basis of the handfast betrothal. A handfast agreement allowed the couple to consummate their union, so it was appealing to the Victorians to have Shakespeare's behavior countenanced in this way. But though Anne Hathaway and William Shakespeare could have had a handfast betrothal, there is no documentation to support this, and it's equally possible that they, like many another young couple, had just let their feelings run away with them.[9]

However binding a handfast agreement might be, a church wedding was necessary to assure a woman her dowry and to ensure that her children would be in line to inherit the family's property.[10] For Anne to have a baby out of wedlock would have brought other grave consequences: her reputation would suffer, she would be socially shunned and even ostracized from her community; not only would her child's right to inherit be in question, but she would have no established right to any income from the father of her child. So Anne's discovery that she was pregnant led to a flurry of activity to arrange her marriage. A wedding normally took place after banns to announce the marriage and to ask the congregation to state any reason the couple should not be married. These banns were called in church for three Sundays in a row. But marriages could not take place during the penitential season of Advent, which was to begin December 2 that year, and Anne's pregnancy was revealed late in November.

So, time being short, Anne Hathaway and William Shakespeare applied for a license to marry that would exempt them from the traditional calling of the banns. The license had to come from the bishop of Worcester, some twenty miles away. Quickly, then, they needed to gain the consent of Shakespeare's father (necessary as William was a minor), the agreement of two friends of the bride who would speak for her (also a requirement as Anne's father was dead), and guarantors for a bond of £40 that would be forfeited if it were later discovered the couple could not legally marry (such a potential discovery being the point of calling the banns).

Anne and William's request for a license is noted in the register in Worcester, dated November 27, 1582, and was written for the marriage of "Willelmum Shaxpere et Annam Whateley de Temple Grafton." The license "dispensed with the full publication of the banns, and was generally addressed to the rector, vicar, or curate, occasionally by name, of the church designated for the marriage, which was not necessarily in the parish of one of the parties."[11] The next day, November 28, the same Fulk Sandells and John Richardson who were mentioned in her father's will, and who showed themselves to be very good friends indeed, "entered into a bond for £40 to exempt the bishop from all liability if there should be any irregularity in the speedy marriage of 'William Shagspere . . . and Anne Hathwey of Stratford in the Dioces of Worcester, maiden.'"[12]

A confusion between the names Anna Whateley of Temple Grafton and Anne Hathaway of Stratford, both of which are connected with a license to marry William Shakespeare, has challenged interpreters ever since these two documents were discovered in the nineteenth century.[13] Anthony Burgess, in particular, in his biography of Shakespeare builds the romantic story of William Shakespeare longing to marry Anna Whateley and forced, instead, to marry Anne Hathaway. However, a close look at the records does not support this fantasy. Realistically, the reason for the differences in Anne's name and residences can best be explained by noting a number of mistakes in the documents written by the clerk who was keeping or copying the registry between 1582 and 1583. The clerk/copyist had written the name Whateley in another entry that day and it was a common name in the area; the name Anne Hathaway in Latin would have been rendered annam hathwey. A look at the documents shows that in his carelessness the clerk ran the two names together virtually attaching the "m" to the following "h." Names were not routinely capitalized; an "m" in the old Latin looks very like a "w," and furthermore a "th" in the spelling was often pronounced "t" at the time. For all these reasons, Whateley and Hathaway were easier for the copyist or subsequent interpreter to confuse than might seem probable to the modern eye.

Some scholars suggest that the documents refer to two different William Shakespeares (the name was not uncommon in the area), a different one for each Anne mentioned. But we would then have two unconnected documents: a license request with no bond, and a bond with no license, a highly unlikely occurrence, as each couple would have needed both. If, as most agree, both William Shakespeares refer to the same man, the Anne in question must also be the same, for the bishop would not have readily accepted a bond for a marriage between William Shakespeare and Anne Hathaway if the day before William Shakespeare had been granted a license to marry another Anne named Whateley. So despite speculations about the differences in Anne's last name and her parish of origin on the license and on the bond, the confusion most logically rests with the carelessness of the clerk.[14]

Much would be clarified if we had the other important documents needed in the application for a marriage license. The first was "an allegation, to which the applicant was sworn, stating the name, residence, and occupation of each of the parties and of the parents, guardians, or friends giving consent, and the reason why the full publication of banns was to be dispensed with or why permission was required to marry in a parish which was not the ordinary residence of the bride or bridegroom." The second was "a letter from some person of position known to the bishop or his officials and to the parties and their friends, certifying that no impediment existed and that the license could safely be granted. The assurance of consent was sometimes included in this certificate."[15] William Shakespeare would have had to present consent from his father, as at age eighteen he was still a minor. Other missing documents include the license itself, and the registry of the marriage in a local church. Lacking the latter, the church where the Shakespeares were married is not known, though Temple Grafton, named in the license request, is the oft-suggested choice.[16] It is in asking why Temple Grafton was mentioned in the license request that leads some scholars to the thought it was the home of Anne's mother and her family.[17]

The marriage was necessary. But the situation was not a happy one for the Shakespeares. John Shakespeare was in financial trouble and would have found it difficult to stand surety for the bond of £40, which may be the reason Fulk Sandells and John Richardson had to step forward as friends to the bride. (And here the timing was lucky as just two months later, in January, the amount of the bond increased to £100.)[18] Given the Shakespeares' financial difficulties, adding a new family to their household would not be easy, for Anne Hathaway and William Shakespeare, so suddenly and so quickly married, likely moved into the Shakespeare family home on Henley Street. Anne, who at twenty-six could have been blamed for entrapping this eighteen-year-old boy into marriage, faced her mother-in-law, father-in-law (whose permission had been necessary for his minor son to marry), three brothers-in-law (one a baby of two), and a teen-aged sister-in-law.[19]

Surely the adjustment to Anne as part of the family was eased by the excitement and joy a new baby brings. On May 26, 1583, William took his new baby daughter Susanna from Anne Hathaway to be baptized at Holy Trinity Church, Stratford. Anne, still recovering from the birth, waited at home until the ceremony was over, after which family and friends gathered to celebrate and congratulate her. Mary Shakespeare would have had fearful memories of her first two baby girls who died in infancy, but Susanna, John and Mary's first grandchild, survived; and twins, Hamnet and Judith, were baptized less than two years later (February 2, 1585). Our sense of Anne and William's social life expands when we note that these children were named for the Shakespeares' good friends Hamnet and Judith Sadler, also parents of young children, who lived nearby.

In taking care of her young brood, Anne Shakespeare had the help of her mother-in-law, Mary, and her sister-in-law, Joan. These important relationships developed over the sixteen years the families shared the same roof and became life-long. Anne had a special need for them when, around 1588, William Shakespeare left Stratford for London to take up life as an actor and ultimately a writer and theatrical producer. It was a strange career choice for a young man from Stratford, and the evidence strongly suggests that he did not take Anne and the children to the city with him. Shakespeare never bought a residential property in London, for instance, but moved at least three times during the years he lived there, from one rental lodging to another. In addition, there is no record of his ever having taken an apprentice to train, though this was the practice of most of his colleagues who had wives and families.

To understand that Anne might not have *wanted* to come with him we have only to compare the life of Shakespeare's London friends and their families with what Anne was used to in Stratford. Shakespeare's colleagues had family-oriented lives, living in large houses with lots of children: Winifred and Richard Burbage had eight children; Henry and Elizabeth Condell, nine; their close friends and neighbors the Heminges (John and Rebecca), fourteen. But they all led busy, big-city lives, and undoubtedly some wives took an active part in their husbands' work. The Heminges had a grocers' license and would have used their wholesale rights to buy produce for concessions at the Globe where their children could sell nuts and oranges and drinks to the audience. Elizabeth Condell had been an heiress and owned twelve houses on the Strand when she married Henry Condell. Winifred and Richard Burbage lived near his brother Cuthbert and their parents on Shoreditch Road, an enclave of London's predominant and most innovative theatrical family for two generations, their homes must have been filled with children, young people, apprentices, actors, and constant theatre talk.[20] What would Anne Hathaway, a farmer's daughter from Shottery, have had in common with these women, these families? Furthermore, Anne would have known that theatres were filled with a riotous public and were frequently closed because of plague. To a woman from the country, the city must have seemed a vast, crowded, dirty, unhealthy place to bring up children. And did Shakespeare want her and the children there? Was it not easier for him to write when he could be alone as much as he wanted to be, in a small and quiet room?

But separation, and Shakespeare's increasingly glamorous life in London, took a toll on the marriage (as indeed consistent cohabitation might have). The passionate sonnets Shakespeare wrote in the early to mid 1590s suggest Anne's husband was involved in the most profound emotional/romantic relationship of his life, and not with her. Some feel the sonnets were just an intellectual or aesthetic exercise, but the poet W. H. Auden asserts "what is astonishing about the sonnets . . . is the impression they make of naked autobiographical confession."[21] Indulged in, regretted, and anguished over in these poems are both the infatuation of an older man named Will with a beautiful young aristocratic man and also the poet's uncontrollable passion for a dark-haired, dark-eyed enchantress.[22] It's possible that Anne Hathaway had no knowledge of the crisis her husband was experiencing. The sonnets were not published until years later, in 1609, and then, seemingly without Shakespeare's permission. Mysteriously, they were withdrawn from sale, not to be published again until 1642, well after his death, leading one to speculate that Shakespeare did not want his private feelings exposed to view—particularly not that of his family, the young aristocrat in question, or the dark lady. Certainly, what the sonnets do not suggest is a satisfying and happy marriage. Anne and Willliam's intimacy is further questioned when we observe that though Shakespeare is thought to have returned to Stratford frequently during the twenty-five or more years of his active career, though Anne had proven herself fertile, and though it was an age when large families were the norm, she and William had no more children.

A sad confirmation that Anne and the children had indeed stayed in Stratford is seen in the Trinity Church records of August 11, 1596. On this mournful day, Anne's son Hamnet, age eleven and a half, was buried. Had they been living in London (as in the case of Shakespeare's younger brother Edmund and Edmund's illegitimate son), death and burial would have occurred in the city. It is doubtful that Shakespeare was with Anne when their son died—the company with which he was a performer was touring in Kent that summer,[23] and who knows when he learned about his little boy's death. The agony of every parent who has lost a child crept into his work, however, when in *King John* (written about this time), Constance rails against those who claim she is "too fond of grief" for her son Arthur:

> Grief fills the room up of my absent child,
> Lies in his bed, walks up and down with me,
> Puts on his pretty looks, repeats his words,
> Remembers me of all his gracious parts,
> Stuffs out his vacant garments with his form:
> Then have I reason to be fond of grief . . .
> O Lord! My boy, my Arthur, my fair son!
> My life, my joy, my food, my all the world!
>   *King John*, act III, scene 4

Distraction, and perhaps comfort, came to Anne the next year, when, in 1597, William Shakespeare bought the second largest house in Stratford, New Place, confirming his intent to move back home one day. This purchase enabled Anne and the children to move from the Henley Street house of her in-laws into their new home. In time the large house was also occupied by Thomas Greene and his family, who in the first decade of the seventeenth century, were invited to live in Shakespeare's house while waiting the construction of their own. Clearly, these families were close friends, for Greene called Shakespeare his children were named William and Anne. So, although her husband was in London most of the time, Anne had company in her grand new home, children for her children to look after, and someone to walk with in the gardens or sit with by the fire at night.

About this time, Anne's sister-in-law Joan Shakespeare married William Hart, a hatter, and in 1600 their first son, William, was born. They resided most of their lives in the house on Henley Street so recently vacated her brother's family, and Joan would likely have had the assistance of Anne with the birth of her children.

Anne Hathaway Shakespeare's stepmother, Joan, died in 1599. She had continued to live at Hewland Farm, Anne's girlhood home, and when she passed on, Anne's brother, Bartholomew, took up residence in the house. So Hewland was always there for Anne to visit. Anne's connection with her original family is further witnessed by the will of Thomas Whittington of Shottery, who had been one of her father's shepherds. The entry from March 1601, filled with the variable spellings acceptable in those days, reads:

> Item I geve and bequeth unto the poore people of Stratford
> 40*s* that is in the hand of Anne Shaxpere, wyf unto Mr Wyllyam
> Shaxpere, and is due debt unto me, being payd to myne Executor
> by the sayd Wyllyam Shaxsperre or his assigns.[24]

It would be odd, as wealthy as William Shakespeare had become, for there to have been a loan made to his wife by a shepherd, particularly a loan not repaid.[25] The 40*s* mentioned, therefore, probably refers to monies given to Anne Shakespeare for safe-keeping. In a day when there were no banks this was a frequent practice, and other monies of Whittington's had been given in trust to members of the Hathaway family.

In September of that year (1601) William Shakespeare's household was shaken by the death of its patriarch. John Shakespeare died at something over seventy years of age and was buried at Holy Trinity Church on September 8. Death blighted the next year as well. The Shakespeares' old friend Richard Quiney died unexpectedly, the result of his interference, as bailiff, in a brawl. His death left his wife, Bess, a widow with nine children to raise. Bess, who was one of Anne's close acquaintances, took up the management of an inn and forged a life that, like Anne's, would probably not have been of her choosing.

In May 1606, Susanna Shakespeare, Anne and William's adult daughter, came into the news. She was brought along with twenty other defendants before the ecclesiastical court for the rebellious act of not receiving communion on Easter

Day. This action often identified one as a recusant Catholic, but it is difficult to confirm this as the reason for Susanna's abstention, especially when, soon after, on the fifth of June, 1607, at age twenty-four, Susanna married John Hall, a known Protestant with puritanical leanings. Hall was the most distinguished physician in the district and would become a good friend to his father-in-law. There must have been a general rejoicing in the family at such a fine match for Susanna. William Shakespeare would undoubtedly have been urged to come home for this important event; his family was now very well-to-do, and we can imagine Anne supervising and preparing a traditional Elizabethan wedding in the house and garden of New Place. Memories of her own hugger-mugger ceremony must have filled her mind as she found herself able to give her daughter the kind of wedding she herself had never had.

The sorrow experienced by Joan Hart and the whole extended family when Joan's little daughter four-year-old Mary died in December must have been at least partially alleviated when on February 21, 1608, Elizabeth Hall, Anne Hathaway and William Shakespeare's first grandchild, was baptized. Mary Shakespeare, who had first welcomed Anne Hathaway into her home twenty-four years before, lived long enough to hold her great-granddaughter in her arms, though the matriarch died soon after. Anne and her sister-in-law, Joan Hart, undoubtedly prepared Mary Shakespeare's body for burial, as was the custom, and accompanied the body to its final resting place in the Stratford churchyard. Anne would have helped Joan prepare the food for the funeral, hosting the neighbors, and comforting her husband and his sister as best she could for the loss of their mother.

In 1610, Bartholomew Hathaway, who had inherited the Hewland house and farm from his stepmother, bought the freehold to Hewland's. Bartholomew did not die until 1624, the year after Anne, so Anne's older brother occupied the house she had been brought up in until after her death. In 1611, William Shakespeare moved back to Stratford to make it his permanent home, but sorrow soon followed with the deaths first of his brother Gilbert (1612) and then of his brother Richard (1613). The funeral ceremonies would have been decided upon and conducted by William and Anne and Joan Hart and her husband. Whether William's purchase (1613) of the only residential property he ever bought in London, and his trips in 1612 and 1613 back to the city, may reflect on his relationship with his wife, indicate a needed distraction from his sorrow at losing his brothers, or reveal a dissatisfaction with country life, it is impossible to say.

For five years Anne led the life of a normal, upper middle-class English country wife, busy with her home, her husband, children, and grandchild. Surely Mistress Ford and Mistress Page, in *The Merry Wives of Windsor*, give us a flavor of that life—eager, sociable, high-spirited, good-humored, energetic. Master Page continually invites his neighbors to eat at his house, and we know from an entry in the accounts of the Stratford corporation that the Shakespeares entertained, notably a local preacher in 1614.[26]

But by January of 1616, all was not well with William Shakespeare or with his family. In all likelihood he was sick with the illness that would kill him that spring, and if Anne and William had had difficulties with Susanna, they were multiplied at this moment by problems with their second daughter, Judith. Judith was over thirty years old and had fallen in love with (or at any rate decided to marry) Thomas Quiney. Thomas was the son of Shakespeare's old friend Richard Quiney, but he was a ne'er do well who had been carrying on an affair with another woman. She was even at this moment pregnant with his child. So Judith's choice of a husband must have been the subject of much conversation between Anne and her husband.

Furthermore, Shakespeare's health was likely not good, as late in January he called for his lawyer, Francis Collins, to draft his will. In February Judith and Thomas Quiney married. It seems, then, Shakespeare's concern about Judith's future caused him to rethink his will. He revised the document in March, and the next month, in April, 1616, at the age of fifty-two, William Shakespeare died.

He had organized a complicated financial settlement for Judith in the revised will and left her a silver bowl. He left his property to Susanna, and, famously, only his "second best bed" to Anne, presumably trusting she would be cared for by Susanna. Indeed, Anne would have been greatly helped and comforted by Susanna and Judith and by John Hall, her physician son-in-law. But despite their care and their company, Anne Hathaway, after a marriage of thirty-four years, had lost forever the husband who had so recently come home to her.

The family suffered greatly at this time, as just the week before Shakespeare died, his brother-in-law William Hart died as well. Twice in less than ten days the sisters-in-law Anne and Joan led a sad train of mourners to Holy Trinity Church.

Six years later, in 1622, the church was the scene of a happier occasion as Anne was to see her husband's bust installed near the altar rail. About the same time the King's Men, her husband's theatre company, came to Stratford. It was the only date the records show them stopping in William Shakespeare's home town. This might have been a chance for Anne to meet his colleagues, to see them perform, and perhaps to see one of Shakespeare's own plays. However, the bailiff of the time and the council paid the company, the King's Men, not to perform in the Guild Hall. The Puritan tide was in full spate in Stratford and the opportunity was lost.

The next year, 1623, at age sixty-seven, Anne Hathaway died. That same year the *First Folio* of her husband's plays was published. Anne was buried in Trinity Church, nearer perhaps to him in death than she had been through much of her life.

In many ways, the marriage of William Shakespeare and Anne Hathaway was far from the norm for the time. The difference in age, the man being eight years younger, while not unheard of, was unusual. And Anne was among the minority (20 percent)[27] of young women of the time who went to the altar pregnant. But most uncommon were the long separations they endured as they lived so much of their lives in different places. A situation that would have been acceptable and understandable for the wife of a sailor, a soldier, a government emissary, would have seemed strange for the wife of an actor, playwright, and theatrical producer. Anne would have lived her adult life trying to understand and come to terms with marriage to a man whose career choice was so different from those of her rural and small town family and friends. The rhythm of marriage and birth and death, however, and in particular the suffering caused by the frequent death of young children, was an experience shared by Anne with all her contemporaries. The closeness she had with her own family and the family into which she married was also normal in the life of the time.

That young William Shakespeare once adored Anne Hathaway is suggested by one of his sonnets, number 145. It is the most primitive of the sonnets in execution, and the tetrameter rhythm (all the others are pentameters), the simplistic imagery, and restricted vocabulary all mark it as an early work. Its connection with Anne, however, comes with the play on words in the next to last line: "hate away" punning on "Hathaway"; and serves as a fitting reminder of his early feelings for her:

> Sonnet 145
> Those lips that Love's own hand did make,
> Breath'd forth the sound that said 'I hate,'
> To me that languishe'd for her sake:
> But when she saw my woeful state,
> Straight in her heart did mercy come,
> Chiding that tongue that ever sweet
> Was us'd in giving gentle doom;
> And taught it thus anew to greet;
> 'I hate,' she altered with an end,
> That follow'd it as gentle day
> Doth follow night, who like a fiend
> From heaven to hell is flown away.
>   'I hate' from hate away she threw,
>   And sav'd my life, saying 'Not you.'[28]

And some think the memory of his frequent walks from Stratford to Anne's home in Shottery resounds in Celia's description to Oliver of the way to her sheep cote in the magical Forest of Arden:

> West of this place, down in the neighbour bottom:
> The rank of osiers by the murmuring stream
> Left on your right hand brings you to the place.
>   *As You Like It*, act 4, scene 3

The inscription on Anne Hathaway's tomb reads (translated from the Latin):

> Mother, to me thou gavest thy breast and milk and life,
> Woe is me! For such great gifts I give a tomb!
> I would far rather that the good angel should
> From its mouth the stone remove
> That like Christ's body thy image might come forth.
> But vain our wishes. May'st thou come quickly Christ!
> And then my mother, though entombed, shall rise again
> And seek the stars.[29]

It is thought to have been written by her daughter, Susanna. Whatever the true relationship between William Shakespeare and his wife, whatever hurt feelings Anne Hathaway may have nursed as she watched her husband repeatedly leave her and their children to live in London, whatever she may have felt regarding her husband's choice of career, or the terse sentence in his will leaving her only the second-best bed, this final inscription tells us she possessed to the end of her life the profound love of a devoted daughter: the child whose conception complicated her early life, the child who caused her hasty marriage, and the child who tied together for all time her parents, Anne Hathaway and William Shakespeare.

8

Shakespeare's Children

Lear: Didst thou give all to thy daughters? . . .
Kent: He hath no daughters, sir.
                    King Lear, act 3, scene 4

Susanna Shakespeare (1583–1649)
Judith Shakespeare (1585–1662)

O Lord! My boy, my Arthur, my fair son!
My life, my boy, my food, my all the world!
                    King John, act 3, scene 4

Hamnet Shakespeare (1585–1596)

SUSANNA SHAKESPEARE (1583–1649)

Susanna Shakespeare was born when her father was barely nineteen. It is hard to imagine that her conception was either intended or desired by Shakespeare; it is rather an affirmation of the ironies he so often saw in life that she was to become the child most like him, the mother of his beloved granddaughter, and the joy and comfort of his retirement years.

Susanna was baptized on May 26, 1583, and was only four or five years old when her father left Stratford to begin his career as an actor and playwright in London. Her little brother and sister were sixteen months younger. From the day their father left Stratford, the children would have seen him at most several times a year, and that for varying and unpredictable lengths of time. But Susanna was far from lonely. In addition to her siblings, her family included her mother and her grandparents, Mary and John Shakespeare, whose youngest son, Edmund, was just two years older than Susanna, more like a brother to her in age than an uncle. Also at home were her uncles Richard, age fourteen, and Gilbert, who in his early twenties was close to the age of her father.

As Susanna's mother was (we think) traditional and uneducated, a great part of Susanna's education would have been in the housewifely arts, with an emphasis on gardening, tending animals, cooking, and needlework of all kinds. But as a child Susanna may well have learned to read; girls often had the same petty school background in ABCs as boys. She could at least write her name,[1] and the sensitivity to words and imagery in the memorial she composed for her mother suggests both intelligence and literacy.[2] Shakespeare's own plays show that at end of the sixteenth century a number of middle-class women could read and write. In *The Merry Wives of Windsor* of 1598, a play that depicts the daily life of a town much like late sixteenth-century Stratford, the reading and writing of letters by Mistress Page and Mistress Ford is taken for granted. The next year, in *As You Like It*, he shows Celia and Rosalind both reading easily the missives with which Orlando decorates the trees; and no surprise is registered by other characters when Phoebe, a country girl, threatens to write the disguised Rosalind "a very taunting letter." Given these examples, and considering the ambitions of her father and grandfather to rise in station, it would be surprising if a young woman of the wit and spirit of Susanna Shakespeare were not given whatever education she desired, if only by being allowed to learn from her uncles and younger brother the lessons they brought home from school.

When Susanna was eleven the Stratford fires of 1594, which damaged their house on Henley Street, must have been a dramatic and shocking experience. A worse trauma followed two years later. Susanna was thirteen that never-to-be-forgotten year when her brother Hamnet died. The body of the family's only boy child would have been washed and dressed at home, prepared by the family for his final rest; and Susanna would have been one of the train of mourners, walking sadly with her sister Judith, her mother, her grandparents, her uncles, and her aunt, following the little boy's coffin down the shaded avenue of lime trees to the grave where he was laid to rest in Holy Trinity Church cemetery. All thoughts would have turned toward his father, but William Shakespeare's company was touring in Kent that summer. It is more than likely he had not even heard of his son's death by the time the boy was buried.

If Susanna craved her father's company she was heartened the next year when William Shakespeare bought a big new house for his family: New Place, across the street from the Guild Hall and the school that Hamnet and his father and his uncles had attended. Soon Anne Hathaway Shakespeare with her daughters, Susanna and Judith, moved from Henley Street, the only home Susanna had known, into this impressive new edifice, the rosy brick house with five gables and the beautiful garden with barns and an orchard behind.

There were times when events of the outside world reverberated in Stratford and touched the Shakespeare family. In 1603, at over twenty years of age, Susanna would have been acutely aware of the death of Queen Elizabeth and the accession of King James, especially as the new king claimed her father's company as his own, making William Shakespeare's company the King's Men. On a more sinister note, a group of men with Stratford connections were leaders of the Catholic recusant-inspired Gunpowder plot two years later that was designed to blow up Parliament and kill the King. Most often failure to receive holy communion on the great festival days was an act of resistance by Catholics, so this terrorist plot inspired a firmer than usual insistence that all citizens prove their loyalty by receiving communion following the Church of England rite the Easter of 1606. Twenty-three year old Susanna Shakespeare did not do this. Punishment was swift. In May of 1606 the ecclesiastical court of Stratford accused Susanna along with twenty other defendants (among them her father's old friends Hamnet and Judith Sadler) of not receiving the sacrament that Easter day. Though Susanna did not appear at the hearing, the Sadlers did, and asked for "time to clear their consciences."[3] Many of the accused were known to be papists, so Susanna's indictment brings up questions about her religious beliefs. There is little other evidence of rebellious Catholicism on the part of the Shakespeares, however, so the reason for this action by Susanna remains undetermined.[4] The case against her was dismissed and one presumes that she, like the Sadlers, ultimately complied with the law by receiving the sacrament according to the Church of England rite.

If Susanna harbored Catholic beliefs they were overcome by the next major event in her life. Around 1600 a new doctor had moved to Stratford. His name was John Hall and he was a Protestant, in fact a "devoted churchman inclined to Puritanism."[5] He soon established a highly respected practice and lived in a large home, Hall's Croft, which was also the site of his apothecary's shop and was located not far from Susanna's home at New Place. John Hall was seven or eight years older than Susanna Shakespeare. Close to the time of her summons by the ecclesiastical court, when he was just over thirty and she approaching twenty-four, he courted her and won her affection. Shakespeare's plays, particularly his comedies, bring alive for us the courtship and marriage customs of the time. In *The Taming of the Shrew*, *Romeo and Juliet*, *A Midsummer Night's Dream*, and *The Merry Wives of Windsor* we see on the one side the concern of the parents for a proper match for their daughter and on the other her need to make her own choice. *The Taming of the Shrew*, *The Merchant of Venice*, *Twelfth Night*, *Much Ado About Nothing*, and especially *As You Like It* are filled with delightful courtship encounters. If art mirrors life these plays illustrate the circumstances and rituals of Elizabethan courtship that suggest ways Susanna and John, a witty young woman and a brilliant man, might have come to know one another. Scenes in *Much Ado About Nothing* and in *Romeo and Juliet* show the excitement about wedding clothes and the dressing of the bride. And in *Much Ado About Nothing* we see the bride brought to church by her father, given to her groom, and the marriage ceremony commenced by the priest.

On June 5, 1607, Susanna Shakespeare and John Hall were married in Stratford's Trinity Church. Of all the Shakespeare family weddings this was surely the most welcomed and celebrated. Susanna's grandparents had been married soon after her grandmother Mary's father's death; Mary's mother had died years before, and John Shakespeare was not likely to have been thought a great catch, giving Mary's stepmother and sisters little cause to stage for her a large, public celebration. Susanna's parents had had a hastily arranged marriage made urgent by her mother's pregnancy, and the marriage occurred when the Shakespeare family was under severe financial pressure. Susanna's aunt Joan married a hatter of no distinction who came back to the family home to live. None of her three uncles married at all. But Susanna, whose father was earning a great deal of money in London, and whose family now lived in one of Stratford's most elegant homes, was marrying the town's most distinguished physician. In *The Taming of the Shrew* we see the feast that celebrates a marriage: the food, the toasts, the speeches. Now that the Shakespeares' oldest daughter was marrying a distinguished man whom she loved, surely similar rituals, feastings, and toasts were organized and rejoiced in on that early June day among the flowers and the trees in the garden at New Place.

Anne Hathaway Shakespeare bore only three children; her daughter Susanna just one. Not quite nine months after her marriage, on February 21, 1608, the Hall's daughter Elizabeth, was christened in the church where her parents had been married, and where all the Shakespeare children had been baptized. One can picture baby Elizabeth, brought home from her baptism by her father and her grandfather, wound tightly in her swaddling bands, to be held in turn by her mother, Susanna (still in bed recovering from the birth); her grandmother, Anne Hathaway Shakespeare; and her great-grandmother, Mary Arden Shakespeare: three remarkable women welcoming to the family a new little girl. But this unusual span of four generations could not last long: in September, Susanna's grandmother, Mary Shakespeare died; an elderly woman of seventy, she had been the matriarch of the family and was the last of her generation.

In 1611 William Shakespeare moved back to Stratford to take up permanent residence in New Place, a block and a half from Hall's Croft, the home of Susanna and his only grandchild. The beginning of the following year, on February 3, his closest brother, who had been part of Susanna's family since she was born, her uncle Gilbert, was buried; and almost exactly a year later (February 4) the last of Shakespeare's brothers, Richard, was also laid to rest. Susanna's father William and his sister, Susanna's aunt Joan, were the only ones left of John and Mary Shakespeare's children.

For a time it is likely that the Halls moved into New Place with William and Anne Shakespeare for, in 1613, they were rebuilding their own home. As they finished construction and planned to move into this new house (the present-day Hall's Croft) Susanna's father returned to London to buy the Blackfriars Gatehouse. One wonders if he needed a refuge from a Stratford now without his brothers and with only Anne and Judith left at New Place.

This same year the most curious event that has come down to us concerning Susanna's life and character occurred. She was accused by a man named John Lane of carrying on an adulterous affair with Ralph Smith at John Palmer's and as a result had "the runinge of the raynes," the old term for gonorrhea. On the 15th of July of that year Susanna brought a suit for slander against Lane.

Her supposed partner, Ralph Smith, was born in 1577 and therefore was about six years older than Susanna. He was a hatter, a haberdasher, and a member of the Stratford town militia. Furthermore he was Hamnet Sadler's nephew, the Hamnet Sadler who was godfather to Susanna's young brother and good friend of her father's since childhood. Smith was a respectable married man who was often called to act as Foreman of the jury at local sessions.[6] Nothing much is known about the John Palmer at whose place the act was alleged to have occurred, but Palmers had long owned the farm that neighbored on her grandmother's old home in Wilmcote, and a John and Elizabeth Palmer had held property near the Shakespeare land in Snitterfield dating back to 1529.[7] Palmers and Ardens and Shakespeares had known each other through several generations.

There was also a long relationship between the Shakespeare and the Lane families: Richard Lane (c. 1556–1613), the slanderer John's uncle, had helped John Shakespeare in his suits concerning the Wilmcote property, and in 1611 was one of a group including William Shakespeare and Thomas Greene to draft a complaint against William Combe (the nephew of Shakespeare's old friend John Combe) stating that he was endangering their holdings by not paying "his share of the mean rent for the tithes he held."[8] To go back even farther, Richard Lane (this uncle of Susanna's slanderer) was the son of Nicholas Lane who had lent money to Henry Shakespeare (William's uncle) and then sued Shakespeare's father for its return. On July 9, less than a week before Susanna sued his nephew, Richard Lane (feeling his end was near) had appointed Susanna's husband John Hall the trustee for his children. To make the relationships even more complex, in 1609 John Lane's sister Margaret had married John Greene, the brother of Shakespeare's good friend Thomas Greene. In 1612 John Greene was Stratford's Town Solicitor and served as Chief Burgess from 1612 to 1615. Several years later, Susanna would deal with John Greene as he was a trustee of part of her inheritance: her father's only London property, the Blackfriars Gatehouse. As a last odd twist, John Lane senior, the slanderer's father, had been married since 1584 to Frances Nash, the aunt of Thomas Nash, who, in 1626, would marry Susanna's daughter Elizabeth.

So the slanderer John Lane (1590–1640) was the grandson to Nicholas (a contemporary of Susanna's great uncle Henry); nephew to Richard (the friend of her father and her husband); brother-in-law to Chief Burgess and Deputy Town Clerk John Greene; and his mother was the aunt of Susanna's daughter's future husband. This young man with the complicated connections was twenty-three when he spread the despicable rumor about the thirty-one-year old Susanna Shakespeare Hall. She did not just let it pass; she retaliated against him in the consistory court at Worcester.

What caused Lane to try to sully both Ralph Smith's and Susanna Hall's reputation remains unknown. At the hearing in Worcester, Robert Whatcott appeared as the primary witness for Susanna. Nothing can be found about him, except that three years later he shows up as one of the witnesses to William Shakespeare's will. As he had no known address in Stratford, yet did these services for the family, it is conjectured he might have been a servant in their household. The tempest in this small town teapot calmed when Lane, the slanderer, failed to appear at the hearing. The court punished him with excommunication, clearing Susanna's name. He was not reformed by his sentence, however, and remained a contentious character: in 1619 he was sued in Star Chamber for riot and for libeling the vicar and various aldermen, and had been at one time accused as a drunkard in the Stratford Church Court; and he had met his match with Susanna Shakespeare Hall, not one to ignore, or excuse his behavior.

Susanna was in her early thirties in January of 1616 when her father sent to Warwick for his old friend Francis Collins to come to write his will, then called him back again in March to revise it. Her father's will reveals Susanna to be the most trusted member of his immediate family, his favored child.

The March changes in the will were caused by Susanna's sister Judith's marriage in February, so the revision first addresses bequests to Judith making precise her dowry or wedding portion. Shakespeare also makes specific individual bequests to family members and friends, and to the poor of Stratford. He then says: "Itim I gyve will bequeath & devise unto my daughter Susanna Hall for better enabling of her to performe this my will & towardes the performans thereof all that capitall messuage or tenemente with thappurtenaunces in Stratford aforesaid called the Newe Place wherein I nowe dwell and twoe messuages or tenements with thappurtenaunces scituat lyeing and being In Henlye streete within the borough of Stratford aforesaied. And all my barnes stables orchards gardens landes tenements and hereditamentes whatsoever sctiuat lyeing and being or to be had received perceived or taken within the townes hamlettes villages ffieldes & groundes of Stratford upon Avon Oldstratford Bushopton &Welcombe or in anie of them in the saied countie of Warr." He adds to this his London property, stipulating that after Susanna's death all should go to the first "sonne of her bodie lawfullie yssueing." The paragraph lengthens as he tries to envision all the possible boy children from either Susanna or Judith or their issue, so determined was he to leave property to a male heir. And at the end he says "All the rest of my goodes chattel leases plate jewels & household stuffe whartsoever after my dettes and legacies paied & my funerall expenses discharged I gyve devise and bequeath to my Sonne in Lawe John Hall gent & my daughter Susanna his wife whom I ordaine and make executours of this my last will and testament." The fact that Shakespeare left nothing but the second-best bed to his wife shows that he felt that Anne Hathaway would be well taken care of by Susanna and her husband and therefore needed no resources of her own. Secure in this belief, within a month of the will's revision, he died and, as Marchette Chute writes: "was carried out of his home in a wooden coffin, and the great bell in the tower of the Guild Chapel, just across the way, had been repaired in time to toll for his burial."[9]

> No longer mourn for me when I am dead
> Than you shall hear the surly sullen bell
> Give warning to the world that I am fled . . . [10]

Did anyone in his family ever know he had written such lines?

As was allowed owners of church tithes (rather than because of his profession or his artistic success), William Shakespeare was buried not in the shady old churchyard that held his parents, his little sister, two of his three brothers, and his little son, but under the pavement of the church itself. A four-line piece of doggerel on the stone slab reveals that Shakespeare feared his bones, as was customary in crowded graveyards, would one day be moved to the charnel house attached to the church, to be dumped willy-nilly with miscellaneous others to make room for the newly dead. The verse, attributed to the poet himself, reads:

> Good friend, for Jesus' sake forbear
> To dig the dust enclosed here.
> Blest be the man that spares these stones
> And curst be he that moves my bones.

Since Shakespeare owned property in more than one diocese, Worcester and London, his will could not be proved locally. It had to be taken up with the archbishop of Canterbury's Prerogative (Probate) Court (whose hearings were held at Doctors Commons in London). John Hall made this journey and proved the will on June 22, 1616. Even though she was the coexecutor, Susanna is not mentioned in the action so it is likely she did not accompany him.

After her father's death Susanna and the Hall family moved back from Hall's Croft into New Place and started to discuss a memorial to William Shakespeare. A commemorative bust was decided upon, the bust that still looks out over the altar rail and chancel of Holy Trinity Church. Susanna, her deceased father, and the family knew well the monument in Holy Trinity Church carved for Shakespeare's friend John Combe by Gheerart Janssen. They chose Janssen as sculptor for this new monument. Janssen was one of four sons of a Dutch immigrant who had established a stonemason's business in Southwark near the Globe theatre where he and his sons worked during the years Shakespeare was acting at the Globe. Janssen was not a fast worker: the bust was installed in 1622, six years after Susanna's father's death. Susanna's and her family's apparent satisfaction with the Shakespeare bust (and the fact that Janssen knew Shakespeare, at least by sight) is our best evidence that this decidedly nonromantic figure represents the way William Shakespeare looked in his retirement years.

In the same year, 1622, Shakespeare's theatre company, The King's Men, made their one and only documented visit to Stratford. They applied to the bailiff for the right to play, but it was denied them. The town council had taken a puritanical turn since the days after Susanna's grandfather first licensed two companies to play, and from 1602 onward there was an act prohibiting plays in the Guild Hall in Stratford. It's pleasant to think, however, that Shakespeare's dear friends Henry Condell and John Heminges, who led the company still, and who were working on editing the plays for the First Folio (to be published the next year) had time while they were in Stratford to see the new bust and to visit with the wife and daughters of the colleague they loved so well—and in Susanna to see the child who was so dear to her father, their fellow Shakespeare.

August 6 of the following year, 1623, a grieving Susanna followed her mother's body to the church. Tradition holds that Anne Hathaway desired to be buried with her husband, and her grave is as near his as was possible. Given the personalities and resources of her two daughters it would seem the moving tribute to their mother seen on her grave was written by Susanna, and translated into Latin (if indeed she lacked that skill) by her husband. The depth of feeling in the tribute shows Susanna grieved deeply at her mother's passing.[11]

Happier days were to come. In 1626 young Elizabeth Hall married Thomas Nash, son to William Shakespeare's friend Anthony Nash.[12] But although Susanna had the joy of marrying her daughter she was denied the delight of grandchildren. There were none in 1635 when John Hall died and none to be. John's death must have come suddenly as he left only an oral will in which he bequeathed his "study of books" to his and Susanna's son-in-law, Thomas Nash. As Hall had inherited the books Shakespeare owned, mixed in with his own medical books may well have been the books Susanna's father had read and prized.

The Nashes in turn moved into New Place, to live with the widowed Susanna. The outside world again exerted pressures on Stratford; seven years later, in 1642, with England in the midst of civil upheaval, Thomas Nash made the largest contribution of anyone in Stratford to the Royalist cause.[13] He also made his will that year, suggesting he felt vulnerable in the midst of England's civil war, though he lived for five more years. And when Thomas Nash died in 1647 he was buried in Trinity Church near William Shakespeare. Susanna must have been there, supporting her widowed daughter, as Elizabeth had stood by her mother at John Hall's burial twelve years before.

During the Civil War years (1642–1648) Susanna sold casebooks written by her husband to James Cooke. Cooke was a Parliamentarian (on the opposite side to the Royalists her son-in-law supported) and a surgeon who would later translate into English a section of the casebooks from John Hall's Latin, entitling the work *Select Observations on English Bodies* (1657). In this book Hall details treatments for himself, Susanna, Elizabeth, and the poet Michael Drayton. But as the casebook begins in 1617 there is no mention of Shakespeare's final illness of the year before. Cooke "tells how in 1642 he visited New Place, when Mrs. Hall thought her husband's Latin manuscript was written by some other doctor, though her own ailments—she suffered from scurvy—and Hall's treatments are recorded."[14]

In July 1643, a thrilling event occurred that would have rejoiced the heart of Susanna's grandfather, the ambitious John Shakespeare. It was in the midst of the Civil War, in which as we have noted, Thomas Nash was an enthusiastic royalist. Queen Henrietta Maria, wife to King Charles I, was making a triumphant march from Newark to Keinton, which brought her through Stratford where she stayed three days (July 11, 12, 13), bringing with her a thousand horses and a hundred wagons, plus a train of artillery. She was met there by Prince Rupert, the head of another body of troops, which was according to Halliwell-Phillipps the most stirring event of the kind the ancient town had ever witnessed.[15] During those three days the Queen of England was the guest of Susanna Shakespeare Hall and the Nash family at Shakespeare's New Place.

Susanna lived just long enough to see Elizabeth remarry a man younger than herself by two years or so: John Barnard, a squire from Northamptonshire. Susanna died and was buried July 15, 1649. On her grave is written:

> Heere lyeth ye body of Svsanna wife to John Hall, gent:
>   ye davther of William Shakespeare, gent: shee deceased ye 1jth of
>   July. A. 1649, aged 66.
> Witty above her sexe, but that's not all,
> Wise to salvation was good Mistris Hall,
> Something of Shakespeare was in that, but this
> Wholy of him with whom she's now in bliss.

This first part of the epitaph is the one most quoted. The latter half is often ignored, but it gives us insight into Susanna's generous and empathetic spirit:

> Then, Passenger, hast nere a teare,
> To weepe with her that wept with all
> That wept, yet set her self to chere
> Them up with comforts cordiall.
> Her love shall live, her mercy spread
> When thou has't ner'e a teare to shed.

Surely these were the thoughts of Susanna's only daughter, Elizabeth, thoughts similar to those Susanna expressed in commemorating her mother, Anne. These women loved and appreciated each other deeply. From his mother to his wife to his daughter to his granddaughter, Shakespeare's women showed themselves to be the loving, strong, bright, counterparts of the fictional women he created in his plays.

JUDITH SHAKESPEARE (1585–1662)

It is hard not to pity Judith Shakespeare. She had the longest but perhaps the most difficult life of all the members of Shakespeare's family.

Judith was born one of twins, her brother, Hamnet, was instantly the hope of the future of the family, the always-desired heir apparent who would carry the family name into the next generation. The little twins were named for their godparents, Hamnet and Judith Sadler. Hamnet had been best friends with William Shakespeare in boyhood; the friendship grew to include their wives, continued through their child-bearing years, and lasted all their adult lives.

Judith and Hamnet were just eleven, constant companions since birth, when in the middle of the summer of 1596 Hamnet suddenly died. The parents and grandparents must have been distraught at the loss of their little boy, the child of their hopes. Judith too must have been grief struck and perhaps turned for comfort to her godmother Judith Sadler, a dear friend of the family who had known the grief of losing seven of her own fourteen children. Perhaps little Judith clung to her older sister Susanna as well. But, though Susanna was undoubtedly saddened at this time, she was the older sister and Judith must often have felt hard pressed to keep up.

There was a brief period of time eleven years later when Judith found herself the only child. Right after Susanna's wedding and removal to Hall's Croft, Shakespeare's New Place was suddenly home to just Judith, her mother Anne Hathaway Shakespeare, and her grandmother Mary. And one of the three, Mary, died in September, just a year and a half later (1608).

Perhaps Judith and her mother then found New Place, the second largest house in town, a bit lonely. In 1609 the Shakespeares invited their good friend Thomas Greene, a man who called himself Shakespeare's "cousin," to live there with Anne and Judith while Greene's house, St Mary's, near the church, was undergoing repairs. Thomas Greene was a man fourteen years younger than Shakespeare and just seven years older than Judith (thirty-three to Judith's twenty-six). He had a wife and two young children, one named Anne (baptized 1603/4) and the other William (1607/8). To have new adults to talk to and children of two and six running around the house and garden must have added energy and joy to Judith and Anne Shakespeare's daily life. The Greenes were with them until 1611 when William Shakespeare himself came home to Stratford to live. He had left home for London nearly twenty-five years earlier and though he had often been in Stratford, it was not to live, day in, day out, year after year. The adjustment to him as a permanent resident in New Place must have been a considerable one for his wife and second daughter.

In February of that year Judith turned twenty-six, the average age for a woman of the time to marry. Her sister Susanna had made a brilliant match when she was just twenty-four and her husband was a distinguished man who rapidly became their father's good friend. They were the parents of a three-year-old girl, the Shakespeare's only grandchild. Susanna was well and happily married, Judith, a spinster at home.

The turning event in Judith's life came five years later when she married Thomas Quiney, the son of Richard and Bess Quiney, longtime friends of the Shakespeare family. Richard had died prematurely in 1602 leaving his widow with nine children under twenty. Bess managed by running a tavern in town. That she was close to the Shakespeares comes clear when she asked Judith to witness a deed conveying a house to William Mountford in December 1611.[16] Judith signed twice with a mark, suggesting that she was less literate than her older sister Susanna. Thomas was the third of the Quiney sons. The oldest, Richard, who was to have a successful career as a London grocer and Virginia plantation-owner, married one of Judith Sadler's daughters, creating another tie between the Quiney, Sadler, and Shakespeare families.[17] Thomas was living on High Street when he married Judith. In July they moved to the corner of High Street and Bridge Street where the building housing The Cage, his new house and wine-business, still bears an identifying plaque.

The commencement of Judith and Thomas's marriage was not promising. The wedding was on the 10th of February during Lent, one of the religious seasons during which marriages were not allowed. They did not get the required special license; Thomas and Judith were summoned before the court on March 12, and when Thomas failed to appear he (and perhaps Judith as well, here the records are unclear) was punished with excommunication by the consistory court at Worcester Cathedral.

Worse, on March 26 the recently married Thomas was charged in the ecclesiastical court in Stratford with impregnating a woman named Margaret Wheeler. The unfortunate woman accused him of fathering her child about the time of his marriage. Undoubtedly she wanted Thomas as her husband, which perhaps pushed Judith to demand his hasty union with her. Margaret Wheeler died along with her child just over a month after Judith married Thomas; both mother and child were buried on March 15. At the hearing ten days later, to the sure and certain embarrassment of the Shakespeare family (and particularly to Judith, his wife), Thomas confessed to having had carnal relations with Margaret Wheeler. Found guilty, he was sentenced to do penance publicly by standing, wearing only a white sheet for three Sundays in a row in church. Before this punishment was carried out it was remitted and Thomas was charged just with paying a five shilling fine for the benefit of the poor. He had only to acknowledge his fault before the minister at Bishopton, a town with no church, only a small chapel, where this could be done in relative privacy; so Thomas was spared further public humiliation.

The marriage of his second daughter inspired William Shakespeare to revise the will he had just had drafted in January. On March 25th he added a new first page addressing Judith's inheritance, now a marriage portion. He left Judith £100 outright and £50 more if she promised to give up any claim to the cottage Shakespeare owned on Chapel Lane. £150 was a handsome amount: New Place was purchased for an initial sum of £60 (an amount that subsequent fees probably doubled). Sentimentally perhaps, as a keepsake, he left Judith his "broad silver gilt bowl." But this does not come close to what he left Susanna, and his fear that Judith married badly is indicated when a second £150 is left her only if "any issue of her body be living at the end of three years. . . . Provided that if such husband as she shall at the end of the said three years be married unto or attain after do sufficiently assure unto her . . . lands answerable to the portion by this my will given . . . then my will is that the said £150 shall be paid to such husband as shall make such assurance to his own use." John Hall, Susanna's husband, Judith's brother-in-law, appears by name in the will. Thomas Quiney is only "such husband."

Within a month of this revision William Shakespeare died. In November Thomas Quiney appeared in church for the baptism of his first child, indicating that the excommunication of eight months before was of short duration. Judith's attachment to her father, her desire to please him, memorialize him, reincarnate him is evident in the name of her first-born son: Shakespeare Quiney. Sorrow followed joy for Judith: this long-desired boy child, so hopefully named, lived only for six months.

Two years later Judith gave birth to Richard Quiney; two years after that to Thomas. Judith must have felt vindicated in her marital choice when her husband's behavior improved enough that Thomas Quiney was chosen a burgess by the town corporation and was named constable in 1617. In 1621 and 1622 he was elected chamberlain (the treasurer for the town corporation), an office once held by Judith's grandfather.

Thomas Quiney's true character revealed itself again in 1630 when he resigned from his position on the corporation council having been fined for swearing and for allowing drunkards in his shop.[18] And though he had been named chamberlain, finances were not his gift. They were ultimately approved, but his accounts for 1622/3 were first voted imperfect. Ten years later, in 1633, the lease on Thomas's vintner and tobacconist shop, The Cage, was signed over to his brother Richard, who gave Thomas a fixed salary of twelve pounds a year.[19] Judith Shakespeare's life had turned from that of the privileged daughter of a wealthy man to one like the hard working, modest life of her mother-in-law Bess Quiney.

Judith's mother Anne Hathaway Shakespeare died in 1623. She was sixty-seven. Judith (now age thirty-eight), Susanna (age forty), and Susanna's daughter Elizabeth (age fourteen) would have cared for her in her last days and have been the chief mourners.

The next decade and a half leave few records of Judith Quiney's life. In 1630 her husband tried to sell his lease on The Cage, but "his kinsmen stopped him, and in 1633 assigned the lease in trust to a triumvirate consisting of Dr. Hall, Hall's son-in-law Thomas Nash, and Richard Watts, now Quiney's brother-in-law and the vicar of Harbury."[20] It must have been galling to Judith to see her sister's husband take over the management of her own husband's business lease. And yet one hopes these were for the most part uneventful years spent helping her husband in the shop, raising her sons, and socializing in the town. Then, in 1639, in one single year, Judith and Thomas suffered the terrible loss of both their remaining sons: Richard barely twenty-one, and Thomas just eighteen. It is thought by Mrs. Stopes that an infectious fever might have taken both their young lives.[21]

One wonders about Judith's place in the visit of Queen Henrietta Maria in July of 1643. While her sister and niece were busy readying New Place for the royal visit and preparing to welcome the sovereign, Judith and Thomas must have rejoiced in the business the arrival of thousands of soldiers must have brought their wine shop.

In 1646 Judith's aunt Joan died, the last of her father's siblings, and three years later she lost her sister Susanna. Judith survived thirteen years longer, working with her husband to keep their tobacco and wine shop going, while the turbulent years of civil upheaval raged through the country. It is unknown when Thomas died: F. E. Halliday says simply, "About 1652 he is supposed to have gone to his elder brother Richard, a wealthy London grocer, and to have died there."[22]

However this same brother made a will in 1655 leaving his brother Thomas twelve pounds.[23] Mark Eccles, on the other hand notes that "Thomas may have died in 1662 or 1663 when there is a gap in the register." Judith lived until 1662, two years after the restoration of Charles II as king of England. That same year a new vicar came to Holy Trinity Church in Stratford, John Ward. Ward left an entry in a notebook indicating the intention "to see Mrs. Queeny." He failed to make the visit before she died and as Ward had a great interest in Shakespeare's life it is regrettable that he never had the chance to interview his daughter.[24] Judith is buried, presumably, in Holy Trinity churchyard, her grave lost to time like that of her twin Hamnet, who had died so many years before.

HAMNET SHAKESPEARE (1585–1596)

The saddest part of the story of Hamnet Shakespeare is that he was so important to the family, yet he had so little time, and left us with so little known of him. One wanders the cemetery of Holy Trinity Church, among the old, lichen-covered, tilting gravestones, looking in vain for where Shakespeare's only son was buried. No one knows.

The boy was baptized with his twin sister, Judith, at Holy Trinity Church, Stratford, on February 2, 1585. The twins were christened by the new vicar, Richard Barton of Coventry, who was described in a Puritan publication as "a preacher, learned, zealous, and godly and fit for the ministry."[25] This would have pleased Anne Hathaway, if, as some suggest, she had Puritanical leanings (a conclusion based partly on the choice of the unusual old testament name Susanna for the Shakespeare's first child). The twins were named for Shakespeare's close boyhood friend, Hamnet Sadler, and his wife, Judith; and one assumes the Sadlers were their godparents.

As William Shakespeare spent most of his time in London, John Shakespeare and his unmarried sons, Gilbert and Richard, must have been strong father figures for the boy. Hamnet would have been especially treasured by the whole family as the only child who would carry the Shakespeare name into the next generation. But this hope was not to be fulfilled.

On July 22nd, 1596, a summer outbreak of plague in London forced a closing of all the theatres. Ian Wilson, in *Shakespeare, the Evidence*, conjectures that this plague might have traveled to Stratford and struck Hamnet Shakespeare (though one would expect if that were the case there would be clearer records of a plague outbreak in Stratford that summer).[26] Whatever caused Hamnet's death, the next mention of the Shakespeares in Stratford after the baptism of the twins, is the noting in the church records of Hamnet's burial on August 11, 1596.

The grief of the family must have been catastrophic.

Samuel Shoenbaum feels it reasonable to suppose Shakespeare was in Stratford for his son's burial. But according to Marchette Chute, as a result of the closing of the theatres, Shakespeare's company had left London to go on tour, and on the 11th of August they were playing at a town in Kent, forty-seven miles from

London.[27] Shakespeare was then a valuable member of the acting company so it seems most likely he was needed on the company tour. If Hamnet's illness were a long one, his father might have been notified in time for him to get home; but there was no way to get word quickly to an actor on tour, and it seems more probable that William Shakespeare did not hear about his loss until after Hamnet's burial.

His friend and colleague Ben Jonson lost two sons as children and wrote directly and movingly of his grief.

> Farewell, thou child of my right hand, and joy;
> My sin was too much hope of thee, loved boy . . .
> Rest in peace: and asked, say: "Here doth lie
> Ben Jonson his best piece of poetry.[28]
> > Ben Jonson, *On My First Son*

Shakespeare, ever personally discreet, never wrote of his son's death. And yet some scholars date the writing of *King John* to 1596 largely because the agony felt by Constance for the loss of her child is so devastating, so intense, that one feels instinctively it must express Shakespeare's own feelings on the death of his son:

> Death, death. O amiable lovely death . . .
> Arise forth from the couch of lasting night
> Thou hate and terror to prosperity,
> And I will kiss thy detestable bones . . .
> > Misery's love,
> O, come to me! . . .
>
> There was not such a gracious creature born:
> But now will canker-sorrow eat my bud
> And chase the native beauty from his cheek,
> And he will look as hollow as a ghost,
> And so he'll die; and rising so again,
> When I shall meet him in the court of heaven
> I shall not know him: therefore never, never
> Must I behold my pretty Arthur more.
> > *King John*, act 3, scene 4

Yet the speeches of Constance are no proof for the dating of *King John*: Shakespeare's genius is such that, experience aside, in his imagination he felt and expressed the grief—and the joys—of the world. Stylistically, *King John* would seem to have been written earlier in the 1590s. How ironic, if Constance had been written before the death of Hamnet; how prescient would seem her words as he read them later, and how painful as he heard them performed in the months and years after he had lost his own son.

Shakespeare's works follow many patterns, one of which is the repeated explorations of a theme or idea, as if the first expression was not enough. We see this in the sonnets; the first seventeen, being a response to a probable commission, have the theme set out for him: the need of a young man to marry and reproduce, and Shakespeare's repeated treatment of the idea is virtuosic. But sonnets 29 and 30 exemplify the need to explore more than once the idea of friendship and love exceeding all other values.

Among the plays, *The Taming of the Shrew* and *Love's Labour's Lost* explore ideas, relationships, and character traits to which Shakespeare returns with greater maturity in *Much Ado About Nothing*; Richard III reappears, deepened and more subtle, in Iago; Antonio, the left out man in *The Merchant of Venice* reappears as Jaques in *As You Like It* and is named Antonio again in *Twelfth Night*. And if Constance explores for the grief of losing a child, she is re-presenting a grief earlier and more baldly expressed by the three queens in *Richard III*.

More importantly, in his grief over the loss of his son, and his search for a world view in which to give it value, Shakespeare moves from the experience of a single character to the structure of an entire play to find meaning for his sorrow. The great play in response to Hamnet's death is not *King John*, not even *Hamlet*, but *Twelfth Night*. It has often been noted that the climactic scene in *Twelfth Night* is not between lovers, as in every other of Shakespeare's comedies, but the recognition scene between a brother and sister, each of whom had thought the other dead. Recognition and resurrection are the twin ideas that lift the heart at the end of *Twelfth Night*. What he could not do in life, bring back his son, Shakespeare could do in the theatre. What he could not give his little girl, Judith, in actuality, he could give her on the stage: her brother alive again.

After *Twelfth Night* Shakespeare would explore the dark night of the soul in his great tragedies. He would look without flinching into the void, and contemplate with tragic apprehension the meaninglessness of life. But his explorations of the human experience did not stop there. His final plays return to the theme he explored so deeply in *Twelfth Night*, they all ritualize for us recognition, renewal, redemption, and resurrection.

9
Shakespeare's Sons-in-Law

I will add
Unto their losses twenty thousand crowns –
Another dowry to another daughter,
For she is changed, as she had never been.
The Taming of the Shrew, act 5, scene 2

John Hall (1575–1635)
Thomas Quiney (1589–c.1662)

JOHN HALL (1575–1635)

John Hall married Susanna Shakespeare in Holy Trinity Church, Stratford-upon-Avon, June 5, 1607.[1] It was a wedding to celebrate, a marriage of equals, and one that gave William Shakespeare a son-in-law who was also a close friend—so much so that in his will Shakespeare made John and Susanna Hall his executors and left them the bulk of his estate.

Not a native of Stratford, John Hall arrived in the town about 1600. Twenty-five years before, John Shakespeare had bought his Henley Street property from an Edmund and Emma Hall and certainly these could be relatives, though the connection has not been proved. Whatever brought him to the market town by the Avon, John Hall at the young age of twenty-five set up a medical practice that rapidly became the most respected in the area. His house, the handsome and comfortable Hall's Croft, was an easy walk from Susanna Shakespeare's home at New Place.

His name was common in the English midlands, so John Hall's origins cannot be determined with certainty. But B. Roland Lewis, in *The Shakespeare Documents*, makes a persuasive case for John as the son of William Hall of Acton, Middlesex. Acton was a village on the road from London to Stratford-upon-Avon via Oxford. Eccles agrees with Lewis, but follows this William Hall to Carlton in Bedfordshire, where he claims Hall lived between 1569 and 1593 and where he fathered eleven children: Elizabeth, Susan, Sara (who would marry William Sheppard, a Leicester physician and graduate of Cambridge), Samuel, Dive, John, Frances (who married Michael Welles, the son of the Carlton rector), Martha, Mary, Damaris, and William.[2]

John was born in 1575, married Susanna Shakespeare in June of 1607, and lost his father to death in December of that year. William Hall left an extensive will that contains an intriguing hint about the nature of John Hall and his practice of medicine, and provides links that help establish his son John as the John Hall of Stratford.[3] Crucial is the fact that William Hall was a doctor, for though John Hall attended university his degrees were not in medicine.[4] Still he was the most esteemed physician in the Stratford area. Therefore he must have learned his art privately, and here we have a father who could have taught him. The fact that his sister Sara married a doctor magnified the opportunities John had to increase his knowledge of the medical practices of the time.

Within a year of their marriage John and Susanna Shakespeare Hall became parents to a little girl, their only child and the only grandchild Shakespeare knew. They named her Elizabeth. Most names for children at the time had family connections, and as Elizabeth was not a traditional name within the Shakespeare/Hathaway clan, the Elizabeth mentioned in William Hall's will suggests another link between John Hall of Stratford and the Acton family.

In his will, William Hall leaves his son John all his books on "physicke" and also his library of books on "Astronomye" and "Astrologie" if he "do intende and purpose to laboure, studdye and endeavor in the sayed Arte." This paragraph tells us much about the medicine of the time. Often, it would seem, physicians treated patients not only with complexly compounded drugs, but also with attention to astrological and astronomical signs. Active in London at the same time John Hall was practicing in Stratford was a famous and successful doctor named Simon Forman. Forman left a confusing and disorganized array of papers: casebooks, an autobiography, a diary, and various notes on his life, which for centuries gathered dust in the Bodleian Library, Oxford. Resurrected by the researches of Dr. A. L. Rowse in the late twentieth century, these papers became the basis for a biography of Forman by Judith Cook.[5] Simon Forman's papers carry fascinating and detailed information about his clients (including Emilia Lanier whom Rowse believes to be Shakespeare's Dark Lady and Maria Mountjoy, in whose household Shakespeare lived in London for a number of years) in large measure because he included astrological analyses as a crucial part of his treatment. Before he prescribed or diagnosed Forman cast and recorded a detailed horoscope of each patient so that his physical treatments could be coordinated with astronomical and astrological information. Most doctors of the age, it would seem, did this. Evidently William Hall is included in this number, as witness his library of books on the topic. But

John Hall shows no signs of incorporating astrology in his work. Perhaps he was of a rigorously scientific bent and saw no value in what he might have deemed a superstitious approach to physical well-being. His own casebooks, and his father's doubt as to whether John intended to study astronomy and astrology, suggest in John Hall's practice a purely physical approach to healing.

He did give credence to the Elizabethan belief that the human body was dominated by four "humours," and that an imbalance in the humours led to specific diseases. Judith Cook (29) gives an example in stating that when confronted with patients with consumption "Dr. John Hall, for instance, prescribed different remedies and treatments for people depending on their humours. For one woman it was a variety of spices and drugs in whine including 'galangal' an aromatic bitter root from China, accompanied by an enema to relieve the body of ill humours and a syrup, the main ingredients of which were cinnamon bark and *Calamus aromaticus*, the dried root of the flag iris. For a young girl in whom the disease was further advanced, he prescribed a ptysan (tisane) made from barley, a restorative cordial composed of purslane and borage, and an enema of cooling herbs. He also recommended for her a light diet of snails, frogs, and river crabs, all of a 'cooling nature.'" Hall left a tantalizing glimpse of Shakespearean family life in the records of his treatments for his wife, Susanna, and his daughter, Elizabeth. He tells us how when Susanna was "tormented with the Cholick" he gave her an enema of flowers, and then "I appointed to inject a Pint of Sack made hot. This brought forth a good deal of Wind, and freed her from all Pain"—and so "Mrs. Hall of Stratford, my Wife was cured."[6] Then, in 1624 he records that on January 5 his daughter Elizabeth suffered from "tortura oris," or convulsions of the mouth, and ophthalmia (severe inflammation of the eye). Her father cured her of this first attack, but in April she made a trip to London and when she returned, on April 22, she had a bad cold and the "tortura oris" returned on the other side of her face. Again "by the blessing of God," reports Hall, "she was also cured in sixteen days." In May she had an erratic fever: "Sometimes she was hot, and by-and-by sweating, again cold, all in the space of half-an-hour." Her father's treatment again healed her; "the symptoms remitted daily till she was well; thus was she delivered from death and deadly diseases, and was well for many years."[7]

John Hall rode miles to treat many of the wealthy, aristocratic families in the area, including the Earl and Countess of Northampton who lived over forty miles away at Ludlow Castle; Dr. Thornbery, the Bishop of Worcester; and Michael Drayton, Warwickshire's other great poet of the time who often visited his close friends the Rainsfords two miles from Stratford in Clifford Chambers.[8] Eccles quotes a Lady Tyrrell writing to a friend concerning her husband's choice of a doctor: "I am very glad to hear: that Mr. halle: Is the mann: of hom: Sr Thomas Tempell hath made choice of: In regard I kno by experience: that hee is most excellent In that arte." And her husband added to the letter, concerning Lady Tyrrell's husband: "Gett mr hale speedily to him."[9] Hall also treated, and lists by name, middle class merchants and local artisans, laborers and farmers, a whole cross-section of Stratford's population. He had an apothecary named Court and lists his wife, Mrs. Grace Court, as one of his patients. Though he was a committed Puritan he responded to the call of Catholics and Protestants alike. Among the famous patients he treated in the area, John Hall undoubtedly tended William Shakespeare, his father-in-law and his friend, in his last illness. Unfortunately the casebooks that survive begin in 1617, the year after Shakespeare's death, and so the nature of the poet's final illness and cause of death remain a mystery.

Leaders of Stratford society were pressured to take on the civic responsibility of serving on the corporation council. Though his grandfather had been mayor of Bedford[10] John Hall (like William Shakespeare whose father had also been civic-minded) had no interest in local town government. Elected a burgess in 1617 and in 1623 Hall was at first excused from meetings because of the pressure of his practice. Elected again in 1632, he was fined at this point rather than excused for not attending meetings. In October 1633 the other councilors expelled him from the corporation for "breach of orders, sundry other misdemeanours, and for his continual disturbances at our Halles."[11]

Hall's disinterest in the civic corporation council was countered by his service to the church. The disturbances alluded to above may have resulted from John Hall's passionate support of the current vicar, Thomas Wilson. The corporation had complained about Wilson to the bishop, and John Hall was at that time the vicar's warden and had joined with the vicar in an action in Chancery against the town, claiming that he had sold tithes "for a hundred pounds less than their worth so that the town might increase the vicar's salary."[12]

His repeated references to the power of God as the true healer mark Hall as a deeply religious man, of partisan beliefs very different from the nondogmatic spiritual instincts of his father-in-law. While he cared for people of all denominations he was himself a committed Puritan who wrote the following prayer after surviving a critical illness:

> Thou, O Lord, which hast the power of life and death and drawest from the gates of death, I confess without any art of counsel of man, but only from thy goodness and clemency, thou hast saved me from the bitter and deadly symptoms of a deadly fever, beyond the expectation of all about me, restoring me, as it were, form the very jaws of death to former health, for which I praise thy name, O most Mercifull God, and Father of our Lord Jesus Christ praying thee to give me a most thankful heart for this great favor for which I have cause to admire thee.[13]

In 1614 John Hall traveled to London with William Shakespeare. One can't help but wonder if on this journey the noted Puritan doctor went to the theatre with his famous father-in-law to witness one or another of Shakespeare's plays, or to meet any of his great theatrical colleagues. One notes as well that in Shakespeare's plays from 1606 onward doctors appear in several plays and are treated with respect: the doctors in *Macbeth* and *King Lear*, and particularly the doctor, Cerimon, in *Pericles* are all sympathetic portraits perhaps influenced by Shakespeare's observations of his son-in-law.

Hall's next trip to London would be just two years later, this time alone and burdened with the sad responsibility of proving the poet's will. In Stratford, after Shakespeare's death in 1616, the Halls moved into New Place from which Hall continued to practice medicine. Furthermore, it would seem John Hall took William Shakespeare's place as the head of the family, as he became a trustee for Thomas Quiney (his brother-in-law, married to Judith Shakespeare) when Quiney's business ran into difficulty.

John Hall's service to the church included being named as church warden in 1628, and being elected as a sidesman the following year, at which time he gave a new and expensive pulpit to the church. In 1633 his long friendship with the Vicar, Thomas Wilson (vicar 1619–1640) was acknowledged when he was named the Vicar's warden.

The doctor died suddenly at the age of sixty in 1635. He had no time to call a lawyer to draft his will; he dictated it, perhaps to the local Puritan curate from the church, Simon Trappe, who was one of the witnesses. The document is very brief and everything about it breathes haste. In it he says:

> I give unto my wife my house in London
> I give unto my Daughter Nash my house in Acton
> I give unto my Daughter Nash my Meadow.
> I give my goods and moneys unto my wife and my Daughter Nash to
>   be equally divided between them
> Concerning my study of Books I leave them (said he) to you my son Nash to
>   dispose of them as you see good.
> As for my manuscripts I would have given them unto Master Boles
>   if he had been here but forasmuch as he is not here present you may
>   (son Nash) burn them or else do with them what you please.
> Witnessed hereunto: Tho. Nashe
>   Simon Trappe[14]

John Hall was buried in Trinity Church near the grave of William Shakespeare. On his tombstone he is honored with the description: "medicus peritissimus."

Odd as it may seem to us, this rural physician was as famous in the area, or perhaps more so, than the writer we revere. After John Hall's death, a doctor named James Cooke, who was surgeon to a Lord Brooke in the Civil War and who haled from Warwickshire, came to call on Mrs. Hall because her husband had been so renowned, and because he had been known to have left books behind intended for publication. Cooke bought these casebooks from Susanna Hall and translated parts of some, which were published in 1657 as Hall's *Select Observations on English Bodies*.[15]

Both William Shakespeare and John Hall came from middle class rural families of the midlands; their fathers had striven to rise in the world: William Hall as a doctor, John Shakespeare as an artisan and public servant. Both their sons had great gifts plus high ambition, and their achievements were recognized and honored in their life-times. Both treasured the woman who united them, Susanna.

They became companions in life and they lie near one another in death: William Shakespeare and his doctor son-in-law, John Hall.

THOMAS QUINEY (1589–C. 1662)

Alas, Thomas Quiney was in many ways the opposite of John Hall. He was a native Stratfordian and his father, Richard, was a schoolmate and friend of William Shakespeare. With the marriage of Thomas Quiney, in February of 1616, to Shakespeare's daughter, Judith, the two families—friends for over sixty years— became related. But Thomas Quiney was a bit of a ne'er-do-well, and of all the Quineys he was probably the last William Shakespeare would have wanted to welcome into his immediate family.

A friendship between Thomas's grandfather Adrian Quiney and Judith's grand-father John Shakespeare began shortly after the latter settled in Stratford around 1550. The connection was documented in 1552 when the two young men were each fined for keeping a muck heap in front of their houses; surely their minds at this youthful beginning of their lives were far from contemplating a marriage between grandchildren as yet undreamt of and unborn. The relationship between the two families reaches even further, both backwards and forwards, when we note that from 1532 to 1533 Thomas's grandfather (also Adrian) lived in New Place, the house William Shakespeare would buy, and Judith Shakespeare would occupy, some sixty-five years later.[16]

The Quineys were successful Stratford mercers (dealers in textiles and other merchandise)[17] and Thomas Quiney's ancestors had been members of the Stratford guild for four generations. After Stratford was given its charter in 1553, Thomas Quiney and Judith Shakesepeare's grandfather both became involved in town politics; Adrian Quiney was in fact the first to be named bailiff under the new corporation charter, while John Shakespeare became a burgess and, then, in 1565, an aldermen, before he, like Adrian, rose to be bailiff. Each was a distinguished public servant, though Mark Eccles says admiringly of John Shakespeare: "No one else looked after town business for so many years."[18]

Thomas Quiney's grandfather, Adrian, lived on High Street near the intersection with Wood. He was married twice and had three children: one of whom was Richard, who would become the friend of William Shakespeare and the father of Thomas. Another child was a daughter, Elizabeth, who married Davy Jones. Jones produced a Whitsunday pageant in Stratford in 1583, the only locally produced theatre event on record in the Stratford of Shakespeare's time and it is hard to believe William Shakespeare did not take some part in its performance. He seems, in fact, to remember the experience when, a decade later, he has Julia, in *Two Gentlemen of Verona*, talk of "Pentecost, / When all our pageants of delight were played,"[19] and toward the end of his career again in *The Winter's Tale* when Perdita says: "come, take your flowers; / Methinks I play as I have seen them do / In Whitson pastorals."[20] Elizabeth Quiney Jones died in 1579 and Davy Jones' second wife was a Frances Hathaway; though one is tempted to connect her with the Hathaway family of Shakespeare's wife, the relationship is hard to document clearly.

Though Thomas's father Richard was six or eight years older than Judith's father William Shakespeare, the men were friends from their childhood until Richard Quiney's death in 1602. Deeply involved in town politics like his father, Richard Quiney has the distinction of being the only correspondent of William Shakespeare's from whom we have a letter addressed to the poet. The letter was written in 1598 and asked the now successful playwright, theatre manager, and actor (addressed as "Dear Countryman") for a loan to cover debts Quiney had incurred going back and forth to London on town business. As the letter was found later in the Quiney papers it would seem it was written and addressed to William Shakespeare but never reached its destination.

Richard Quiney married a woman named Elizabeth (Bess) and they had eleven children, of whom nine survived infancy and of whom Thomas was the second surviving son.[21] Edgar Fripp points out that of the eleven there were two Williams, one Mary, one John, and one Anne—all Shakespeare family names, reemphasizing the close relationship between the two families. After years as a successful merchant and public servant, Richard was wounded in a town riot in early May, 1602, and died before the month was out, the only Stratford bailiff to die while in office.[22] Thomas was thirteen years old when his father died. His mother, Bess, took to running a tavern to support her nine children. A document dated December 4, 1602, reveals Bess taking charge of her own life after the death of Richard and also shows an early closeness between Judith Shakespeare and her future mother-in-law. On that day Thomas Greene (Shakespeare's cousin then living with Anne Hathaway Shakespeare and her two daughters at New Place), his wife, Lettice, and seventeen-year-old Judith Shakespeare signed as witnesses to a deed made by Elizabeth Quiney and her oldest son, sixteen-year-old Adrian.[23]

Following the lead of his tavern-keeping mother, Thomas became a vintner and, in 1611, when he was twenty-two years old, he moved into a home he had leased on High Street a few doors from Wood Street.[24] Judith Shakespeare and Thomas Quiney knew each other their entire lives, but judging from their marriage date, romance between the two did not flower until Judith was thirty-one and Thomas twenty-seven.

Their wedding was recorded at Holy Trinity Church, Stratford, on February 10, 1616. The date indicates they were married during Lent, a forbidden season requiring that they get a special license from the Bishop of Worcester (as Shakespeare was compelled to do for his hasty marriage to Anne Hathaway). But Judith and Thomas had not received such a license and were summoned to the Worcester consistory court twice to answer for their neglect—they ignored both summons and for this defiance they were excommunicated on March 12.

Worse, barely a month after Judith's wedding, on March 15, a woman named Margaret Wheeler and her illegitimate child were buried from Holy Trinity Church. Thomas Quiney was accused of fathering the child and on March 25 he was brought to trial at Holy Trinity's ecclesiastical court and charged with carnal copulation.

Thomas was found guilty and sentenced to appear in church for three weeks in succession wearing only the white sheet of a penitent. Though the penance was commuted to a single act of contrition in a church in Bishopton outside Stratford, plus a five-shilling fine, the news that Thomas had been fornicating with another woman at the time he was courting Judith Shakespeare would have been known throughout Stratford.

The most famous of all the Shakespeare documents—the will—reveals Shakespeare's attitude to the marriage between Thomas Quiney and Judith. Edgar Fripp attributes even the making of Shakespeare's first will in January, 1616, to Judith's and Thomas's decision to wed.[25] But their wedding and the scandal of Margaret Wheeler surely prompted the revision in March. In both the first draft and the revision, Susanna, the older daughter, was named the primary legatee, and she and her husband, the executors. Judith was left 150 pounds, with another 150 to come "if she, or any issue of her body be living at the end of three years. . . . Provided that if such husband as she shall at the end of the said three years be married unto or attain after do sufficiently assure unto her . . . lands answerable to the portion by this my will given . . . then my will is that the said 150 pounds shall be paid to such husband as shall make such assurance to his own use." Ian Wilson, in *Shakespeare the Evidence* (389), points out how cold the reference sounds, calling Thomas Quiney "such husband" when Shakespeare referred warmly elsewhere in the will to Susanna's husband as both "son-in-law" and "John Hall" by name. But Quiney was still delinquent in the matter of assuring his wife lands to the value required, so Shakespeare, Fripp says, "revised his will, with the object of ensuring Judith an immediate income at his death and future prospects without admitting her husband to more than a conditional benefit."[26]

Judith's father did not have long to endure Thomas Quiney, a scofflaw, an excommunicant, and a fornicator as a member of his family. In less than five weeks after revising his will, William Shakespeare died. He never knew his grandchildren from this marriage. Little Shakespeare Quiney, whose name seems to represent Judith's eagerness to cement the union of both families and to honor her father's memory, was born in November of 1616 and died the following May. In 1618 the Quineys had a second son, Richard, and a third, Thomas, in 1620. Both these boys died the same year, 1639, perhaps from one of the frequent infections that plagued the town.

In July 1616, Thomas Quiney established both his winery and tobacco shop in "The Cage" on the corner of Bridge Street and High Street where a plaque still marks the building. One could claim he improved somewhat with age. Though he was never made an alderman, following the pattern of public service established by his grandfather and his father, he was chosen burgess and named a constable in 1617, and became chamberlain of Stratford, responsible for the city accounts, from 1621 to 1623. His "accompt," presented January 9, 1624, was in his own handwriting and included a French motto, written with pride but filled with senseless grammatical errors.[27] The account was at first voted incorrect and only subsequently approved, indicating Thomas Quiney was no more a meticulous man of business than he was a careful linguist.[28] In or around 1630 Quiney was fined for swearing and for permitting tippling; some wine he had bought in Bristol prompted a lawsuit; and after trying to sell his lease of "The Cage," he turned it over to a trust to benefit his wife and sons. The trustees were John Hall (Shakespeare's good son-in-law), Thomas Nash, and Richard Watts; finally, in 1652, the lease was taken over by Thomas's brother Richard who had become a successful London grocer.

Thomas was still alive in 1655 when Richard left him an allowance of twelve pounds a year for income and five more for his burial.[29] There is no record of his death, but, noting a gap in the Trinity Church records in 1662 and 1663, Mark Eccles suggests Thomas Quiney may have died at that time. Judith lived until 1661/2, when she died at age seventy-seven. Except for his granddaughter Elizabeth, who would die childless nine years later, she was the last of Shakespeare's immediate family.[30]

10

Shakespeare's Grandchildren

This oracle of comfort has so pleased me
That when I am in heaven I shall desire
To see what this child does, and praise my Maker.
Henry VIII, act 5, scene 5

Elizabeth Hall: Granddaughter (1608–1670)
Thomas Nash: Elizabeth Hall's First Husband (1593–1647)
John Bernard: Elizabeth Hall's Second Husband (1604–1674)

Shakespeare, Richard, and Thomas Quiney: Grandsons

ELIZABETH HALL NASH BARNARD (1608–1670)

Elizabeth Hall was christened in Holy Trinity Church, Stratford, on February 21, 1608. The daughter of Dr. John Hall and Shakespeare's favored daughter, Susanna, Elizabeth was three years old when her grandfather came home to Stratford to live and just eight when he died. One imagines the joys she gave him as he watched her grow from the enchanting ages of three to eight and wonders what memories she carried into adulthood about her famous grandfather.

Eight years following William Shakespeare's death, an entry in Elizabeth's father's medical books gives us a hint about a possible relationship between Shakespeare's family in Stratford and his friends and work in London. As with other incidents in Shakespeare's biography, a small group of facts inspires a conjecture that becomes one of the threads leading us through the maze of his life.

First, because of John Hall's records, we know that Elizabeth made a trip to London in 1624 (he reports that she came down with a bad cold on her return and details the treatment he gave her).[1] This was a trip that took three days of hard riding each way, one frequently made by the male leaders of the town who had business in the capital, but not as often made by women.[2] So one wonders what took Elizabeth to London at the young age of sixteen?[3] Too young to travel on business, she must have gone for pleasure. But what were the circumstances of the trip? I suggest a connection between this trip and the appearance of Shakespeare's acting company in Stratford, which had occurred some eighteen months before.

In 1622 the King's Men, Shakespeare's troupe, made their only stop on record in the poet's hometown. The monument to Shakespeare had just been installed in Holy Trinity Church, and one infers that his friends, John Hemings and Henry Condell, who were even then at work editing the plays for the First Folio, might have wanted to view the sculpture of their friend (made by an acquaintance from London) and perhaps meet the wife and daughters of their beloved colleague. Does it not seem likely the two leaders of the company, both of whom were happily married with large families in London, would offer to return any hospitality shown them with an invitation to Shakespeare's relatives to visit them?

This is admittedly a conjecture. The next *fact* is that not long after this visit Anne Hathaway Shakespeare died, her burial duly recorded in the Trinity Church records of August 8, 1623. The epitaph on her tomb shows the affection her daughter Susanna felt for her. But the death of her elderly mother, for whom she felt love and consequently responsibility, freed Susanna to take her daughter on a trip to London. It freed her as well from any uneasiness about displeasing her mother by visiting colleagues of her father's, workers in the theatre.

With no way of knowing Anne Hathaway's attitude toward her husband's work, we observe that through her life she seems to have remained separate from it. If one reads autobiography into the content of Shakespeare's *Sonnets*, an emotionally traumatic and sexually tormented experience was part of Shakespeare's life in the city—not an experience to share with a provincial wife, and yet not one he found possible (at least for a time) to control. It's hard to imagine that going to London to visit William Shakespeare's colleagues, the men who represented the hold city life and the theatre had over her husband, would have pleased Anne Hathaway. Such a trip, however, would likely have seemed thrilling to her sixteen-year-old granddaughter, and highly interesting to the girl's mother, Susanna, who demonstrated herself throughout her life to be intelligent, eager, active—a woman with many of the qualities of her cosmopolitan father.

Two years after her return from the trip to London, on April 22, 1626, Elizabeth Hall married Thomas Nash, the son of her grandfather's friend Anthony Nash. She was eighteen years old, a very young age for a middle-class woman to be married at the time, and he was thirty-two, above average age for a man. The church record reads: Mr. Thomas Nash to Mrs. Elizabeth Hall, the titles, according to Lewis, being important honorifics designating they came from excellent families of the gentry.[4] As is true now, the fourteen-year age difference was unusual but not unheard of. The fact that their marriage of twenty-one years was childless, causes one to wonder about the limited fertility of this line of Shakespeare's women. His wife, Anne Hathaway, in an age of very large families, had borne only three children; Anne's daughter, Susanna, had only one; and Susanna's daughter, Elizabeth, none at all.

According to the official guide to The Shakespeare Houses,[5] the newly married Nashes did not live in Nash House, but next door at New Place with their in-laws the Halls, continuing a long tradition of Shakespeare family members living together in extended groups. New research shows that the timbers in Hall's Croft date to 1613,[6] meaning that for some time Elizabeth's parents, Susanna and John Hall probably also lived with the Shakespeares at New Place, awaiting the building of their new house. Assuming the Halls took possession of their own house in 1613 they occupied it only three years, for when William Shakespeare died in 1616 the Halls moved back to New Place to live with the widowed Anne Hathaway. They stayed there for the rest of all of their lives.

In 1635 Elizabeth's father died very suddenly. His dictated will reads as if executed in breathless haste. In it he leaves to Elizabeth ("my Daughter Nash") a house Hall owned in Acton, his meadow, and half his goods and money (the other half to go to his wife). He died soon after and was buried the next day, the haste suggesting that his death came from a contagious disease. John Hall's unexpected death and quick burial must have left his wife and daughter in a state of shock. Susanna Hall would have been comforted by the presence of her daughter and son-in-law in the house with her.

Four years later another tragedy came. In 1639 Elizabeth's cousins, the two surviving sons of Judith Shakespeare, died. Richard was only twenty-one and his brother, Thomas, just nineteen; it is surmised one of the virulent infections common at the time took them both. With their death and because they left no issue, the part of Shakespeare's estate that had originally been destined for them came, following the dictates of Shakespeare's will, to Elizabeth. This created a legal dispute following the death of Thomas Nash when his brother Edward claimed rights to the property, including New Place. Elizabeth and her mother successfully contested this claim, showing both these generations of Shakespeare's women, daughter and granddaughter, to be determined, assertive, and resourceful (as his mother had a been and as are so many of the women characters in his plays).[7]

The new head of the household, Thomas Nash, was a royalist during the Civil War. We are reminded of the status the Shakespeare family had attained when, from July eleventh to thirteenth of 1643, Queen Henrietta Maria visited Stratford on her way to join her husband Charles I. She brought with her over 2,000 infantrymen, 1,000 cavalry, and 100 wagons to meet Prince Rupert there: according to Halliwell-Phillips, "The most stirring event of the kind the ancient town has ever witnessed."[8] For those three days the Queen stayed at the Shakespeare/Hall home, New Place.

Thomas Nash died in 1647, and two years later Elizabeth made a second marriage (June 5, 1649), this time to a widower, John Barnard, from the town of Abington in Northamptonshire. John Barnard's wife had died in 1641, three weeks after the birth of their eighth child. Five half-grown children survived to whom

Elizabeth became stepmother.[9] She had barely settled into her newly married life when, a month later (July 16, 1649), her mother died. As her mother had done for her grandmother, Elizabeth wrote (we would suppose) the admiring and affectionate tribute for her mother's grave, a tradition connecting three generations of Shakespeare's women. The epitaphs emphasize their mutual affection and individual strength, sensitivity, and intelligence.[10]

Like Elizabeth's first husband, John Barnard had supported the King in the Civil War, and after the restoration of Charles II he was created a Baronet (November 25, 1661) making his wife Lady Barnard. How this elevation in rank would have pleased her great-grandfather, John Shakespeare, the son of the tenant farmer who came to Stratford determined to improve his family's lot, and her grandfather the actor/playwright who helped his father reestablish the family fortune and gain a coat of arms. But so capricious is life that less than three months later Elizabeth received the news that her aunt Judith, her mother's sister and the last of William Shakespeare's children, had died. Though possessed of a new husband and stepchildren Lady Elizabeth Barnard was bereft of original family: no aunts or uncles, no parents, no children, no siblings, she was the last of William Shakespeare's immediate family. Only her cousin Thomas Hart, the son of Shakespeare's sister (Elizabeth's great aunt Joan), would survive to carry on that branch of the family, and some cousins to continue the Hathaway side. She stayed connected to these last cousins. When it came her time to die and to divest herself of the last of William Shakespeare's belongings she left cousins on both sides bequests in her will. Included were Judith, Joane, and Susanna, daughters of her cousin Thomas Hathaway; and to her cousin Thomas Hart, grandson of her Aunt Joan, the property on Henley Street, now known as the Birthplace, half of which was then the Hart's dwelling, the other half an inn called the "Maydenhead."[11] In disposing of New Place she requested it be sold and the money used for the legacies she dictated; her "loving cousin Edward Nash" was to be given the right to the first offer on the house, indicating that the difficulties in contesting Thomas Nash's will (that had left the property to Edward) had been smoothed over with time.

Elizabeth's first marriage had settled her not only in Stratford, but perhaps for a time in New Place with her parents and in Nash House next door. Her second marriage, however, took her some distance from the town of her birth to the manor house of Abington, fronting on the road from Northampton to Cambridge.[12] With this move the family was broken by space as well as by death and time. Except for Shakespeare's brother Edmund, Elizabeth Hall Nash Barnard was the only one of Shakespeare's immediate family whose final resting place was outside Stratford. And so with her the diaspora of the family from Stratford begins.

THOMAS NASH (1593–1647): SHAKESPEARE'S GRANDSON-IN-LAW

Though William Shakespeare did not live to see his granddaughter married, he knew well the man who was to marry her: Thomas Nash. Thomas was the oldest son of his good friend Anthony Nash, and nephew to his equally good friend John Nash,

Anthony's brother.[13] The family was from Old Stratford and nearby Welcombe, and they came to own the house next door to Shakespeare's grand residence, New Place. Thomas Nash was nearly twenty-three years old when Shakespeare died, and the poet would have seen him grow and develop from infancy to adulthood.

It is a pity Shakespeare never knew of his granddaughter's marriage, for Thomas Nash was an admirable match for young Elizabeth Hall. A gentleman born, he never needed to work for his living. Though at the time he was years older than some of the students matriculating with him, at the age of twenty three he started attending law school at Lincoln's Inn, perhaps recognizing the usefulness of a law background for the management of the inheritance that would be his. When his father died in 1622, Thomas Nash inherited two houses, a piece of land, the Bear Inn on Bridge Street, and a good deal of money.

When his father-in-law died suddenly in 1635 we have a vivid and unexpected snapshot of Thomas Nash and the Shakespeare family. John Hall dictated his will and Thomas Nash was a witness and a legatee. After bequests to his wife and daughter, John Hall's will says: "Concerning my study of Books I leave them (said he) to you my son Nash to dispose of them as you see good. As for my manuscripts I would have given them unto Master Boles if he had been here but for as much as he is not here present you may (son Nash) burn them or else do with them what you please." The "study of books" would have included what remained of Shakespeare's own library. The direct address ["you may (son Nash)"] conjures an image of Nash beside the dying Hall, the scribe writing quickly, with Hall so near death that "do with them what you please" suggests an inability to say more. The words set down (words—Shakespeare's own medium) paint a portrait as vivid as an artist could have done with paints and canvas. When John Hall was buried the next day Thomas Nash, who had been at his side at death and who had witnessed his will, became the head of the family. As such he made certain assumptions. One was that what belonged to his wife was his to dispose of.

During the Civil War that convulsed the country at this time, Thomas Nash was a royalist. When funds were needed for the King's cause (1642) Thomas Nash's contribution as recorded in nearby Warwick totaled "plate or money" worth a hundred pounds, by far the largest amount from any other local donor.[14] Perhaps it was in acknowledgement of this donation that Queen Henrietta Maria made New Place her residence for three days the following year.

Sometime after 1639 when the two sons of Judith Shakespeare died Thomas Nash made a will. In an indenture, dated 1642, Nash speaks of New Place as being in his own occupation; and in a document dated March 14, 1646, he alludes to "my mother-in-law Mrs. Hall who lives with me." In his will he also treated Elizabeth's property as his own. One supposes he expected to outlive them both.

But when Thomas Nash died, in 1647, it was a shock to his young widow and his mother-in-law that in his will he presumed to leave New Place "together with all and singular howses, outhowses, barnes, stables, orchards, gardens, etc, esteemed or enjoyed as thereto belonging . . . also fower yards of arable land meadowe and pasture . . . in old Stratford . . . " to his brother Edward.

This was not tolerable. On the basis of William Shakespeare's last testament Elizabeth and her mother contested the will of Thomas Nash. They won their case, for following William Shakespeare's will of 1616, "an indenture confirmed the Shakespeare family estate to Elizabeth Hall-Nash, his wife, and him for life, subject to the life interest of Susanna Hall." The women recovered the use of New Place for their lives and the ownership of it and the other properties for their heirs forever.[15]

Thomas Nash was buried in Holy Trinity Church, in the chancel beside Shakespeare, his tombstone reading: "Heere resteth ye body of Thomas Nashe Exq. He mar. Elizabeth, the daug. and Heire of John Halle, gent. He died Aprill 4, A. 1647. Aged 53."[16]

JOHN BARNARD (1604–1674): ELIZABETH HALL'S SECOND HUSBAND

Elizabeth Hall Nash was left a widow not yet thirty-nine years old. Eighteen months after Thomas Nash's death she took the unusual step of marrying a man who lived some distance from Stratford. How did they meet? Mrs. Stopes reports that during the month of her husband's death, this now being in the midst of the Civil War, Elizabeth Nash had soldiers quartered at New Place.[17] John Barnard, from Northamptonshire, was an ardent royalist, knighted by Charles II in 1661 for "he had done the state some service during the Civil War."[18] The connection between John Barnard's war service, Thomas Nash's well-known support for the royalist cause, and the quartering of soldiers at New Place gives a possible reason for the meeting of John Barnard and Elizabeth Nash. Or perhaps John Barnard simply came through town as part of a general increase in mobility of the population during this time of war.

John Barnard was an eligible man: a gentleman of means whose family lived in Abington Manor near the church on the road to Cambridge. Perhaps of appeal to the childless Elizabeth were the five surviving children from John's first marriage. He had had four sons and four daughters, three of whom had died; and he had lost his first wife in 1641 shortly after the birth of their eighth child.[19] So John had been a widower some eight years before he met and married Elizabeth. In 1649 he was forty-three years old; she, thirty-nine. He was a wealthy gentleman, she an heiress of a good family. Following the oft-observed custom of Shakespeare's women (Mary and John Shakespeare who likely married in Aston Cantlow; William Shakespeare and Anne Hathaway who married probably in Temple Grafton; Joan Shakespeare and William Hart whose marriage was not registered in Stratford), they were married at Billesley, four miles from Stratford, for reasons no one knows. According to F.E. Halliday (61), the Barnards lived at New Place "for a time," not moving to Abington until 1653.

After another childless marriage of twenty-one years, Elizabeth died in February of 1670. She left no bequests to any Barnard family members in her will, nor did she mention her husband more than was legally necessary. She did not make him the executor of her will, giving the impression that the marriage was perhaps not a happy one, The Abington Parish Register reads: "Madam Elizabeth Bernard, wife of Sir John Bernard, Knight, was buried 17th Feb., 1669–70." No one noted that she was the last of the direct line of the poet William Shakespeare.

Sir John Barnard died four years later in 1674, and though there is a memorial slab in the Abington Church, beneath it there is a vault belonging to another family. The place of his burial is unknown.

SHAKESPEARE QUINEY (1616–1617), RICHARD QUINEY (1618–1639), AND THOMAS QUINEY (1620–1639)

As with William Shakespeare's own son, Hamnet, the saddest aspect of the lives of the grandchildren by his second daughter, Judith, is that there is so little known and so little to say. There were three Quiney sons. The first was born within a year of William Shakespeare's death, a child who lived less than a year. He was named Shakespeare and foreshadows the many descendents of Shakepeare's sister, Joan Hart, who, so that the connection to the family would not be lost among a welter of different last names, often chose to give Shakespeare as a first name to their male children.

The grief caused by the death of Judith and Thomas Quiney's first son was mitigated by the birth shortly after of a second, named Richard. Two years after Richard's birth came Thomas, evidently named for his father. The boys survived until 1639 the year Richard turned twenty-one and Thomas nineteen. Then, most likely because of one of the frequent infections that swept with deadly effect through communities at that time, both boys suddenly died.

The grief of the parents must have been extreme. They had no other children. When these boys died they left Elizabeth Hall Nash, their cousin, the last descendent of William Shakespeare.

Part III
Shakespeare's Extended Family

11

Shakespeare's Aunts

Rise up, good aunt . . . .good aunt, stand up.
Richard II, act 5, scene 3

Shakespeare's Arden Aunts
Agnes Arden Hewyns (John; then Mrs. Thomas Stringer) (d. by 1569)
Joan Arden Lambert (Edmund) (d. 1593)
Katherine Arden Edkins (or Etkyns, Thomas) (d. by 1578)
Margaret Arden Webbe (Alexander; then Mrs. Edward Cornwell) (d. 1614)
Elizabeth Arden Scarlett (or Skarlett) (d. 1581)
Joyce Arden (Dates Unknown)
Alice Arden (Dates Unknown)
Shakespeare's Shakespeare Aunt
Margaret Shakespeare (d. 1597)

As Mary Arden Shakespeare was one (the youngest) of Robert Arden's eight daughters, William Shakespeare had seven aunts on his mother's side of the family. In contrast, his father's only sibling Henry was married rather late in life to a woman named Margaret, William's only paternal aunt.

Information about the seven Arden aunts comes largely from their father's will and its consequences.[1] Provisions in this will played out over a generation or more, and on more than one occasion directly affected William Shakespeare and his parents.

William's eldest aunt, Agnes, died when he was about five; a second, Katherine, when he was fourteen. Of two others, Elizabeth and Joyce, so little is known that it is hard to trace with any certainty where or even how long they lived. Mrs. Stopes suggests that Joyce as an unmarried woman might have gone into service for the wealthy Ardens of Park Hall as "The registers there record the death of a 'Mistress Joyce Arden' in 1557,"[2] but no other mention helps to confirm or deny this speculation. A younger sister, Alice, seems to have lived at the farm in Wilmcote as indicated in her father's will. Alice was perhaps nearest to Mary in age, but the records suggest that Mary Arden Shakespeare remained closest to her sisters Joan and Margaret: she named daughters for them, and went to them and their families for help in the Shakespeare family's financial difficulties. Joan lived fifteen miles away in Barton-on-the-Heath, so they could not have seen each other easily, but Margaret was in the old Shakespeare family home in Snitterfield. Though neither lived in Stratford itself, because of their closeness to his mother, one might assume that of all his aunts Joan and Margaret were the two William Shakespeare knew the best.

AGNES (ANNE) ARDEN (DIED 1569)

Agnes, the oldest of the eight Arden sisters, married John Hewyns (Hewins) with whom she lived in nearby Bearley and by whom she had two children, Thomas and Margaret. Hewyns died sometime before 1550 as in that year Agnes married her second husband, Thomas Stringer. Mary Shakespeare was just a child when her oldest sister left the farm at Wilmcote to live with her first husband and she was still young when all of Agnes's children were born.

With her second husband Agnes Stringer had a daughter, Alice, who died an infant (1552), and two sons, John born in 1554 and Arden (1555/6).[3] She was settled some distance away from Stratford at the home of the Stringers, in Stockton, co. Salop,[4] but this distance did not put her entirely out of memory or reach of family. In February 1569, after Agnes had died, Thomas Stringer devised (bequeathed) to Alexander Webbe (husband to Agnes's sister Margaret) his share of the Snitterfield property that had been left to his wife by her father and that at her death had come to him. John Shakespeare was one of the witnesses to the indenture. Two years after Agnes's death John and Mary Shakespeare had a daughter they named Anne, most likely in memory of Mary's oldest sister. Seven years later (1578), Thomas Stringer along with his sons John and Arden sold all their rights to the inheritance of Robert Arden's widow (also named Agnes).[5]

His aunt Agnes died before William Shakespeare was five, and as she lived outside of Stratford, he would have heard talk of her, but not seen her often. As he grew he would have known his Hewyns/Stringer cousins but perhaps not closely as they were all much older than he. His uncle-by-marriage, Thomas Stringer, had property in Bearley and Snitterfield as well as in Stockton, so he was in and around the area even after his wife had died.

JOAN ARDEN (DIED 1593)

The second daughter, Joan, married Edmund Lambert sometime before 1550 and had one son, John. Joan must have been a favorite sister to Mary as Mary twice named daughters Joan (the first having died an infant). In addition the youngest Shakespeare son was named Edmund, undoubtedly for Joan's husband. The Lambert family lived in Barton-on-the-Heath, a small village about fifteen miles south of Stratford, close to the borders with Gloucestershire and Oxfordshire.

As the years passed the relationship between the Lamberts and the Shakespeares became difficult, with who knows what affect on the feelings of Mary for her sister Joan. The story is as follows.

Mary, apart from all her older sisters, had inherited from her father a property called Asbies. Mrs. Stopes makes three interesting observations concerning this property: "What I wish to suggest," she says, "is that Asbies was to the family the cherished heirloom, the visible link of connection between their branch and the historic family from which they sprang, and that some family jealousy may have arisen through its being absolutely left to the youngest child."

She goes on to say: "It is perfectly certain it was intended to be the inheritance of William Shakespeare, and that he was prepared to be a small farmer, for which reason he was not trained to any profession, nor apprenticed to any trade."[6]

She even goes so far as to assert: "Now it cannot be too carefully considered, that it was the private discussions and decisions about the return of Asbies, that were the deciding factors in John and William Shakespeare's life." (44)

What happened was that in 1578 John Shakespeare was experiencing such severe financial difficulties that he needed to raise a good deal of ready money. He and Mary made the agonizing decision to mortgage her Asbies property, and though Mrs. Stopes suggests they might have preferred to go to Robert Webbe, the son of her sister Margaret, for the loan, Robert had just bought his Aunt Agnes's Snitterfield share and was therefore short of money. So the Shakespeares went to Joan and Edmund Lambert. An indenture was drawn up for the sale of Asbies to the Lamberts for £40 with the proviso that if the money were to be repaid by Michaelmas Day, 1580, the sale would be void. Unfortunately this condition seems to have been a verbal understanding between the two parties and was not written into the contract.

Now probably because Mary had inherited Asbies she not been given shares in the Snitterfield property on the death of her father. However, when her older sisters died some of their shares came to her. Therefore when the deadline for the mortgage loomed in 1580 and the Shakespeares still lacked the money, they sold two Snitterfield shares to Robert Webbe thinking they would pay the Lamberts and redeem Asbies.[7] But it seems that John Shakespeare had borrowed other monies from Edmund Lambert, for Lambert said that he would not accept the £40 for Asbies unless the other debts were paid as well.

At this moment relations between the Lambert and Shakespeare families must have been at a low ebb. Here is where the jealousy noted by Mrs. Stopes might have come into play: she suggests that Joan had never felt it right that Mary had inherited Asbies for herself alone, and that perhaps she, Joan, had had as much right to it as her younger sister.[8] Or perhaps that was Edmund Lambert's point of view. The Shakespeares must have had some hope of reclaiming the land as at the very time they were trying to pay back the money and cancel the mortgage (1580) they named their youngest son Edmund, presumably after Edmund Lambert.

The case was still unsettled when Edmund Lambert died in April of 1587. The Asbies property passed to his son, John, and in September of that year the Shakespeares tried once again to redeem the property. William's name is added to those of his parents in the Bill of Complaint this time filed in Chancery in London. As Mrs. Stopes points out, alive to the irony, this means that the very first time William Shakespeare's name was written in London was not in document connected with the theatre or with the publishing world, but in a court of law.[9] John Lambert showed himself to be fully as stubborn as his father had been and the Shakespeares learned to their cost that verbal agreements were unpersuasive in a court of law. Despite what they claimed was their agreement with Edmund Lambert, they were unsuccessful in regaining their property.

The date of 1587 is important if Mrs. Stopes's assertion is true that Shakespeare expected to farm Asbies as his career, for in 1587, most unusually, five acting companies played in Stratford. If the loss of the Asbies property left William Shakespeare without an occupation, how tempting it must have been to follow one or another of these companies to London to establish a different career altogether, one that surely he had desired all along.

William Shakespeare's aunt Joan Lambert died in 1593 when her nephew was not quite thirty. By then he had become a highly successful London actor and writer. Perhaps all animosity toward the Lamberts had faded, for in *The Taming of the Shrew*, written early in his career, Shakespeare calls Christopher Sly in the Induction "old Sly's son of Burton Heath," a nod to Barton-on-the-Heath, a town he knew well because it had been home to his Aunt Joan.

KATHERINE ARDEN (DIED BY 1578)

Three of Mary Arden's older sisters married about the same time, when she was probably between eight and ten, for in 1550 Katherine Arden married Thomas Edkins (Etkyns) who came from their own village of Wilmcote. Eccles notes that she and her husband "sold their reversion to Thomas Stringer" (19), a curious move as Stringer had bequeathed Agnes's share of the Snitterfield property to Alexander Webbe nine years before.[10] Katherine and Thomas Edkins had one son, Thomas. She seems to have died by 1578 when William Shakespeare was about fourteen years old. The properties of Katherine Edkins and her sister Elizabeth Skarlett virtually adjoined the Arden farm, so though these sisters moved out of the house they were not far away.[11]

MARGARET ARDEN (DIED 1614)

Margaret Arden was close to her sister Mary as the Shakespeares named their second little short-lived daughter after her in 1562. Margaret lived longer than any of her sisters, not dying until 1614 just two years before the death of her famous nephew. William Shakespeare was living in Stratford at the time of her death; he would have known this aunt very well as there were continuous financial dealings between the families, and the loss of this last of his aunts must have brought with it many memories.

Sometime before 1550 (fourteen years before the birth of her poet nephew) Margaret Arden had married Alexander Webbe of Bearley (variously referred to as Saunder and Elyxaunder). Webbe was the brother of Margaret's stepmother Agnes and was therefore Margaret's step-uncle as well as her husband.

In 1560, Agnes Arden, Robert Arden's widow, left her Snitterfield land to her brother Alexander Webbe. In May of that year Alexander Webbe leased the two houses and property in Snitterfield that had been occupied by Richard Shakespeare, John Henley, and John Hargreve. After Richard Shakespeare's death the next year (1561) it seems the Webbes moved into the Shakespeare house in Snitterfield: at least two of their children were baptized in the Snitterfield church (Edward on July 30, 1562, and Sara on April 23, 1565) and Alexander Webbe was buried there April 17, 1573. Therefore when William Shakespeare's family went to visit aunt Margaret and uncle Alexander they went to the house in Snitterfield where William Shakespeare's grandfather had lived and where his own father had been brought up.

Margaret and Alexander Webbe had six children in all: Robert, Edward, Anne, Elizabeth, Mary, and Sara all of whom Alexander mentioned in his will of 1573, asking that they be "vertusly brought up."[12] John Shakespeare, Margaret's brother-in-law, was one of the overseers of the will and Margaret was named executrix. William Shakespeare was nine years old at the time, two years younger than his cousin Edward, a year older than his cousin Sara. The young Shakespeares must have looked on with awe and curiosity at their young cousins whose father had just died.

Within a year or so of Alexander Webbe's death Margaret took as a second husband Edward Cornwell. Cornwell was serving as a Snitterfield constable in that year, 1574, when Henry Shakespeare (Shakespeare's uncle) assaulted him and was constable again in 1578 when, according to Mark Eccles (21), "Edward Grant, gentleman, assaulted him twice, once with a dagger and once with a staff." Furthermore Cornwell was fined for "frays" on two other occasions in 1581 and 1583. Either he was unduly confrontational in his job as constable, or the peace was hard to keep in Snitterfield at the time.

During this time (1560–1600) there were a number of financial dealings between the families of Shakespeare's aunts.[13] For instance, in 1576 Edward and Margaret Cornwell "bought a reversion," that is, purchased the rights to the inheritance of Agnes (Anne), from Thomas Stringer. Stringer was the husband of aunt Agnes who had evidently died. As the property of Robert Arden had been left to his daughters in parts, much of the financial dealing between surviving sisters and their in-laws had to do with keeping the estate together or reestablishing it in larger entities. The frequency with which John Shakespeare was called as witness speaks to the respect and trust felt toward him by his wife's family. The reversion bought by Edward and Margaret Cornwell was sold, along with all of Edward Cornwell's goods, to Margaret's oldest son Robert Webbe in 1578, the year of the death of her sister Katherine.[14] At this time William Shakespeare was fourteen years old, absorbing the news of the death of his aunt Katherine, and witnessing the financial difficulties of his parents causing havoc in their lives.

ELIZABETH ARDEN (DIED C. 1581)

Elizabeth Arden married a man whose last name was Skarlett or Scarlett[15] and Mark Eccles lists a number of Scarletts in Aston Cantlow, the parish of Wilmcote, suggesting Elizabeth, having married one of them, lived there.[16] From this marriage she had one son, John. Elizabeth had made a good marriage, for, though tracing exact relationships is difficult, among the Scarletts in Aston Cantlow parish one John had a household of fourteen persons, and an Adam Scarlett of Wilmcote died in 1591, the richest yeoman in the parish.[17] She died sometime before March 18, 1581/82 for on that date her son sold his share of land in Snitterfield to his cousin Robert Webbe. At the time of her death William Shakespeare was not quite eighteen.

JOYCE ARDEN (DATES UNKNOWN)

Joyce is listed in her father's settlement and will. She then disappears from sight. As noted above, Mrs. Stopes suggests she might be the Joyce Arden whose death in 1557 is recorded in the registers of the Ardens of Park Hall, but this woman seems to have been married, giving even Mrs. Stopes pause. Edgar Fripp states: "Joyce disappears—possibly she went to reside with relatives, the Ardens of Pedmore, near Stourbridge, and died there in 1557."[18]

ALICE ARDEN (DATES UNKNOWN)

Alice was listed as coexecutor with Mary Arden (Shakespeare) of their father's will, so she must have been a capable woman. But Alice did not get on well with her stepmother, Robert Arden's second wife Agnes. Robert's will says: "Allso I give and bequethe to Agnes my wife vi li xiiis iiid upon this condysion that she shall sofer my dowghter Ales quietly to ynjoye half my copyhold in Wyllincote during the tyme of her wyddewoode; and if she will nott soffer my dowghter Ales quietly to occupy half with her, then I will that my wife shall have but iii li vis viiid, and her gintur in Snytterfelde."[19] When Agnes, Robert's second wife, died in 1580 she was still living on the Wilmcote property, so it seems she and Alice came to terms. Alice might have been a maiden aunt whom the Shakespeare children visited when Mary brought them to the farm and to whom the Shakespeare children were dear, but she died without a will and without a record of her burial, so she remains a mystery.

MARGARET SHAKESPEARE (DIED 1597)

Margaret Shakespeare married Shakespeare's uncle Henry when he was about fifty and was bearing their children in Ingon or Snitterfield at the same time her nephew by marriage, William, and his wife Anne were having their three in Stratford. With this in common and with the records that show John Shakespeare was in frequent contact with his brother we can assume William Shakespeare knew this aunt and uncle well. Henry and Margaret's little son James died young (in 1589 at the age of four) and William must have known and shared their grief; no one knows what became of their daughter Lettice. Henry died in 1596, the same year William Shakespeare lost his own son, and his aunt Margaret died the following February.

SHAKESPEARE AND HIS AUNTS

The Shakespeares remained closely connected in geography (none of the Arden aunts as far as we know left Warwickshire) and in relationship with Mary Arden's family. They were important figures in William Shakespeare's extended family. Concerning the numerous financial dealings between William Shakespeare's family and those of his aunts as they contested up to Chancery court the Asbies estate, and inherited, bought, and sold the shares of Robert Arden's Snitterfield property, Mrs. Stopes says: "The whole series of documents, taken together, teach us a great many important points regarding the poet's family and surroundings. It lets us picture the house abutting on the High Street where John Shakespeare was doubtless born, the extent of the united properties, and the stretches of the common fields which the poet doubtless haunted in his youth. . . . But, above all, it answers conclusively the question, so mockingly put by the Baconians, Where did the Stratford man learn his law? There are more legal documents concerning this Snitterfield property than were drawn up for any other family of the time in Warwickshire . . . and as few of his relatives could write, it is possible they could not read. William Shakespeare may have had but little Latin, but he was very likely esteemed as the scholar of the family, and doubtless had all these deeds by heart through reading them to his anxious and careful relatives. . . . The law papers of the Ardens, and the litigation of his father, prepared him alike for his many later personal associations with the law, and for the conduct of the Chancery case which he hugged to his heart during ten years at least."[20]

12

Shakespeare's Cousins

O coz, coz, coz . . . my pretty little coz—
As You Like It, act 4, scene 1

How fares our cousin?
Richard III, act 3, scene 1

Children of Shakespeare's Arden Aunts
Agnes Arden Hewyns (John; then Mrs. Thomas Stringer)
Thomas Hewyns
Margaret Hewyns
Alice Stringer (b. 1552 died as an infant)
John Stringer (b. 1554)
Arden (b. 1555/6)
n.b. Agnes died before 1569
Joan Arden Lambert (Edmund)
John Lambert
Katherine Arden Edkins (Etkyns, Thomas)
Thomas
Margaret Arden Webbe (Alexander then Mrs. Edward Cornwell)
Robert Webbe
Edward Webbe (b. 1562)
Anne Webbe
Elizabeth Webbe
Mary Webbe
Sara Webbe (b. 1565)
Elizabeth Arden Scarlett (or Skarlett)
John

Joyce and Alice seem not to have married

Children of Shakespeare's Uncle Henry Shakespeare
Lettice and James
Thomas Greene (c. 1578–1640)

THE COUSINS

William Shakespeare's mother was one of eight sisters so he had a number of cousins on the Arden side of the family. It is difficult to trace the birth dates of all the cousins as the sisters moved with their marriages to villages where records have not survived, but since Mary Arden Shakespeare was the youngest, the children of her sisters were for the most part much older than their cousin William. For instance, Agnes (who died when William Shakespeare was only five) had five children by two husbands the youngest of whom was born nine years before the poet. As far as can be determined, in addition to Agnes Arden's five children, Joan Arden Lambert had one child, John; Katherine Arden Edkins also one, Thomas; Margaret Arden Webbe six, four girls and two boys; and Elizabeth Arden Scarlett one, John.[1]

On the Shakespeare side William had two cousins, Lettice and James, who, born late in life to his father's brother, were the contemporaries of his own children. Though his uncle Henry and aunt Margaret lived closer than most the aunts and uncles to the Shakespeares in Stratford, and though one of their children, James, died very young, William Shakespeare's relationship with these children was more that of an uncle than a cousin.

We can be sure William Shakespeare was aware of all these relatives and that he had a strong sense of a large extended family, but he would have seen his cousins only from time to time; none lived close enough for daily companionship, and family bequests in his will were restricted to his immediate family members.

There was interaction, however, and as the younger generation grew up two of the cousins had a direct impact on the life of the Stratford Shakespeares: John Lambert, the son of Joan Arden and Edmund Lambert, and Robert Webbe, the oldest son of Margaret Arden and Alexander Webbe.

JOHN LAMBERT (ACTIVE 1587–1602)

According to Mark Eccles (19) Joan Arden and Edmund Lambert were married by 1550, and had one son, John, the date of whose birth is not known. Edmund, husband and father, died in 1587. The next year John acted with his mother to defend the Lambert's right to keep the Asbies estate that was Mary Arden Shakespeare's inheritance, but that the Shakespeares had mortgaged to the Lamberts in 1578. When John Shakespeare brought suit to reclaim the estate he identified his nephew John Lambert as "a man of great wealth and well friended."[2]

The situation, which must have brought much familial anguish, was as follows. John Shakespeare suffered financially, likely from a downturn in the wool trading business, from 1576 until his son's success in London had reestablished the family's position twenty years later. The extremity of John Shakespeare's sad position is notable when on November 14, 1578, John and Mary mortgaged their house and land in Wilmcote to Edmund Lambert of nearby Barton-on-the-Heath. These were lands inherited by Mary Arden from her father, lands that would have been a primary inheritance for their oldest son, William. Undoubtedly, in borrowing monies against this property from their brother-in-law, John and Mary hoped to regain the land when they had the money. The sum raised was £40. The due date for the mortgage was Michaelmas (September 29), 1580, at which time it was not paid.[3]

In fact it was nine more years before the Shakespeares were in a position to try to reclaim the land, by which time Edmund Lambert had died. So it was against John Lambert, the son, that John Shakespeare filed a complaint in Queen's Bench in 1589, asking for recompense for the Wilmcote property originally mortgaged to John's father. In the complaint John Shakespeare alleged that on September 26, 1587 John Lambert had offered an additional £20 to purchase the land outright from John, Mary, and their eldest son, Willliam, but then reneged.[4] Lambert denied this claim.

No settlement is noted for this complaint. Ten years later, November 1597, in Chancery, the Shakespeares tried again to get the Asbies property back from John Lambert, insisting that they had offered Edmund Lambert the £40 they had borrowed, only to be spurned, because the Lamberts had insisted that the Shakespeares still owed them additional money from a previous loan.

The repeated attempt to reestablish ownership of this property over the period of two decades reveals how important it was to the Shakespeares to hold the family land. However, they were never successful in regaining the property. In the mid-twentieth century, Mark Eccles discovered a record from Easter term, 1602, showing that John and Margery Lambert sold forty-six acres of land in Great Wilmcote to Richard Smyth for forty pounds.[5] So, it would seem, the property passed from the hands of the Shakespeare family. At this time William Shakespeare could easily have bought it. Was it sold away from him deliberately? Was William Shakespeare never given a chance to purchase it? Did he or they refuse a sale out of pride or spite? Or with his father's death the year before, had William Shakespeare simply ceased to care? No one knows. The family relations can only be speculated upon. John Lambert never shows up in any other situation concerning his cousin William Shakespeare.

ROBERT WEBBE (ACTIVE 1576–1597)

Robert Webbe was another cousin involved in financial dealings with John and Mary Shakespeare during the time of their troubles. In November of 1578, the same time John Shakespeare was mortgaging some of Asbies to the Lamberts, he also conveyed eighty-six additional acres in Wilmcote to Thomas Webbe, connected to the Shakespeares by the marriage of Alexander Webbe to Margaret Arden. The Shakespeares also held, via the complicated Arden inheritance, one-ninth of two houses and one hundred acres in Snitterfield, acreage that was leased to Alexander Webbe. The Shakespeares sold this one-ninth part in 1579 to Robert Webbe, Shakespeare's cousin, for a mere four pounds.

Mark Eccles points out that Robert Webbe left more records than any of Shakespeare's other cousins. When we look carefully at the pattern we see that while the Shakespeares were losing their hold on family property, Robert Webbe, starting in 1576, was carefully putting the family holdings back together.

In 1576 he bought the lease his mother and stepfather held from Agnes Arden and their share in her estate after her death. In 1578 he bought the shares his parents had purchased from the Stringers and Thomas Edkins (his aunt Agnes's and aunt Katherine's inheritance). As noted above, in 1579 he added the Shakespeare's share for £4 and two years later, in 1581, he bought Joan and Edmund Lambert's share for £40. Later that same year (1581/2) he purchased his Aunt Elizabeth's share from her son (probably), his cousin John Skarlett, for 20 marks (about £14).

Having consolidated the inheritance of five of the Arden daughters (Agnes, Katherine, Joan, Margaret, and Mary), Robert defended his ownership of other properties in court, and finally, on his marriage to Mary Perkes, leased two houses to his father-in-law for £35. Mr. Perkes promised to welcome Robert, his wife, any children they might have, plus Robert's mother Margaret and her husband Edward Cornwell into these dwellings. Both houses must have been full as Robert and Mary had seven children.

Other court records name Robert as a "common player at bowls," and fined him (like Shakespeare's Uncle Henry) for not wearing a woolen cap to church.

Robert Webbe seems to have lived his whole life in Snitterfield, where he died in 1597. His goods were valued at £51.[6]

THOMAS GREENE (c. 1578–1640)

The only cousin about whom we know a great deal is Thomas Greene, the son of Master Thomas Greene, mercer, in the High Pavement, Warwick.[7] No one knows quite how Thomas Greene is related to William Shakespeare except that Greene (spelled variably with and without the final "e") repeatedly refers to William Shakespeare as his cousin. He says, for instance, in his "Diary and Correspondence," "My cosen Shakspeare has commyng yesterday to towne; I went to see him how he did."[8]

The terms for relationship in Shakespeare's day were as variable as the spelling of their names. In his will Shakespeare calls his own granddaughter his niece, so though Greene called himself Shakespeare's "cosen" it's quite possible there was no blood relationship between them. In fact, Greene called other men "cousin" to whom he was not related. But it is undeniable that William Shakespeare and Thomas Greene were very close; for a number of years they lived in the same house; the Greenes named their children William and Anne; and Shakespeare's name appears more in the diary and letters of Thomas Greene than in any other single Stratford source. He was a worthy friend and/or cousin, for, according to Mr. Fripp,

Thomas Greene "was probably, next to the Poet and Doctor Hall, the ablest man in the town."[9]

Fourteen years younger than Shakespeare, Greene trained as a lawyer, entering Middle Temple in 1595, where his guarantors were the playwright Marston and Marston's father.[10] Mark Eccles notes a mention in the Stratford records of a letter to Marston, probably to be signed by July Shaw the bailiff, concerning some conveyances between citizens of Stratford and Marston's father, "late of the Cytie of Conventrie."[11] Between the Marstons in Coventry and Michael Drayton who was often in Clifford Chambers, it would seem the Stratford area was not a complete cultural backwater.

When Thomas Greene arrived in London as a seventeen-year-old law student William Shakespeare was a member of the newly formed Chamberlain's Men, the finest theatre company in the city, and was one of the its most celebrated playwrights. In the half-dozen or more years since his arrival in London, William Shakespeare had written the three parts of *Henry VI*, *Richard III*, *Titus Andronicus*, *The Comedy of Errors*, *The Taming of the Shrew*, *Love's Labour's Lost*, and *The Two Gentlemen of Verona*. His epic poems *Venus and Adonis* and *The Rape of Lucrece* had recently been published. He could claim the acquaintance of a number of great aristocrats up to and including the Queen herself, and while Thomas Greene studied law at the Middle Temple his fellow Stratfordian was unleashing his great lyric gifts in writing *Richard II, A Midsummer Night's Dream, Romeo and Juliet*, and *The Merchant of Venice*. Who would not want to be William Shakespeare's cousin?

But Thomas Greene had gifts of his own. Before he had even come to the bar, in 1601, he was named solicitor for Stratford. He supported Shakespeare's friend Richard Quiney in his claims against Sir Edward Greville and was called to the Bar in 1602.

Beginning about 1603 Thomas Greene and his wife Lititia lived with the Shakespeares (Anne, Susanna, and Judith) at New Place.[12] The same year he was appointed Steward of the Court of Record for the town (September 7), an office he held until 1610, when under the new charter granted the town by James 1 (July 8) there was created the office of Town Clerk. Thomas Greene immediately stepped into this office, which he held until 1617.

In 1604, the Greene's daughter Anne was born at New Place. The Greenes had bought a house called St. Mary's House that was located just beyond Hall's Croft, but the owner was slow to leave and the Greenes had extensive plans for remodeling, so they were still in residence at New Place with the Shakespeares when Susanna Shakespeare married John Hall on June 5, 1607, and when the Greene's son William was born in 1608.

In 1609, Thomas Greene noted in his diary that he had agreed to let George Browne stay another summer at St. Mary's and sow his garden: "Seeing I could get no carriage to help me here with timber, I was content to permit it without contradiction: and that rather, because I perceived I might stay another year at New Place" (Sept. 9, 1609).[13]

Greene did ask Browne to vacate the house by the 25th of March, 1610, so that he could use the timber he mentioned for his remodeling. He wanted to move into his new house by September 29. This indicates he planned to leave New Place by that date, and gives us a possible date for Shakespeare's retirement, as it would seem likely Greene was moving out because Shakespeare was coming home to stay. According to Marchette Chute, "During the next six years, Greene spent the enormous sum of four hundred pounds on his new residence, converting it into what he himself called a "gentlemanlike" home, but it could never have had the social connotations that were attached to New Place."[14]

The year after the Greenes moved to St. Mary's House, their second daughter, Elizabeth, was born. The connection with the Shakespeares remained close as Elizabeth was the name of Shakespeare's granddaughter born four years before.

Furthermore, records show a lawsuit in Chancery brought by both William Shakespeare and Thomas Greene concerning tithes, in 1611 (an explanation of this complicated issue is discussed by C.C. Stopes in her collection of essays entitled *Shakespeare's Environment* [pp. 82–84]).[15] Two years later, even though Shakespeare had retired to live in Stratford, the draw of London was strong enough to induce him to buy the Blackfriars Gatehouse. Here he chose as one of his secondary trustees not Thomas Greene, interestingly, but his brother, John Greene.

Thomas Greene spent time in London during his years as counsel for Stratford, but in 1614, much of his effort was expended on a home town concern. Arthur Mainwaring and young William Combe were threatening to enclose the nearby Welcombe common fields. These fields represented common arable land farmed historically by local farmers and subject to tithes. Therefore the enclosure would affect the tithe income of those who had invested in the land. Greene worked diligently (and recorded his efforts) to organize a protest of tithe holders and other concerned citizens, including William Shakespeare. At issue was not the earlier tithes purchased as such and about which the suit had been brought in 1611. This time the concern was 107 acres of arable land and 20 acres of pasture Shakespeare had recently purchased from William Combe himself and his uncle John Combe who had just died.

William Combe sent Mr. Mainwaring along with a Mr. Replingham to reassure Shakespeare and Greene that they would not lose materially by the enclosures; in fact Combe was willing to offer a deed saying he would make up any losses to the investors himself. According to Mrs. Stopes, "The poet seems to have allowed them to do this, and one touch of his personal affection for Thomas Green incidentally appears in his insisting that the security should include his cousin Greene."[16]

The enclosure threat prompted several entries in Thomas Greene's papers, including an indirect record of one of Shakespeare's conversations: on November 17, 1614, Greene noted: "My cosen Shakspeare commyng yesterday to towne, I went to see him howe he did; he told me that they assured him they meant to enclose noe further then to gospel bushe, and so upp straight (leaving out part of the dyngles to the field) to the gate in Clopton Hedge and take in Salisbury's peece;

ant that they meane in Aprill to survey the Land, and then to gyve satisfaction and not before, and he and Mr. Hall say they think there will be nothing done at all."

In the next entry, December 23, he says: "Letters written, one to Mr. Mannering, another to Mr. Shakspeare, with almost all the Companyes hands to either: I alsoe wrytte of myself to my Cosen Shakespeare the coppyes of all our oaths made then, also a note of the inconveniences wold grow by the Inclosure."

Concerning Shakespeare's feelings, the entry of September 1615 in Greene's notebook says, "W. Shakespeares telling J. Greene that I was not able to beare the encloseinge of Welcombe."[17] The lack of punctuation has made this entry difficult to decode but it possibly represents a quote from Shakespeare himself.

Greene was in an awkward position. On the one hand he dealt with Combe and his representatives on Shakespeare's behalf, accepting the reassurance that they would not suffer from enclosure and therefore making Shakespeare and Greene amenable to the idea of enclosure. On the other hand Greene represented the town of Stratford that was, on behalf of its citizens, determinedly and violently opposed to enclosure. Mrs. Stopes says: "Yet during the whole of the struggle Thomas Greene honestly threw himself into the duties of defending the rights of the town which had reposed trust in him."[18]

In the spring of 1616 Thomas Greene finally notes that "[a]t Warwick Assises in Lent 1615–1616 my Lord Chief Justice willed im [i.e. W. Combe] to sett his heart at rest he should neyther enclose nor lay downe any earrable, nor plowe any auncient greensward." It was in that same spring that Shakespeare died.[19] The very next year Thomas Greene resigned as Town Clerk of Stratford, sold his house, and retired to Bristol for the rest of his life. William Combe tried for two more years to defy the Stratford corporation and the will of the Lord Chief Justice, not giving up his idea of enclosure until 1618–1619.

Thomas Greene was an amateur poet. Fripp attributes to him the following sonnet complementing the Warwickshire poet Michael Drayton. The poem was included in Drayton's collected poems of 1605 and though some credit an actor Thomas Greene with the sonnet, Fripp attributes it to Thomas Greene of Stratford:

> What ornament might I devise to fit
> Th'aspiring height of thy admired spirit?
> Or what fair garland worthy is to sit
> On thy blest brows, that compass in all merit?
> Thou shalt not crowned be with common bays,
> Because for thee it is a crown too low;
> Apollo's tree can yield thee simple praise –
> It is too dull a vesture for thy brow;
> But with a wreath of stars shalt thou be crown'd,
> Which, when thy working temples do sustain,
> Will like the spheres be ever moving round
> After the royal music of thy brain:
> Thy skill doth equal Phoebus, not thy birth;
> He to Heaven gives music, thou to earth.[20]

He could equally well have written the encomium to his cousin. For of all his Stratford friends and relatives Thomas Greene seems the most likely to have seen and appreciated William Shakespeare's work: he traveled to London frequently; he was extremely close to the poet at the height of the latter's writing career; he was free of John Hall's Puritanical beliefs; and he had literary interests. One wonders, then, that this intimate friend, and perhaps family member, was not mentioned in Shakespeare's will. Did something distance them at the end of Shakespeare's life? Thomas Greene's diaries are silent on this matter. No private papers from Shakespeare family survive. We wonder, but likely we shall never know. But Thomas Greene wrote to the Stratford corporation a year after moving to Bristol, telling them that his years in Stratford when he had been their clerk were the "golden years." "We cannot doubt that it was the Poet's friendship and kinship which made these days of strenuous labour 'golden' and his death which turned sunshine into night."[21] For the rest of his life Thomas Greene traveled from Bristol to his work as a barrister in London. He died in 1640.[22]

13

Shakespeare's In-Laws: The Hathaways

'I hate', from hate away she threw,
And saved my life saying 'not you.'
Sonnet 145

Joan Hathaway: Step-Mother-in-Law (m. 1565–1599)
Bartholomew Hathaway: Brother-in-Law (b. circa 1554–1624)
Thomas Hathaway: Half Brother-in-Law (b. 1569)
John Hathaway: Half Brother-in-Law (b. 1574)
William Hathaway: Half Brother-in-Law (b. 1578)
Catherine Hathaway: Sister-in-Law (b. 1563)
Margaret Hathaway: Half Sister-in-Law (b. 1572)
Richard Hathaway: Nephew (b. 1583)

THE HATHAWAYS

In John Shakespeare's day the Shakespeare and the Hathaway families were friends, for in 1566 John Shakespeare, William's father, had offered security for loans representing a large amount of money to Richard Hathaway, Anne's father. This was when William and his future wife, Anne, were just children. Richard Hathaway died in 1581 at the time William was courting his daughter, but the year before they married. Hathaway left his daughter ten marks (£6.13s.4d.) to be paid on her wedding day. This could indicate he knew of her plans to marry William Shakespeare, but everything else points to their marriage being unplanned and unknown to their parents. Most likely the bequest ensured that whenever and whomever Anne married, she would have the traditional dowry.

After the marriage between William Shakespeare and Anne Hathaway there came to be an estrangement between William Shakespeare and his in-laws. Though Anne Hathaway's brother Barthomew lived nearby and was an upstanding citizen, and though his son, Shakespeare's nephew Richard, had a distinguished public career and a thriving family, none of the Hathaways are mentioned in Shakespeare's will. Furthermore, though Shakespeare contemplated at one point buying property in Shottery, his wife's hometown, no business dealings of the kind that were so common with branches of his own family connect him with any of the Hathaways. The coolness many scholars have adduced when observing that the only legacy William Shakespeare left his wife was their second-best bed has often been remarked upon. But that this coolness should have spread to the rest of the Hathaway family, and lasted a lifetime, has not so often been noted.

The gap was bridged by Anne herself and by the younger generation. One assumes that while William Shakespeare was working in London Anne kept in close touch with her own family who lived in her childhood home, an easy walk from Stratford. She was, in fact, mentioned in the will of the Hathaway's shepherd, Thomas Whittington (Marcy, 1601), who said, "I give and bequeath unto the poor people of Stratford xl*s*. that is in the hand of Anne Shaxpere wife of Wyllyam Shaxpere."[1] This probably indicates that he had asked her to care for the money, the entrusting of money to other people being a common practice at the time when banks were unknown.

Shakespeare's son-in-law and good friend, John Hall, was close enough to Bartholomew Hathaway (Anne's brother) that Hall was named the overseer for his will. And though William Shakespeare did not leave any legacies to Hathaway relatives in his will, his grand-daughter, Elizabeth, remembered the son of her cousin Thomas Hathaway in her will at the end of the seventeenth century, showing that though William Shakespeare chose not to be close to them, the Shakespeare/ Hathaway families remained connected through four generations.

JOAN HATHAWAY (M. 1565, D. 1599)

In his book *1599, A Year in the Life of William Shakespeare,* James Shapiro notes that one of the events in the fall of that year that might well have brought William Shakespeare to Stratford from London was the death and burial of his step-mother-in-law, Joan Hathaway.[2] Joan was the second wife of Richard Hathaway, to whom she gave a second family of children: a baby Joan who died in infancy, then Thomas (b. 1569), Margaret (b. 1572), John, (b. 1575), and William (b. 1578). The older children had been born to a first wife in all likelihood named Anne as that was the name of the first-born daughter. Two little boys, both Richards, had died soon after they were born, but Anne's older brother Bartholomew (b. 1554) and sister Catherine (b. 1563) were part of the family when Joan married Richard Hathaway in 1565.[3] From 1565 when Anne was nine or ten until 1599 when Joan died, Joan Hathaway was Anne's mother. She would have been intensely concerned with Anne's marriage so soon after her own husband had died, and the birth of

Anne's daughter Susanna six months after the marriage would have given Joan Hathaway her first grandchild. This grandchild was just four years younger than Joan's own youngest, and coincidentally bore the name William. So Anne and Joan were raising young children together during the 1580s.

Joan came to Hewlands, the house we now know as Anne Hathaway's cottage, when she married Richard Hathaway in 1565 and lived there the rest of her life. In 1581 she was named executrix to her husband's will and saw him to his grave that year. In 1590 she was recorded as having two and a half yardlands[4] (more than forty acres) probably her inheritance as a residual legatee in her husband's will; she was mentioned again in 1595 where we are told the household comprised six people, which probably included her sons John and William and her shepherd Thomas Whittington.[5] It was probably because his mistress Joan Hathaway had died in 1599 that Whittington gave the monies noted above in keeping to Anne Shakespeare.

In marrying Richard Hathaway Joan had married well and in a prudent, traditional, and accepted fashion. In contrast, her stepdaughter Anne found herself pregnant before wedlock and compelled to marry an eighteen-year-old boy. Though no records exist (no letters, diaries, or journals) that would give us an insider's view into the family emotions, the following conjectures are based on the mores of the time. For instance, however much in love her stepdaughter might have claimed to be, Joan could not look with favor upon the young man who had gotten her stepdaughter into trouble. Though William Shakespeare came from a good local family he was young, untrained in any craft or trade, unable to support a wife and children, and his family was experiencing serious financial difficulties, reversals that were known throughout the community. If there was coolness between the Hathaways and the Shakespeares it might have started here, an understandable reserve or distain on Joan Hathaway's part vis-a-vis her new son-in-law. If (as is also a reasonable conjecture) Shakespeare was not altogether happy with having to get married at the age of eighteen he would have had little incentive to develop a close relationship with a family who had little choice but to condemn his actions. His own resentment at marrying Anne could have been displaced, projected onto her family. And these early reactions could easily have hardened into unbreakable habits of thought and feeling.

BARTHOLOMEW HATHAWAY (ANTE 1560–1624)

Anne's brother Bartholomew Hathaway's exact birth date is unknown. Roland Lewis concludes he was born about 1554, a year or two before his sister Anne, both of them children of Richard Hathaway and his first wife. This date of birth makes Bartholomew about ten years older than his brother-in-law, William Shakespeare.[6]

In his father's will Bartholomew was left the use of some of his farmland and was asked to serve as a guide to his stepmother in matters of farming the property left to her, and to comfort the younger children. Perhaps a year of supervision was enough, for in November of 1582 (the same month of the same year that Anne married William Shakespeare), Bartholomew married a woman named Isabella Hancocks of Tredington and moved from Shottery. For his stepmother, Joan, this meant that within a year her husband had died and her two oldest stepchildren left Hewlands farm. Bartholomew's oldest child, Richard, was born in Tysoe where he and his wife evidently lived for their first year of marriage.

Bartholomew seems to have returned to Hewland Farm by the time his daughter, Anne, was born in 1584. John followed in 1586, and infant who died nameless in 1588 and a last child, Edmund, in 1590. His sister Anne had her first daughter in 1583—Susanna Shakespeare and Richard Hathaway, therefore, were cousins of exactly the same age; the Shakespeare twins, Hamnet and Judith, followed in 1585, in between Bartholomew's Anne and John. Whenever Anne Hathaway Shakespeare walked her children over to her childhood home to visit her step-mother or her brothers and sisters, she would see her sister-in-law Isabella and could watch their children play together.

In 1586 Bartholomew was taking his place in the adult world of the time: that year he was asked to and helped to appraise the goods of William Sych, a neighbor in Shottery; in 1599 he would have taken charge of the funeral and burial of his stepmother Joan; and after these events he succeeded to his father's copyhold of Hewlands.[7]

From 1605 to 1609 Bartholomew Hathaway was churchwarden at Trinity Church, Stratford. In 1608 he was asked again to appraise an estate—this time the goods of Alice Burman of Shottery. In 1610 Francis Collins drew up a deed for transfer of property, confirming the sale of Hewlands Farm and some few other properties to Bartholomew Hathaway for £200. This considerable amount of money confirms Bartholomew's position as a wealthy and successful citizen. It was at this time that Bartholomew added ten rooms to the house at Hewland's Farm, giving "Anne Hathaway's cottage" dimensions it has today. The proper-ties Bartholomew bought in 1610 remained in the Hathaway family until 1838.

Bartholomew Hathaway matched the profile of the men who were Shakespeare's friends in his maturity: he was a prosperous farmer, family man, successful neigh-bor, appraiser of goods, church warden, brother to Shakespeare's wife, friend to Shakespeare's son-in-law—but not a man close to the dramatist William Shake-speare, not a favorite of his famous brother-in-law.

THOMAS HATHAWAY (B. 1569), JOHN HATHAWAY (B. 1574), WILLIAM HATHAWAY (B. 1578)

Thomas, John, and William Hathaway were the younger half-brothers of Anne Hathaway. They were children when Shakespeare married into the family: Thomas, thirteen; John, seven; and William, four. Anne, at twenty-six, was of an age to have been as much mother as sister to them; and the change in the household that came with the death of their father, followed within a year by the marriage of their older sister and brother, must have seemed to these young boys a major up-heaval in the family. Little is known of these men except that John is probably the

John Hathaway listed as "a soldier at musters in 1596 and 1599."[8] William Shakespeare must have known them well, but they seem to have played a negligible part in his Stratford life, though John Hathaway's military experience might have been useful to him as a source for the military details in *Henry IV Parts 1 and 2*, and *Henry V*. But Shakespeare had no business dealings that we know of with Thomas, John, or William, and they were not remembered in his will.

CATHERINE HATHAWAY (B. 1563), MARGARET HATHAWAY (B. 1572)

William Shakespeare had two sisters-in-law. Catherine Hathaway was born in 1563, was, like Anne, the daughter of Richard's first wife, and was just about Shakespeare's age. Margaret, born in 1572, was a half-sister, born of the second wife, Joan, and eight years younger than her brother-in-law.[9] We know very little about these two women except that both were mentioned in their father's will: Catherine was left ten marks, as was her older sister Anne, to be paid upon her marriage; Margaret was to receive the same amount when she turned seventeen.[10] Richard Hathaway made certain the girls had their dowries, but except for Anne, who married William Shakespeare, we know nothing of what happened to Richard Hathaway's daughters.

RICHARD HATHAWAY (B. 1583)

What a pity William Shakespeare was not close to his nephew Richard Hathaway, whose civic life in Stratford is reminiscent of that of Shakespeare's own father. Richard was the oldest son of Bartholomew Hathaway, Anne's brother. Born in 1583 he was the same age as Shakespeare's daughter Susanna—the two must have been brought up in parallel: Susanna in Stratford and Richard just a mile away in Shottery. Richard did not stay on the farm, however; he became a baker with a shop in town on Bridge Street. From the day William Shakespeare returned to live in New Place (1611) he would have seen his nephew Richard in and around town and been aware of his activities: by 1614 Richard was a Stratford councilman, and two years later, following in his father's footsteps, churchwarden; he would therefore have been active as churchwarden at the time of his uncle William's funeral in 1616 and undoubtedly attended that sad event. He was named chamberlain in 1617, alderman in 1623[11] (the year his aunt Anne died), and finally bailiff of Stratford in 1626,[12] two years after the death of his father.

14
Shakespeare's Hart Nephews and Niece

My lord, your loving nephew now is come.
Henry VI Part 1, act 2, scene 5

God knows I loved my niece.
Much Ado About Nothing, act 5, scene 1

William Hart (1600–1639)
Mary Hart (1603–1607)
Thomas Hart (1605–before 1670)
Michael Hart (1608–1618)

William Shakespeare had one niece and three nephews on his own side of the family. These were the children of his sister Joan and her husband, the hatter William Hart, a family who, even after Joan's marriage, continued to live in the Shakespeare family home on Henley Street. When William Shakespeare moved back to Stratford about 1611 his own two daughters were grown women. His little niece Mary Hart had died, and his nephews were young children. The oldest, William, was about eleven, Thomas six, and Michael, three, the same age as Shakespeare's granddaughter.

Life for the Hart family in the Henley Street house was different from William and Joan Shakespeare's childhood there. After the death of Shakespeare's father in 1601, most of the double property was leased out to Lewis Hiccox and (according to Park Honan) his busy and quarrelsome wife. They ran an inn called the Maidenhead that took up ten rooms, a kitchen, cellar, and brewhouse, reducing the living space for the Harts to a mere three rooms.[1] The Maidenhead Inn lease passed from

Hiccox's nephew Henry to a John Rutter around 1640, so the property remained primarily an inn until Shakespeare's grand-daughter left the entire double-house property to Hart descendants in 1670.

When he died in 1616, William Shakespeare had left his sister a life-tenancy in the Henley Street house, and left each of her sons £5; plus, after Joan's death he stipulated in his will that "£50 pounds shall remain amongst the children of my said sister." During his lifetime and after his death, William Shakespeare supported his family.

WILLIAM HART (1600–1639)

William Hart was christened in Stratford's Holy Trinity Church on the 28th of August, 1600. Listed as the son of William Hart, this record is the first indication we have of Joan Shakespeare's marriage. F.E. Halliday writes that William was an actor, mentioned as one of his Majesty's comedians playing at the Blackfriar's in London. He goes on to acknowledge the legend that this William Hart was the father of the actor Charles Hart who was a member of Killigrew's company following the Civil War, playing Hotspur, Othello, and Brutus, training Nell Gwyn to act, and becoming her first lover.[2] This fascinating history is disputed by Mark Eccles, however, who says William Hart of Stratford was not the actor William Hart. The latter was another man altogether who lived and performed in London and died not in 1639 but in 1650.[3]

MARY HART (1603–1607)

Joan Hart's second child was a little girl she named Mary after her own mother. The family had four years with the little girl before she died. Her older brother William (named undoubtedly for his uncle) was seven at the time of her death, her younger brother, Thomas, two. Mary Shakespeare, the grandmother, had lost two little girls as infants, and one daughter, Anne, at the age of seven. More than once the Shakespeares and now the Harts suffered, as did most families of the time, the devastating grief that comes with the loss of a child.

THOMAS HART (1605–c. 1670)

To Thomas Hart is traced the survival to the present day of William Shakespeare's family. Born in 1605, he lived until sometime around 1670, surviving the Civil War and living ten years into the restoration. In 1633 he married a woman named Margaret, with whom he had two sons.[4] The Harts lived all their lives in the birthplace house on Henley Street, for though the house was left to Shakespeare's daughter Susanna Hall, Joan Hart was given the right to live there at a very modest rate for her lifetime. Joan died in 1646 and Susanna continued to let Thomas live there. When Susanna Shakespeare Hall died, she left the property to her daughter Elizabeth Barnard, and when Elizabeth died in 1670 (about the same time as Thomas Hart) she left the Henley Street house to Thomas's two sons, Thomas (born 1634) and George (1636–1702). George became a tailor; he and his family occupied the house, which eventually passed to his son Shakespeare Hart, a plumber, then on to Hart descendants until it was sold in 1806 to a man named Thomas Court and so, after two hundred and fifty years, passed out of the hands of the Shakespeare family.[5]

MICHAEL HART (1608–1618)

Little is known of Michael Hart. He was born the year his grandmother Mary Arden Shakespeare died. That year his cousin Susanna Shakespeare had her only daughter, Elizabeth, so the grand-daughter of William Shakespeare and the son of his sister would have been the same age, would have played together, and known each other well. As fine a doctor as John Hall (Elizabeth's father) was, he could not help young Michael who died a little boy, age ten. Joan's grief would inevitably bring back to Joan memories of the death of her little daughter Mary eleven years before, and of Hamnet Shakespeare twenty years before that. But William Shakespeare, and indeed Joan's own husband, both had died in 1616, two years before Michael, and were spared this family sorrow.

15
Conclusion

When walking, as one may do easily in Stratford today, from the birthplace house in Henley Street to the site of New Place and on to Hall's Croft, we seek an experience with Shakespeare and his family. These are the very houses in which the family lived; surely they will reveal some secrets. And indeed to one who looks closely they show, from generation to generation, the change in the Shakespeares' status. Each home becomes a symbol illustrating the Shakespeares' rise from middle class to gentry during this dynamic period in English history. Shakespeare's grandparents lived in homes where the fire burned in the center of the room, with smoke wafting freely up to the thatched roof. Shakespeare's father brought his mother to a home with fireplaces and chimneys. However, though the birthplace house was modern in its heating, the windows are comparatively small; in the later Hall's Croft we see an increasing use of glass in larger and larger windows: "The general opening up, and out, of English life, enlightened to some degree by social conscience, was wonderfully symbolized by the new and abundant use of glass, which adorned so many of the houses of the time. Every manor seemed to have its own windowed hall and oriel, flooding the rooms with light—as one lord gently complained, 'You cannot always tell where to come out of the sun.'"[1] To go from Mary Arden's house in Wilmcote, to the Henley Street birthplace, to Hall's Croft or Nash House is to feel William Shakespeare and his family taking part in these changes in domestic architecture, to see their status rise, and to see their lives open up. It is not hard to see a parallel with Shakespeare's contribution to the Elizabethan theatre: his work opened it up, heated it up, and illuminated it to an extraordinary degree. But however compelling his work in London, Shakespeare sustained close ties to these dwellings, to Stratford, to Warwickshire throughout his life. His roots there ran very deep. By examining his background, each of his family members, and his relationship to them we learn about the personal life out of which (in concert with his imaginative genius) his plays and his poetry grew.

When and why did William Shakespeare leave Stratford? The timing of William Shakespeare's move to London is illuminated by reconsidering C.C. Stopes observation that it was about 1587–1588 that the Shakespeares lost Mary Arden Shakespeare's inherited property of Asbies[2] that, Mrs. Stopes believes, was intended as an estate for William Shakespeare. His life's work would be to farm it. The conjunction in timing between the loss of Asbies and the appearance in Stratford in 1587 of five companies of professional actors seems Jungian in its synchronicity, an omen of what Shakespeare was destined to do. Surely this was the time that he followed his instincts to leave Stratford and the life of a small-town farmer and to attempt a theatrical career in London.

Success was not immediate. Those left at home must have had two or three anxious years. But once William Shakespeare started acting and writing for the theatre, one is overwhelmingly impressed by the extent to which he took on the support of his entire family: his parents, his three brothers, his sister, her husband and their children, his wife, and his own children. He worked to release his father from more than a decade of indebtedness. Furthermore, since the family had been unsuccessful at regaining his mother's property at Wilmcote, he set himself to acquire other property, in and around Stratford, to replace it and thereby reestablish the Shakespeares' position as landowners. Although his brother Gilbert was mentioned as a haberdasher in London, we read about him mostly as an aide to William, facilitating property deals when William could not get to Stratford from London. Of his other brothers, Richard seemingly had no profession, and Edmund was an undistinguished player in London, neither contributing substantially to the family income. When his sister Joan married a seemingly unsuccessful hatter, William gave her and her husband housing at a negligible rate in the Henley Street property where the Hart family lived their entire lives. In 1596 William helped his father gain the coat of arms John Shakespeare had always desired, and after his father's death he cared for his mother until she died, probably at New Place, the fine home and garden in Stratford to which he himself returned to live out his last five years. Shakespeare's success and his support of the family, indeed, brought them to a whole new social level: he and his father were now gentlemen and able to display their coat of arms.

The records concerning his father John and his uncle Henry, his uncle Alexander Webbe, and his cousin Robert Webbe, his aunt Joan and uncle Edmund Lambert and their son John, show the degree to which business and work, lands and leasings, loans and money matters, were kept within the family circle. This could not but intensify familial bonds. Among the family's legal records, a number expose the fiscal and temperamental differences between Shakespeare's father and his uncle Henry, which are intriguing, and the possibility of Henry as an early Falstaffian prototype to whom young William Shakespeare played "Prince Hal" looks self-evident, though it has not been suggested elsewhere to my knowledge.

That John and Mary Shakespeare had three unmarried sons out of four has been noted casually in Shakespearean biography but not deeply analyzed or speculated upon. Bachelors were not unknown, but three in a family was an unusual condition for the time and should be appreciated as such. Furthermore the complications to Shakespeare's life in London by the presence of his youngest brother there to pursue a career as a player—and not having much success—is worth deeper contemplation as we try to gain a picture of Shakespeare's day to day life in the city. Frequent travel back and forth between London and Stratford reveals itself to be more constant than one might have thought for the time and conditions. Travel involving Shakespeare, his family, and friends of his family, most often concerned business for the town. This traveling (of John Shakespeare, Richard Quiney, and Thomas Greene in particular) increases the likelihood that Shakespeare's Stratford friends and his family were very well aware of his activity and success in London, and that some might have witnessed his plays and performances there.

Shakespeare's dedication to his family's welfare indicates a close, continuing, and loving relationship with his parents and siblings, but also a willingness, determination, and ability to shoulder great responsibility. In turn, the family must have been of inestimable comfort when the most devastating blow for Shakespeare came: the death of his eleven-year-old son, Hamnet. Since, as we have observed, neither of his Stratford brothers married (and his youngest brother who had come to London died soon after his own illegitimate son was buried), Hamnet's death marked the end of the Shakespeare male family line, a fact that added to the family's grief at the personal loss. After the turn of the century, the death of his father, the death of his mother, and that of all his brothers must have been heavy blows.

The devotion to his own relatives heightens, by contrast, the cold shoulder William Shakespeare showed his wife's family. He established no business relationships with either Bartholomew Hathaway or Bartholomew's son Richard; he mentions no Hathaway in his will, and left all relations with the Hathaways (as far as we can tell) to his wife and daughters. Here another date is suggestive: the year 1613. New research shows that many of the timbers in Hall's Croft date to 1613, though there was a structure preceding the current one on the land.[3] It is most likely then that after her marriage to John Hall in 1607 Susanna Shakespeare and her husband moved into their own home for a few years, then perhaps into New Place in 1613 while her house was being rebuilt. During the time Shakespeare's residence at New Place likely overlapped with the Hall's (1612–1613) Shakespeare enjoyed the daily company of his favorite daughter and watched his grand-daughter Elizabeth grow from three to five years old. Then, in 1613 it became possible for the Hall family to move to their own home, Hall's Croft. That same year Shakespeare, who had never owned property in London, bought the Blackfriars Gatehouse and took care that it be inherited not by his wife but by his daughter Susanna. Perhaps this was just coincidence. But it's equally possible that consciously or unconsciously this action underscores a dissatisfaction with his marriage, a discomfort in having to live in Stratford with his wife alone, their relationship mediated only by their problematic daughter Judith.

And yet one cannot say categorically that Shakespeare did not love his wife. A marriage of so many years goes through many phases; the wooing years are different from the child-bearing years, feelings between spouses come and go and modify and change. His last years with Anne may have been serene, comfortable, and affectionate. But that Shakespeare might have once wished for a more fulfilling union is probable. Persistent themes in the sonnets (most likely written between 1592 and 1594) include obsessive love for an unattainable and/or unworthy object, anguished jealousy, disgust with sex, and two of the most often quoted (29 and 30) reveal feelings of profound depression relieved only by the thought of a loved one. And with his own family three days journey away in Stratford, during his time in London he continually observed the happy marriages, child-filled homes, and busy domestic lives of his best friends, John Hemings, Henry Condell, and Richard Burbage.[4] Here there seemed to be true partnerships between husbands and wives. Furthermore, as if to express his own state, a deepening element of the mature comedies is the creation of the left-out man: the Antonios, Feste, Don Pedro, and Jaques who watch the others pair off and dance while they observe, alone.

In fact the plays themselves suggest a great arc in Shakespeare's personal and inner philosophic life. The first quarter of his career, when he was a young man newly come to London, filled with ambitions and dreams that had been suppressed or dammed up by his early marriage and familial responsibilities, he wrote plays filled with action, drive, and energy: the three parts of *Henry VI*, *Richard III*, and the farcical comedies: *The Taming of the Shrew*, *The Comedy of Errors*, *Two Gentlemen of Verona*, as well as the gruesome, *Titus Andronicus*. The plague of 1592–1594 closed the London theatres and gave William Shakespeare a chance to try his hand at serious, publishable poetry. Perhaps at the home of his patron, Henry Wriostheley, the Earl of Southampton, he wrote the epic poems *Venus and Adonis* and *The Rape of Lucrece*. He also began the sonnets. These intense poems in particular reveal the emotional crucible he was experiencing at the time. They released a lyric gift only suggested in his first plays. But writing them also confirmed that Shakespeare was a theatre man first and foremost. As soon as the theatres reopened he left the world of literature and channeled his lyricism into the great plays of the mid-1590s: *Love's Labours Lost*, *A Midsummer Night's Dream*, *Romeo and Juliet*, and *The Merchant of Venice*, while the lyric *Richard II* opened the door to his next phase, turning his vision back to English history. Here lyricism was replaced by humor, variety of character and class, culminating in the creation of the immortal Falstaff in *Henry IV, Part 1*, *Henry IV, Part 2*, and *Henry V*. Shakespeare's London and Stratford life came together uniquely when the request of Queen Elizabeth (as tradition has it) for a play about Falstaff (the fat knight) in love resulted in *The Merry Wives of Windsor*, a representation of English village life reflective in a great number of ways of Shakespeare's own Stratford.

By the end of the 1590s Shakespeare's son had died. Soon after the turn of the century his father died. The plays between 1596 and 1606, even the comedies, *As You Like It, Much Ado About Nothing,* and *Twelfth Night,* carry a dark thread, while the history *King John* (of undetermined and perhaps earlier date) holds a lament for a dead child so poignant we feel Anne and William Shakespeare themselves grieving at the loss of their Hamnet. About this time it would seem a great void opened before William Shakespeare; looking into it unflinchingly he wrote *Julius Caesar, Hamlet, Othello, King Lear,* and *Macbeth* as well as the bitter, problematic "comedies" *Measure for Measure, All's Well That Ends Well,* and *Troilus and Cressida.* A further look into classic sources produced *Timon of Athens,* and with a deeper, healthier breath of air, *Antony and Cleopatra.*

Shakespeare's final plays however do not leave us with a dark, grim, or bitter vision. At the end of his career (which approached all too nearly the end of his life) his last four comedy/romances, *Pericles, Cymbeline, The Winter's Tale,* and *The Tempest* have a common and powerful theme of recognition, reconciliation, and re-demption. William Shakespeare was nondogmatic in his writing and a law-abiding member of the church of England in his personal life. The result of searching for evidences of Catholic or non-Catholic, Puritanical or non-Puritanical, atheistic or non–atheistic beliefs in his life and work will always prove inconclusive. But the man as revealed in the great arc of his plays shows to be resurrectional in his ultimate philosophy: life emerges from death, rediscovery from loss, reconnection from separation. From the energy and dreams of youth through the comedic and tragic developments forged in his maturity to an ultimate statement of love and restitution—this is the movement of Shakespeare's collective work. And though we cannot date each play with precision, it is the generally accepted order of his plays that produces this observation.

At the end of his life, judging from his will, his homecoming to Stratford gave him his closest relationship to his daughter Susanna: how like Pericles and Marina, how like Prospero and Miranda. Along with Susanna and her husband John Hall his greatest delight may have been provided by their daughter, Elizabeth. Susanna was "witty beyond her sex"; she was called Good Mistress Hall and she had "something of Shakespeare" in her according to the epitaph on her tomb. Shakespeare's other daughter Judith's marriage gave him problems, though he revised his will in such a way as to protect her inheritance and financial interests, and left her, for a valuable and tangible keepsake, his silver bowl. Whereas it is always conjecture to create links between the characters in Shakespeare's plays and the people in his life, the importance of his own daughters is reflected in the picture he develops between the fathers and daughters in many of his plays. From Aegeus and Hermia in *A Midsummer Night's Dream* to the Duke and Celia in *As You Like It,* from the father-king in *Love's Labours Lost* whose death so deeply affects his daughter, to Lord Capulet and Juliet in *Romeo and Juliet,* to Polonius and Ophelia in *Hamlet,* to Prospero and Miranda in *The Tempest,* Pericles and Marina in *Pericles,* to Lear, Regan and Goneril and (most moving) Lear and Cordelia in *King Lear,* these relationships are complex, nuanced, and deeply explored. Here, indeed, Shakespeare's imagination was fed by his own profound experience.

William Shakespeare was a family man who spent twenty-three years of his adult life (1588–1611) away from home. This made his family relations (as intense and constant as his business dealings show them to have been) different from most families of the time. Surely it is true, however, that a family—any family—while unique in itself, is always of its time. The Shakespeares were Elizabethan/Jacobeans and fully a product of their era. William Shakespeare shared with his father, John, and his grandfather, Richard, a drive toward upward mobility that was encouraged and stimulated by Elizabethan culture. A willingness to take risks, a capacity to work hard, and a practicality of temperament were family traits that helped William Shakespeare thrive in the contentious religious and political era in which he lived.

Part IV
Shakespeare's Families
in His Work

16
Family Relationships in Shakespeare's Plays

Family relationships appear in thirty-five of the thirty-seven commonly accepted plays by Shakespeare.[1] There are too many to analyze all in detail, but information can be gleaned from even a summary look. Presented here is a brief overview of a number of these relationships, with commentary on the most important examples and, wherever appropriate, a reminder of connections between the relationships in the plays and the family experiences of Shakespeare's own life.[2]

Only *Love's Labour's Lost* and *Timon of Athens* (one written in the exultation of early, youthful and independent success, the other in the cynicism of a mid-life crisis) lack family members in the cast of characters. Yet *Love's Labour's Lost* is one of three plays where a family member is named, is spoken of frequently, and is so crucial to the plot that one is surprised to find the character never appears. In *Love's Labour's* this character is the King of France, father to the Princess, whose death casts a pall over the end of the play; similarly, in *As You Like It* Orlando's father, Sir Roland de Boys, takes on a tangible personality as Orlando cries out in his father's defense. In *All's Well that Ends Well*, Helena's father, the physician Gerald de Narbon, is so crucial to her capabilities and actions that, once again, it is hard to believe he is never seen onstage. A search throughout the plays would doubtless find other examples of what we might call vital offstage characters.

The cast lists of the plays specify the following relationships a dozen times or less: uncles and nieces (six times), mothers and daughters (seven times), sisters (three times), cousins (eight times), in-laws (ten times), great-uncles and nephews (three times), grandparents (also three), aunts and nephews (also twice). In greater numbers we find brothers and sisters (nine occurrences), uncles and nephews (twenty-five), mothers and sons (twenty-two), fathers and daughters (thirty-two), brothers (thirty-six), husbands and wives (forty-four), and far more numerous than any other relationship, fathers and sons (an astonishing sixty-six).[3]

The father-son, uncle-nephew, and brother-brother scenes are numerous largely because ten of Shakespeare's plays are English histories where extended families bicker, fight, and war over the succession to the crown. Each contending family contains fathers and sons and uncles and nephews and cousins, in confusing proliferation. Using the Chronicles of Holinshed as his primary source, to a large extent Shakespeare had his cast set for him every time he chose this familiar and documented historical subject matter.

Casts were similarly predetermined for most of Shakespeare's Greek and Roman plays. But in the comedies and the romances Shakespeare more freely chose and created his various characters. In the histories, how Shakespeare develops his given characters fascinates; in the comedies, the great tragedies, and the late romances, our interest is equally in the development of characters he borrows from fictional or historical sources and those he invents.

The dominance of male characters throughout the canon reflects the fact that Shakespeare was limited to an all-male company of actors, and the reality that men took a more active part in Elizabethan society, publicly but also domestically. Female parts were relegated to trained boy apprentices and perhaps by young men still able to convince as women. In light of these restrictions, Shakespeare's genius was apparent not only in the undeniable richness of his male characters but in the number, diversity, and depth of his female creations.

HUSBANDS AND WIVES

Forty-Four Instances in Twenty-Three Plays

The married relationship, happy or sad, compatible or stormy, supportive or competitive, is presented forty-three times in the plays of Shakespeare. The presence of married couples is divided about equally through the groups of plays: in the English histories we find thirteen couples, in the Roman/Greek plays, six; in the comedies, seven; in the tragedies eleven; and in the late romances, six.

With his antenna ever-sensitive to powerful dramatic conflict, Shakespeare does not draw back from showing the misery marriage often brings. In *Richard III*, for instance, Lady Anne can (and does) reap nothing but agony from her marriage to the seductive but evil king. Queen Margaret is volubly miserable in her political marriage to Henry VI (*Henry VI Parts 2* and *3*), and Octavia has no hope for happiness when she is forced by her brother into a political marriage with Mark Antony, a man who, despite his courtesy to Octavia, is known throughout the Roman world to be besotted by Cleopatra (*Antony and Cleopatra*).

But sometimes unhappiness is brought simply by character weakness in the partners: Antipholus of Ephesus (*The Comedy of Errors*) is careless of his wife, Adriana, who in turn becomes shrewish and so pushes him away when she most wants him near her. In *The Taming of the Shrew*, Bianca and Lucentio show hints at their wedding feast that they will in all likelihood have a similarly tart and quarrelsome union.

Sometimes Shakespeare acknowledges the unhappiness in marriage triggered by male dominance: in *Romeo and Juliet* Lady Capulet is so frightened by her tempestuous husband that she cannot defend her weeping daughter when he berates her. Emilia (in *Othello*) is similarly terrified by her husband, the vicious and demanding Iago; Alice Ford suffers from a jealous husband and speaks of envy for her good friend Margaret Page whose husband is easy-going "You are the happier woman" (*The Merry Wives of Windsor*, act 2, scene 1); while Caesar's status, ego, and pride in *Julius Caesar* cow the worried Calphurnia. Though not afraid to speak her mind to him, Calphurnia recognizes instantly the moment she must draw back.

Happy couples, or possibilities for happiness in marriage, are not rare in Shakespeare's world view. However, in the serious plays, couples who begin with every experience or hope of happiness, through the action of the play, often come to grief: the Montagues (*Romeo and Juliet*) are destroyed by the tragedy that consumes their son Romeo; and Romeo and Juliet, who in other circumstances might have had a happy life, have only one night of marital bliss. In Denmark, had there been no older brother to challenge his ambition and lust, Claudius and Gertrude might have enjoyed years of happiness (*Hamlet*). Gertrude seems to have found happiness with each of the brothers, until the guilt of Claudius becomes undeniable in the last scene. The imperative of politics in *Julius Caesar* keeps Brutus from his beloved Portia, separates Cordelia from the honorable King of France in *King Lear*, and parts the loving Macduffs in *Macbeth*. Witnessing the sad ending death brings to the marriages of Hotspur and Lady Hotspur (*Henry IV Part 1*), Othello and Desdemona (*Othello*), Antigonus and Paulina (*The Winter's Tale*)—to say nothing of the Macbeths—we are the more grateful for the happy couples Shakespeare creates; for the domestic compatibility shown by the Duke and Duchess of York at the end of *Richard II* as they sit and chat (happiness broken only temporarily, we can imagine, by their argument over their rebellious son); for the joy of the reunited Aegeon and Aemilia at the end of *The Comedy of Errors*; or for the happy future that Katharina can hope for with Petruchio (*The Taming of the Shrew*), Imogen will find with Posthumus (*Cymbeline*) and the reformed Leontes is granted with the resurrected Hermione, a reunion which brings a moving close to one of Shakespeare's last and most hopeful plays, *The Winter's Tale*.

PARENTS AND SONS

Fathers and Sons

Sixty-Six Instances in Twenty-Five Plays

Whether his stories were determined by history, suggested by fictional sources, or completely invented, Shakespeare recognized the father/son dynamic as one filled with dramatic possibilities that he explored to the full. From *The Comedy of Errors*, where Aegeon searches with heart-breaking determination for his lost son, to Alonso grieving for the son he believes dead in the shipwreck that opens

The Tempest; from the deaths of young Talbot and his father in *Henry VI Part 1* to the outburst of jealousy Leontes shares with his young Mamillius in *The Winter's Tale*; from Vincentio seeking the son he had sent off to university in *The Taming of the Shrew*, to the unutterable anguish of Macduff hearing from Ross of the slaughter of his children in *Macbeth*; in other words from the very beginning of his career to the very end, Shakespeare illuminated the relationship of fathers with their sons.

The most complex, developed, and nuanced treatment of the father/son relationship comes in Shakespeare's great middle period (1596–1606). He had reached his maturity as an experienced playwright, and the observer might conclude he had achieved success in his personal life as well. Though in 1596 he suffered the inestimable loss of his young son, Hamnet, his family had emerged from years of financial need. The Shakespeares were granted their longed-for coat of arms in 1596 and William Shakespeare purchased New Place, his grand house in Stratford, the next year. Professionally he was at the top of his form and dove with gusto into the writing of *Henry IV Parts 1* and *2* where he turned his genius to making alive the relationship between the wild young Prince Hal and his kingly father, Henry IV. To do so he juxtaposed the father-king and son-prince to the mock father-son relationship existing between Prince Hal and Falstaff; and to the idealized relationship the king envisioned as existing between the Earl of Northumberland and his son the heroic but volatile "Hotspur," Henry Percy.

From his earliest histories (*Henry V, Parts 1, 2, 3*) Shakespeare discovered the power of juxtaposing similar situations: in *Henry VI Part 1* the moving relationship between Talbot and his young son is counter pointed by the relationship between the Master Gunner of Orleans and his son. And it was ever Shakespeare's tendency to explore and then re-explore an idea or technique that intrigued him. In this early attempt (*Henry VI Part 1*) at using two examples to express an idea, Shakespeare simply shows a scene in Act 1 concerning the gunner and his boy, then in Act 4 shows a more expanded scene between Talbot and his son. By the time he comes to *Henry IV*, however, his skills find expression in a more complex architecture; here he has constructed something akin to a Gothic cathedral in the complex structural patterns connecting the fathers and sons: fathers have scenes with their sons; fathers have scenes apart form their sons, the sons have scenes apart from their fathers (Hal with his disreputable friends, Hotspur with his wife); the king anguishes to himself and to others over the behavior of his son, speaking with envy of Northumberland and his noble off-spring; Prince Hal is given soliloquies and asides to shade and complicate his motives; and in an exhilarating stroke of genius Shakespeare has Hal and Falstaff act out for the denizens of Eastcheap an imagined encounter between Hal and his father, with the two changing roles, giving both Falstaff and Hal a chance to play at being king and son.

Equally masterful is the parallel relationship of fathers and their children that Shakespeare explores nearly a decade later in *King Lear*. Now we have a father with daughters (a relationship that Shakespeare will explore in each of his last works) juxtaposed with a father and his sons (Gloucester): three daughters for Lear, two sons (one a bastard) for Gloucester. In both *Henry IV Parts 1 and 2* and in *King Lear* the father character starts with a false evaluation of a son. And the progression of the sons, Hal (in *Henry IV*) and Edgar (in *King Lear*), throughout the action of the plays is toward the ultimate care and concern for a dying father. But the line of development in the earlier *Henry IV* is straightforward compared to *Lear*, where Gloucester begins as a character with a flawed relationship to one of his sons (bragging of the illicit and casual sex that resulted in Edmund's birth, for example) and where the father takes a far more harrowing journey to enlightenment, a journey that will involve torture, blindness, and total dependency on the son he believed had plotted against his life.

To analyze all the father/son scenes in Shakespeare would require a book of its own. Even a cursory look, however, produces an undeniable observation: all the father characters are positive. Even when Leontes (*The Winter's Tale*) has a crazed out-pouring of jealousy expressed in the presence of his young son Mamillius, or Vincentio complains about his son spending all his money at university, or the Duke of York fulminates against his traitor son, or Henry IV speaks of his wish that his dissolute son were more like the noble Hotspur, they are concerned fathers overwhelmed momentarily by illness and/or emotion triggered or compounded by a stressful situation. The dramatically explosive scenes do not represent their whole being. Fathers in Shakespeare show infinite love and concern for their sons: they want them to marry for love (Alonso in *The Tempest*), they want them to leave the dangers of the field of battle (Talbot in *Henry VI Part 1*) or the perils of an attack (Banquo in *Macbeth*), they search for them at the cost of endangering their own lives (Egeon, *The Comedy of Errors*), they grieve immeasurably when told their children have died (Macduff in *Macbeth*), they come looking for them when they haven't heard from them (Vincentio in *Taming of the Shrew*), they trust them to avenge their deaths and care for their mothers (Ghost in *Hamlet*).

It is hard to imagine a man who had a negative relationship with his own father creating this galaxy of admirable father characters, impossible to believe that these men are not in some way a gift to Shakespeare (and to us) from the fine man who was his own father.

Mothers and Sons

Twenty-Two Instances in Thirteen Plays

Shakespeare must have had the talents of several extraordinary boy or young male actors to meet the demands of the mother characters who exist in thirteen of his plays. We know Shakespeare had an unusually able mother of his own, giving him daily experience with the intelligence and capabilities of a traditional, domestic woman; in London he viewed first hand the behaviors of Queen Elizabeth as a powerful woman in public life; in between were all the mothers he must have known in his home and working life. In creating his "mothers" Shakespeare reflects qualities of them all.

Mistress Page in *The Merry Wives of Windsor* is one with the middle-class women Shakespeare knew growing up in Stratford, or with the competent wives of his colleagues in London; but though Mistress Page has a son, Shakespeare gives her no scene with him. In other plays the scenes between mothers and sons are frequently brief (though telling), such as the tiny scene in *Romeo and Juliet* where Lady Montague worries about her Romeo's depression, an important foreshadowing as later we hear she has died, her husband says, from her worries over her beloved son.[4] In *Richard III* we have a confrontation between an agonized mother and her evil, unreachable child, her last resort being to curse him: "Bloody thou art, bloody will be thy end; Shame serves thy life and doth thy death attend" (*Richard III*, act 4, scene 4).

Two powerful royal mothers appear in *King John*: the king's mother Elinor who does not hold back from criticizing and hectoring her kingly son, and Constance, whose son Arthur is the rallying figure for Philip of France to make claim to the British throne. Here we observe again Shakespeare's technique of counter pointing two similar relationships in a single play. The action begins with John and his mother, Elinor, arguing about the threat from France. Elinor in fact blames the ambitions of Arthur's mother, Constance, for the current situation:

> What now, my son? Have I not ever said
> How that ambitious Constance would not cease
> Till she had kindled France and all the world,
> Upon the right and party of her son?

She then blames her own son, John, for lacking in diplomacy:

> This might have been prevented and made whole
> With very easy arguments of love,
> Which now the manage of two kingdoms must
> With fearful-bloody issue arbitrate
>   *King John*, act 1, scene 1

Constance and Arthur represent a continuing exploration of the relationship between mother and powerful son that Shakespeare had already presented between the Duchess of York and Richard III and that he would explore with more complexity a few years later in *Coriolanus* between Volumnia and her son. Constance, a favorite role with nineteenth-century actresses, has more scenes *about* her son than *with* him and her greatness of found in act 3, scene 4 where she voices her agonizing grief for the loss of her Arthur:

> I am not mad. I would to heaven I were,
> For then 'tis like I should forget myself:
> O, if I could, what grief should I forget!
> Preach some philosophy to make me mad. . . .

It has often been observed that Shakespeare might have channeled his grief at his own son's death through the passionate, grieving speeches of Constance in *King John*.

In a completely different key, the fifth act of *Richard II* shows the Duchess of York defending her son, discovered to have been a traitor, in a scene, to some scholars, so out of character to the rest of the play that they question its authenticity as Shakespeare's writing. This is the judgment of literary minds, however, minds desiring in a play consistency of language and tone, and therefore unable to recognize the dramatic brilliance of giving an audience a moment of heightened energy and comedy in contrast to Richard's complex prison soliloquy to come. The Yorks' son Aumerle is revealed to be part of a conspiracy to kill the new king at Oxford, and his father, the Duke of York, determines to expose him to the king no matter what the cost. The Duchess, fearing for her son's life, races to reach the king first to beg for mercy for her son. The contesting pleas of father and mother to their nephew-king on behalf of their child, the king's cousin, bring aspects of domesticity to bear on a crucial political issue and illustrate that the power and interest of Shakespeare's family scenes often comes from the connecting, or juxtaposing of public and private life.

As interesting as the above scenes unquestionably are, Shakespeare's great scenes between mothers and their sons are those between Gertrude and Hamlet (*Hamlet*), Volumnia and Coriolanus (*Coriolanus*), Lady Macduff and her small son (*Macbeth*).

Gertrude seems to have had a long and close relationship with her son, Hamlet. A loving but not deeply insightful woman, she is shocked and horrified by Hamlet's treatment of her when she calls him to her room to reprimand him for his behavior. She is so stunned by Hamlet's comparison between Claudius and Hamlet senior that one wonders if Hamlet's perception of his father's character was not a far cry from Gertrude's experience of the man. In their scene, commonly called the "Closet Scene" we see the son bitterly critical of his mother's actions, and see as well that the young man has grown beyond any hope of his mother's controlling him. He frankly describes sexual activities between his mother and his uncle:

> Nay but to live
> In the rank sweat of an enseamed bed
> Stewed in corruption, honeying and making love
> Over the nasty sty –

and

> Let [not[the bloat king tempt you again to bed,
> Pinch wanton on your cheek, call you his mouse,
> And let him for a pair of reechy kisses,
> Or paddling in your neck with his damned fingers
> Make you ravel all this matter out . . . "
>
> *Hamlet*, act 3, scene 4

These descriptions shock her as much as his accusations and hatred of her new husband appall. Horrified by Hamlet's murder of Polonius, Gertrude ends the scene distraught at the vision of her beloved son gone mad. To whatever extent one chooses to interpret Hamlet's actions and feelings as the externalization of an Oedipal complex, the tie between Hamlet and his mother is deep, emotional, and passionate and the scene speaks with a powerfully modern voice.

Volumnia in *Coriolanus* is a very different character. She is the incarnation of all-ambitious Roman women whose self-worth depends on the heroic behavior of their male children. She still exerts control over her adult son, Coriolanus. As Dover Wilson has pointed out, "Throughout the whole of the first movement of the play there runs a female and domestic thread binding it together, though completely lacking in the biography . . . The drama of Coriolanus is built up around two crises that arise from situations in which the hero finds himself forced to choose between his duty as a man of honour and his duty as a son. It is the clash of wills between mother and son that marks the culmination of both movements."[5] When, in the first instance, Volumnia demands her son act against his own integrity, she has only to shame him: "At thy choice then. /To beg of thee, it is my more dishonour/ Than thou of them"—and out of his childlike need to please her, he agrees. In the second instance, at the end of the play, she tries again to persuade him to act against his desire. She is pleading for an action that will spare her own life and that of his wife and children, a question of Nature that outweighs his need for Honor. Again he gives way to her, though he intuits it will be at the cost of his own life. The force and power of women working in men's lives, of mothers working through their sons, is a great theme enacted between Volumnia and her son in *Coriolanus*.

For pure horror, however, nothing in Shakespeare exceeds the scene in *Macbeth* between Lady Macduff and her little son, chatting and teasing away their apprehension and their need for Macduff while, unknown to them, murderers stalk the corridors of their castle, closing in. The murderers attack; the boy Macduff's gallant defense of his mother is heartbreaking, and her anguish at witnessing his death just before her own, unbearable.

The mother scenes in Shakespeare's plays stand out for the dramatically divergent characters they present. Gertrude, Volumnia, Lady Macduff, the Duchess of York, Elinor, and Constance can hardly be more different—until we include the barbaric Tamora (*Titus Andronicus*), Cymbeline's Queen and her dreadful Cloten (*Cymbeline*), the Countess of Rousillon and Bertram (*All's Well That Ends Well*), and the holy Aemilia (*The Comedy of Errors*). The boys who performed these roles—so unique, so colorful, so multifaceted—must have been gifted, indeed.

PARENTS AND DAUGHTERS

Fathers and Daughters

Thirty-One Instances in Twenty-Two Plays

From Roman times onwards comedy has concerned itself with love relationships: the wooing and courtship, trials and hardships of young couples are its primary content. And it has often been observed that while tragedy ends in death, comedy ends in marriage. Shakespeare was schooled in these traditions as were his audiences, so in all of his comedies women at last carry a central role. Their fathers do as well, since to arrange a good marriage for his daughters in both the classic world and in Shakespeare's day was a father's responsibility. Conflict often comes, not surprisingly, when a daughter in a comedy does not want to marry the man of her father's choice. Though in his early career Shakespeare treated fathers and daughters following this theatrical convention, by the end of his writing life the relationship between fathers and daughters was a theme he chose to explore in far greater depth.

Except in the "easy-going" plays, where the fathers are less insistent and the stakes less deadly (the Duke of Milan vis a vis his daughter Silvia in *The Two Gentlemen of Verona*, George Page vis a vis his daughter Anne in *The Merry Wives of Windsor*, and Duke Senior in *As You Like It*) the early plays begin with an enormous problem created by the father's assumption that the daughter is his property. She must accept his rulings and obey his dictates. The father is blind to his daughter's identity as a person and assumes that she has no feeling or thoughts worthy of consideration. This reflects the position codified in patriarchal Elizabethan (and all other Western pre-modern) society. But in each Shakespeare play that follows this convention, the daughters' rebellions force their own growth, and by the end of the play the young women compel the respect of their fathers and of their audience as well.

To register this change, Shakespeare gives us Lord Capulet trying to compel his daughter, Juliet, to marry Count Paris, and thereby changing the play from the comedy of the first half to the tragedy of the second. In a lighter vein, the surprised Egeus discovers his daughter asleep in the forest at the end of *A Midsummer Night's Dream*, Duke Senior recognizes his daughter Rosalind at the end of *As You Like It*, and (most symbolically) Hero returns from the dead and newly appreciated at the end of *Much Ado About Nothing*. In other comedies when the father is not there, other male figures stand in; they register astonishment as Viola is recognized by Sebastian at the end of *Twelfth Night*, and as Portia reveals herself to have been the young lawyer in *The Merchant of Venice*.

Regan and Goneril in *King Lear* are contrasted with Cordelia not only by the way they behave, but by the way their father perceives them and treats them. Their true characters emerge in relationship to him. Lear is at first unable to recognize the true worth of his daughters, valuing the ones who lie and dissemble in order to comply with what he and society expect of a woman, and refusing to acknowledge the value of the one who, secure in her own personhood, identity, and values, speaks honestly her own mind. His example is symbolic of the Western view of males toward women of the time. And Lear shows the danger of this willful dominance. His misreading of women comes near to destroying him. He is redeemed in the end by the daughter he had scorned, barely saved from destruction by the monsters he, the patriarch, had created.

After *King Lear*, all four of the late romances celebrate the special relationship that can exist between a father and a daughter whom he truly loves and values.

In *Cymbeline* we start again with the father who misinterprets his daughter and condemns her marriage. Within a fairy-tale framework, *Cymbeline* is a king whose journey, like Lear's, will be through agony to rightful perception. A variation on this theme is worked out in *The Winter's Tale*, where the flawed Leontes would happily have seen his new-born daughter dead. A loving father figure here, however, emerges in the person of the old shepherd who finds Perdita abandoned on the beach and raises her as his own. We see in the sheep-shearing scene how the adoptive father trains his beloved daughter to take her place as a woman in company:

> Pray you, bid
> These unknown friends to's welcome, for it is
> A way to make us better friends, more known:
> Come, quench your blushes, and present yourself
> That which you are, Mistress o' th' Feast. Come on,
> And bid us welcome to your sheep-shearing
> As your good flock shall prosper.
> *The Winter's Tale*, act 4, scene 4

And we feel that such is the integrity of these simple people that once Perdita has returned to Bohemia, married her Florizel, and come into her own as Leontes' daughter, she will not forget the father who raised her.

On the other hand, Prospero's thoughts and plans as he creates his tempest are all for his daughter. He recognizes the need to guide her into the world that will be hers after his death, and takes care that she will come into the inheritance that is rightfully hers, and will be loved and honored as well. In the same way Pericles has never forgotten the baby Marina, the creation of his love with Thaisa, and his rediscovery of his daughter and their reconciliation is the climax of the play that bears his name.

Surely the remarkable stories Shakespeare spun about fathers and daughters relate in some way to his experience with his own daughters. From his will we know that Susanna, his elder daughter, was special to him. From his will we also conclude that his second daughter, Judith, was more difficult. Shakespeare is sympathetic with the fathers of the daughters in his plays, as he is sympathetic to the young women. The fathers are not perfect. Needing to control their daughters, in the early plays they more often erupt in uncontrollable anger at the girls than fathers in Shakespeare ever do with their sons. But the outbursts are filled with understanding. Even Shylock (*The Merchant of Venice*) is pitiable as the efforts he makes to protect his daughter, Jessica, work against him. She is his property. He loves her in his way but he has no appreciation of her needs and no awareness of his own cruelty. Nor does he have any way of anticipating that the force of her desperation will lead her to steal from him and run from home. When he discovers her escape he explodes violently against her as Lord Capulet (*Romeo and Juliet*) does against the rebellious Juliet; Egeus threatens Hermia with death or seclusion in a nunnery if she doesn't marry the man he chooses for her (*A Midsummer*

Night's Dream); Leonato (*Much Ado about Nothing*) berates, nay almost beats, his daughter when she's accused of impurity on her wedding day—yet these are but single, climactic scenes in plays where, by the end, each father but one shows his fundamentally decent character, his care for his child. Shylock, the exception, is the most to be pitied. He is the one father in Shakespeare who ends embittered rather than enlightened by his relationship with his daughter.

Mothers and Daughters

Seven Instances in Seven Plays

In three plays, Shakespeare's mother-daughter relationships involve directly the marriage of the daughters: this is true for the Queen of France and Katherine in *Henry V*, Mistress Page and her daughter Anne in *The Merry Wives of Windsor*, and Lady Capulet and Juliet in *Romeo and Juliet*. In two other plays the subject is presented less directly: in *All's Well that Ends Well* the scenes between the Widow, her daughter Diana, and Helena are essential to set the bed-trick that will gain Helena the husband she desires and Diana the dowry she needs; and in *Cymbeline*, the mother-daughter relationship is one-step removed, for the wicked, duplicitous queen is not mother but stepmother to Imogen. Here marriage is still the issue, however, as the Queen intends to gain Imogen as wife for her son, Cloten, despite Imogen's love and loyalty to her husband, Posthumus.

To return to the first plays mentioned: at the end of *Henry V* we see a marriage being brokered to unite two warring kingdoms. The Queen of France is dignified as she faces the English conqueror Henry V. She must be relieved to have seen in Henry a polite, courteous man and king as she accedes to his request for a private conference with her daughter, an encounter that everyone hopes will lead to marriage and the union of two kingdoms. How different the atmosphere in Windsor, a small town in England, where each of Anne Page's parents have chosen a suitor for her; and where she has chosen one for herself. Despite her mother's wish that she marry the local doctor, Anne is successful in gaining her own love, Fenton, at the end, and (*The Merry Wives of Windsor* being a light and delightful comedy) everything suggests she and her mother will continue to enjoy each other as Shakespeare's mother and wife and daughters did.

In *Romeo and Juliet,* Lady Capulet is much to be pitied. Though she seems to have a decent relationship with her husband, he is subject to violent outbursts when thwarted. His determination that Juliet marries Paris places his wife directly between her husband and daughter, and when a crisis erupts Lady Capulet fails to support her daughter, prompting the ensuing tragedy. The mother-daughter relationship in the Capulet household is triangulated by the presence of the nurse. Juliet seems to have had two mothers—the nurse who raised her day-to-day, and the mother who saw her only whenever she desired. The cost to intimacy in the mother-daughter relationship when a full-time nurse is brought in to care for the child is evident in this play.

The last two instances involve not marriage but return and recognition: in *The Winter's Tale* and in *Pericles* the mothers and daughters are returned to each other after a lifetime of separation. In *Pericles* the major focus is on the father-daughter recognition and we are given only the briefest scene between Thaisa, the mother, and Marina, her child. In *The Winter's Tale* Perdita also meets her long-lost mother, Hermione, just before the story ends. Knowing each of them as we do from the events of the play, we rejoice at the vision of the close relationship for this mother and this daughter that Shakespeare makes possible at the end of the play.

SIBLINGS

Brothers

Thirty-Six Instances in Sixteen Plays

Brotherhood looms large in the history plays, and the relationship is often not exclusive: those who are brothers on the one hand (like John of Gaunt and the Duke of York, like Richard III and Clarence and Edward) also exist as uncles to each other's children, and sometimes have roles in the same plays as husbands or cousins as well.

Royal brothers existed in a predetermined and fixed relationship to the throne. If a brother were ambitious for the crown and evil, as Richard III was presented by Shakespeare to be, any brother in his way was in danger for his life. So Clarence, innocent of his brother's evil nature until just before his murder, dies in a vat of wine at the hands of assassins hired by his brother.

Sometimes the reason a brother turns evil is illegitimacy. In *Much Ado About Nothing*, for instance, John the Bastard is the good Don Pedro's scheming half-brother, with no excuse for his vile behavior except (we surmise) his anger at his bastardy. In *King Lear* this rationale is made explicit: "Now gods, stand up for bastards!" Edmund cries out. His jealousy of Edgar's legitimacy prompts much of the evil action of that play. Interestingly, however, while John in *Much Ado* is unrepentant to the end, Edmund experiences a near-death conversion to good at the climax of *King Lear*. This sudden turnabout may seem unconvincing but it is a glimmer of the themes of hope, repentance, recognition, and reconciliation that will carry Shakespeare out of the darkness of the great tragedies and into the redemptive last plays of his career.

Sometimes, however, the case is reversed. In *King John* the hero, the liveliest and most idealistic character in the play, is Philip the Bastard, half brother to Robert Faulconbridge. And in one play, *As You Like It*, two sets of legitimate brothers show the inexplicably villainous behavior of a brother toward an innocent sibling: in one set, Duke Frederick, for unknown reasons, hates his brother, Duke Senior, and has usurped his lands and power, forcing the kindly Duke Senior to take refuge in the Forest of Arden. Similarly, on a nearby estate the heir, Oliver, has cultivated a violent dislike toward his younger brother, Orlando. Threatened by his brother and fearing for his life Orlando flees into the forest where he joins Duke Senior. Such is the power of nature, and the optimism of Shakespeare's comedic spirit, that Frederick and Oliver both find their way to transformation by the end of the play.

Brothers in Shakespeare are at times shown to be each other's greatest support. Agamemnon was called upon by his brother, Menelaus, to sail to Troy to re-capture his wife Helen, who had eloped with the young Trojan prince, Paris. Agamemnon and Menelaus with their Greek warriors set sail and the brothers find themselves embroiled in ten years of war with Troy (*Troilus and Cressida*). In *Macbeth* Malcolm and Donalbain cling to each other in the chaotic and threatening aftermath of Macbeth's murder of their father, Duncan. The little Princes in *Richard III* go to their doom in the Tower supported by nothing but each other.

One of the earliest genial flights of Shakespearean invention involved brothers and came in response to Plautus's Roman comedy *The Menaechmi,* the story of a pair of twins. Shakespeare, the father of twins himself, took Plautus' idea and developed it into *The Comedy of Errors*, adding a second set of twins who are servants to the first. The delight he seemingly takes and the skill he exhibits in exploring the complications the double set of twins offer marked him in this, one of his earliest plays, as a comedic genius. The recognition of the long-lost brothers at the end of the play is most sweetly and movingly expressed by the servant twins both named Dromio. They end the play agreeing as they exit:

> We came into the world like brother and brother:
> And now let's go hand in hand, not one before another.
> > *The Comedy of Errors*, act 5, scene 1

Brothers and Sisters

Nine Instances in Eight Plays

Of the nine brother and sister relationships Shakespeare delineates, most are of minor importance: Lady Elizabeth Grey, for instance, and her brother, Lord Rivers in *Henry VI Part 3* and in *Richard III*, or the Dauphin of France who has no connection specified at all with his sister, Katharine, in *Henry V*. In *The Winter's Tale*, Perdita is not even born until after the death of her brother Mamillius, though a rather charming relationship is suggested with her adopted brother, identified only as the Clown in the second half of that play. Finally, Octavia is kept a virtual shadow, merely a pawn of her powerful brother Octavius in *Antony and Cleopatra*.

But brother-sister relationships are crucial to the structure and themes of three great plays, written in relatively close proximity at the height of Shakespeare's powers between 1599 and 1604: *Twelfth Night, Hamlet,* and *Measure for Measure*.

In *Twelfth Night* the brother and sister, Viola and Sebastian, are twins, fraternal twins like Shakespeare's own had been, twins who have lost each other in a shipwreck. Believing each other dead as the play opens, each winds up in Illyria, thus giving Shakespeare a chance to rework in his maturity the comedy of mistaken identity he had so delightfully explored in *The Comedy of Errors*. In *Twelfth Night*, however, the twins' discovery of each other at the end of the play is a moment of breathtaking loveliness, slowly played out, fearfully and tentatively explored, and when at last believed and found to be true, profoundly moving.

Sebastian
I had a sister,
Whom the blind waves and surges have devoured . . .
Of charity, what kin are you to me?
What countryman? What name? What parentage?
Viola
Of Messaline: Sebastian was my father –
Such a Sebastian was my brother too:
So went he suited to his watery tomb:
If spirits can assume both form and suit
You come to fright us.
Sebastian
A spirit I am indeed,
But I am in that dimension grossly clad,
Which from the womb I did participate.
Were you a woman, as the rest goes even,
I should my tears let fall upon your cheek
And say 'Thrice welcome, drowned Viola?'
Twelfth Night, act 5, scene 1

The romantic relationships that await Viola with Orsino and Sebastian with Olivia pale in comparison to the importance of this reconciliation. Even so, all else in Shakespeare's life would have paled could he have brought back to life his dead son, Hamnet. If in Shakespeare all the world's a stage, so at times he must have felt the stage to be the world, where all that was most true in life could be created by his most potent art. If so, each time Viola looked and saw her lost brother on the stage so aptly named the Globe, at that moment Shakespeare could see evoked the resurrected presence of his son.

Written close to the same time as *Twelfth Night*, *Hamlet* also gives us as sister and brother in Ophelia and Laertes. The first scenes between them paint an intimate picture of two siblings, happy and affectionate in their relationship. As Laertes leaves to return to France they part with good-byes filled with teasing, serious advice, and gestures of love. Clearly the two form an alliance of youth and understanding against their loquacious and controlling father, Polonius, yet each has a strong and loving relationship with the father. The caring, recognizable, normal relationship between brother and sister, father and children heightens the tragedy of the play. And Ophelia's unconditional love for her father is particularly touching. Both the father and brother try to warn and defend the vulnerable young girl from Hamlet's advances; the father is killed by the maddened prince; the daughter is driven mad by Hamlet's rejection and her father's death; the brother finds himself too far away to protect his family until it is too late. We grieve for the deaths of these troubled but decent people, for the tragedy that has come unbidden and undeserved into their lives.

In *Measure for Measure* Claudio and Isabella are a far more distant sibling pair. Their personalities and experience of the world have led them in opposite directions, and circumstances make it difficult for them to understand each other. Claudio is an active and vigorous young man, in no way evil, but caught by an unyielding government edict against unmarried sex. He has impregnated a young woman, whom he fully intends to marry. The intent does not absolve him—he is imprisoned and faces death. Isabella is a postulant nun close to taking her final vows. Angelo, the acting Duke of Vienna, lusts after Isabella and offers Claudio's life in exchange for Isabella's sexual compliance. The scene in prison between the brother and sister, a scene with his life at stake, illustrates the radical difference between these two young people. At first sympathetic with his sister, Claudio finds the dread of death overcoming him:

> Ay, but to die, and go we know not where,
> To lie in cold obstruction and to rot
> This sensible warm motion—to become
> A kneaded clod; and the delighted spirit
> To bathe in fiery floods, or to reside
> In thrilling region of thick-ribbed ice . . .
> > *Measure for Measure*, act 3, scene 1

He asks himself, and her, What is the sacrifice of her virginity compared to the loss of his life? Isabella's commitment to purity, to principal, to honor, to a vision greater than the material world is everything to her, and is incomprehensible to him. Their impasse is one only the self-exiled Duke can negotiate—they can come to no meeting of the minds themselves. At the end of the play Shakespeare seems uneasy about Isabella; when the Duke asks her to marry him, Shakespeare gives her no reply. It is as if even he does not know what Isabella will do. It is evident, however, concerning her relationship with Claudio that this is one sibling pair too different in essence to be close.

Sisters

Three Instances in Three Plays

Three sets of sisters in only three plays: this is a small number compared with the plethora of brothers, yet to be expected for reasons stated elsewhere: a company of male actors, a primacy of men in the action of the private and public worlds, a privileging of male interests in the plots of plays. There are other female relationships—friends and cousins, mothers and daughters, for instance—but the only sisters Shakespeare gives us are Adriana and Luciana in *The Comedy of Errors*, Katherine and Bianca in *The Taming of the Shrew*, and Regan, Goneril, and Cordelia in *King Lear*.

Adriana and Luciana, in the early *The Comedy of Errors*, are the least differentiated. Adriana is more volatile, angry, jealous; Luciana calmer, more reconciling, and understanding. Otherwise they are two similar attractive young women, alluring to men and speaking easily and quickly in iambic verse.

Katharina and Bianca, however, are very different and developed to a far greater degree—in fact through the course of the play they completely exchange roles. At the beginning, Katharina, the shrew, is easily infuriated, explosive, ready to take offence, sharp, violent, witty, and deeply wounded. In contrast, Bianca, the younger, seems sweet and compliant, but her pretty face belies a clever, manipulative nature. They are opposites, and the story is a moral tale, redemptive only for Katharina who comes to know and value herself through the love of Petruchio. There seems little hope of reformation for Bianca. Whatever closeness the sisters will achieve after their marriages will come only from Katharina's new generosity of spirit, and will likely never be understood by her small-minded younger sister.[6]

Regan, Goneril, and Cordelia give Shakespeare the opportunity to contrast three sisters: two of narrow, selfish, and unkind disposition, the third a personification of love, honesty, and generosity of spirit. Having established the characters of the three sisters in the first two scenes of the play, Shakespeare sends Cordelia off to France and focuses on the two elder sisters. From scene to scene and act to act they move, often in support of each other, from selfishness to viciousness to violence and at last to unspeakable cruelty. Their soul-destroying actions become cannibalistic as, each, in pursuit of the duplicitous Edmund, finds any affection they had for each other consumed by their mutual jealousy and hatred. No one could mourn their well-deserved deaths at the end of the play.

Their younger sister, Cordelia, has seen her sisters' characters clearly from the beginning. She arrives from France to help her beleaguered father, but it is too late. The misperception of Lear, however, that began at the start of the play is corrected in the end. He sees and knows Cordelia, and through her sacrificial love for him he achieves redemption for his own soul.

UNCLES, AUNTS, AND NEPHEWS

Uncles and Nephews

Twenty-Five Instances in Eleven Plays

Aunts and Nephews

Two Instances in Two Plays

As noted above, the history plays abound in male familial relationships, including a number of uncles and nephews who come to the fore as related factions vie for the throne of England. Shakespeare himself was uncle by marriage to Richard Hathaway, born in 1583, the same year as Shakespeare's daughter, Susanna, and he became the uncle of young nephews again in the first decade of the seventeenth century when his sister Joan had three sons in fairly close succession.

This was a dozen years after he had written one of the most chilling scenes in theatre history: that between an evil uncle, Richard III (Gloucester), and his young nephews, the boys who would come to be remembered as the little princes in the Tower. The images of these boys would have come to Shakespeare from his own little son (around seven), his young brother, Edmund, his nephew (about nine), the children of his colleagues, and the sons of his friends. The boys, York, younger and more innocent, the older, Edward the Prince of Wales, more aware and more stoic, confront their cruel and ambitious uncle who is determined to sequester them in the Tower of London:

> Gloucester
> My lord, will't please you pass along?
> Myself and my good cousin Buckingham
> Will to your mother, to entreat of her
> To meet you at the Tower and welcome you.
> York (to his brother)
> What, will you go unto the Tower, my lord?
> Prince
> My Lord Protector needs will have it so.
> York
> I shall not sleep in quiet at the Tower.
> Gloucester
> Why, what should you fear?
> York
> Marry my uncle Clarence' angry ghost:
> My grandma told me he was murdered there.
> Prince
> I fear no uncles dead.
> Gloucester
> Nor none that live, I hope.
> Prince
> An if they live, I hope I need not fear.
> But come, my lord; so with a heavy heart,
> Thinking on them, go I unto the Tower.
> *Richard III*, act III, scene 1

The irony as the boy prince confronts his evil uncle directly, saying, "An if they live, I hope I need not fear," is infinitely poignant. We never see the boys again.

Half a dozen years later Shakespeare revisits the idea of an evil, ambitious uncle wanting to destroy a nephew barring his way to the throne in *King John*. Here the king, Arthur's uncle, contracts the boy's murder in a single chillingly shared iambic line:

> K. John
>   Death.
>   Hubert
> My lord?
>   K. John
>   A grave.
>   Hubert
>   He shall not live.
>   K. John
>   Enough.
> *King John*, act III, scene 3

But the boy Arthur has been friends with Hubert. That Hubert now intends torture and maim him (putting out both his eyes with hot irons), terrifies Arthur, and he is so eloquent in his appeal that Hubert cannot find it in his heart to hurt the child. Instead he lets him go and Arthur, bravely trying to escape, dies leaping from a cliff.

After Shakespeare matures out of his delight in creating these villainous uncles, wanton destroyers of youth and innocence, he produces three in-depth relationships between uncles and grown nephews: that between the Duke of York and John of Gaunt with Richard and Bolingbroke in *Richard II*; and that between Claudius and Hamlet in *Hamlet*.[7]

Richard II is the play that begins the Henriad, four plays—*Richard II, Henry IV Part 1*, *Henry IV Part 2*, and *Henry V*—that track the ascendancy of the Lancaster family in the struggle for the English throne during the early years of the fifteenth century. An important theme in *Richard II* is the divine right of kings; the overriding question in the play is: does one have the right to overthrow a legitimate and anointed sovereign who has proved himself to be a bad king? Richard's selfish, venal nature comes out in his treatment of his uncle, John of Gaunt. When he hears his uncle is dying, Richard's wish is that he may die quickly in order that Richard might take all his possessions to fund his ill-considered wars in Ireland:

> Richard
> Now put it, God, in the physician's mind,
> To help him to his grave immediately!
> The lining of his coffers shall make coats
> To deck our soldiers for these Irish wars....
> Come, gentlemen, let's all go visit him,
> Pray God we may make haste and come too late!
> *Richard II*, act 1, scene 3

Richard's other uncle, York, is caught firmly in the middle when Gaunt's son, Bolingbroke, comes back from exile in France to protest Richard's treatment of his dead father and to reclaim his inheritance. Those who disapproved of Richard's behaviors rally around Bolingbroke, wanting him to take over as king. York cannot condone the overthrow of an anointed king and thunders at the returning Bolingbroke:

> Bolingbroke
> My noble uncle. (he kneels)
> York
> Show me thy humble heart, and not thy knee,
> Which is deceivable and false.
> Bolingbroke
> My gracious uncle!
> York
> Tut, tut!
> Grace me no grace, nor uncle me no uncle,
> I am no traitor's uncle, and the word 'grace'
> In an ungracious mouth is but profane. . . .
> Bolingbroke
> My gracious uncle, let me know my fault,
> On what condition stands it and wherein?
> York
> Even in condition of the worst degree—
> In gross rebellion and detested treason.

After Bolingbroke explains that he has come back from exile only to retrieve his father's property, the Duke, confused between ideological imperatives and familial bonds, gives way:

> York
> If I could, by Him that gave me life,
> I would attach you all and make you stoop
> Unto the sovereign mercy of the king;
> But, since I cannot, be it known unto you,
> I do remain as neuter. So, fare you well,
> Unless you please to enter in the castle,
> And there repose you for this night.
> *Richard II*, act 2, scene 3

A half-dozen years later, Shakespeare moves the uncle-nephew relationship to the center of the plot in the first of his greatest tragedies, *Hamlet*. The connection between Hamlet and his uncle, between a reluctant protagonist and extraordinarily powerful antagonist, anchors the play. Whatever the quality of the relationship between the two characters might have been before the play begins, it is destroyed completely when Claudius marries Hamlet's mother. This triggers in Hamlet an anger and jealousy fed by the young man's conviction that his mother betrayed his father by marrying his uncle. The efforts of Claudius to establish a loving relationship with his nephew are revealed as monstrously hypocritical when we learn Claudius has indeed killed the older Hamlet in order to gain his throne and his wife. Hamlet's hatred of Claudius grows with the revelations of the Ghost, who tells Hamlet that his own brother Claudius killed him and then requires Hamlet to avenge his death. Throughout the action of the play uncle and nephew pursue, challenge, and taunt each other and the climax of the play finds Hamlet, the nephew, at last able to kill his primary antagonist, the king, his uncle.

Only twice did Shakespeare write of aunts and nephews: in *Romeo and Juliet* where Lady Capulet has a deep relationship with her nephew, Tybalt, a young man who seems to be living in the Capulet household, and in *Richard II* where the Duchess of York makes no bones about appealing strenuously, as his aunt, to the new king Henry IV. Each situation is deeply revealing of character: Lady Capulet is emotional, voluble, and courageous as she demands vengeance for Tybalt's death from the Prince; the Duchess is equally peremptory in demanding of her nephew turned king his pardon for her son. The one situation is tragic, the other comedic. The plays were written at about the same time and it would be interesting to know if the same boy played both parts.

These scenes with nephews in Shakespeare's plays are charged with his imaginative genius. As is customary with his plays, no one character can be tied with assurance to any one person in his life (as has been mentioned elsewhere in this book, his own uncle Henry seems as possible an inspiration for Falstaff as for any of the uncle characters). But the nephew relationship appears often in the plays and it was much experienced by Shakespeare in his life, with his Arden aunts, with their husbands, and with Henry Shakespeare, his father's brother.

UNCLES, AUNTS, AND NIECES

Uncles and Nieces

Six Instances in Four Plays

Nieces are given short shrift, numerically, compared to nephews. And yet the nieces are some of Shakespeare's most lively and delightful characters. In *As You Like It*, for instance, Rosalind unwittingly triggers the ire of her uncle, Duke Frederick. She escapes to the forest of Arden, where her father, uncle to her companion, Celia, lives in exile. In *Much Ado About Nothing*, Antonio is uncle to both Beatrice and Hero, his brother (Leonato) father to Hero but uncle to Beatrice. The affectionate relationship between these uncles and nieces is one of the delights of the play. Cressida in *Troilus and Cressida* is niece to Pandarus, who helps both create and destroy her romance with Troilus. With only the venal Pandarus to relate to, Cressida is a weak girl, to be pitied for her lack of a caring family. Less central to the action of plays are the relationships of Antonio, Prospero's brother in *The Tempest* who meets with his niece, Miranda, as a result of the opening shipwreck in that play, and King John who is uncle to Blanche of Spain in the play that bears his name.

There are no aunts and nieces in all the plays of Shakespeare, except for one curiosity: in *Much Ado About Nothing*, in the quarto printing of 1600, the first entrance of characters lists an Innogen as Leonato's wife. In Shakespeare's original idea, then, Hero had a mother and Beatrice an aunt Innogen. But there was no room for Innogen in the development of the story, and so she faded away and no longer appears in the cast lists of modern texts.[8]

IN-LAWS AND COUSINS

In-laws

Ten Instances in Seven Plays

Other relationships given a nod by Shakespeare are those between in-laws and cousins.

Volumnia, mother-in-law to Virgilia, wife to her son Coriolanus, struggles to make Virgilia like her in managing Coriolanus, an impossible task as their temperaments are completely opposite. In *Henry IV Part 2*, the Duke of Northumberland is confronted by the grieving Lady Percy who so passionately loved the son she felt he, the father, had betrayed. Desdemona's father, Brabantio, admires Othello as a man and a military hero, but cannot get past his own racism when confronted with his daughter's marriage to him. Baptista, who feared at the opening of *The Taming of the Shrew* that he would never see his daughters married, finds himself at the end of the play the father-in-law to two young men, Petruchio and Lucentio. King Lear has one vicious son-in-law (Cornwall) who takes sadistic delight in blinding the king's old friend Gloucester, and one, Albany, so decent he gives a glimmer of hope for a better world at the end of the play. Lear's inability at the start of the play to distinguish between the value of the two is typical of the egocentricity and blindness that doom him to the play's horrendous action. In two other plays, in-law relations exist but have no bearing on the action of the stories. These include Aegeon and Aemilia, unwitting parents-in-law to Adriana in *The Comedy of Errors*, and the Capulets and Lord Montague who discover in the tomb of their dead children that they are in-laws to the tragic Romeo and Juliet.

Cousins

Eight Instances in Six Plays

Of cousins there are eight sets. Achilles and Petroclus are cousins in *Troilus and Cressida*, and though much is made of their love and friendship, little is mentioned of their cousinly relationship. Richard II and Bolingbroke are also cousins in *Richard II*, but here the relationship, doomed by Richard's flaws and Bolingbroke's position in line for the throne, is constantly fraught. The cousinly relationships in the play are augmented by Aumerle, who is the son of the duke of

York and consequently finds himself caught between loyalties as cousin to both Richard, the anointed king, and to Bolingbroke, the usurper.

The closest cousins are presented almost as close as siblings in three plays; their affection and support for each other heart-warming. Interestingly of the three sets, two are young women. The first brotherly cousins are Benvolio and Romeo in *Romeo and Juliet*, cousins and the closest of friends; the sister-like cousins whose love runs very deep are Hero and Beatrice in *Much Ado About Nothing*, and Celia and Rosalind in *As You Like It*: "O coz, coz, coz, my pretty little coz," cries out Rosalind. "If you knew how many fathoms deep I am in love!" When one particularly loved a family member or a dear friend in Shakespeare's day, one often called them "cousin" or the sweet diminutive, "coz."

Shakespeare's plays would exist and have their immense value without any knowledge of the writer. But once another artist, the American painter Edward Hopper, wrote, when asked to explain the style and meaning of his paintings: "The man's the work. Something doesn't come out of nothing."[9] (Ah, yes, the echo of King Lear: "Nothing comes from nothing.") William Shakespeare wrote thirty-seven plays, two epic poems, some miscellaneous poetry and collaborative works, and one hundred and fifty-four sonnets, all of which are read and treasured to this day. The man is the work. Something doesn't come from Nothing. It is my hope that this book will help in the search for the man from whom this extraordinary body of work came.

Appendix A: Family Relationships in the Plays

Note: *indicates an unusual relationship.

GRANDPARENTS

> *Richard III*: The Duchess of York and Edward, Prince of Wales and Richard, Duke of York, son of Clarence, daughter of Clarence, their grandmother
> *Coriolanus*: Volumnia and Marcius, her grandson
> *Pericles*: Simonides, father to Thaisa and grandfather to Marina

FATHERS AND SONS

> *Henry VI Part 1*: Lord Talbot and John Talbot; Master-Gunner of Orleans and his son
> *Henry VI Part 2*: Richard Plantagenet, Duke of York, Edward and Richard, his sons; Lord Clifford and Young Clifford, his son
> *Henry VI Part 3*: Henry VI and Edward, Prince of Wales, his son; Richard Plantagenet, Duke of York and Edward, Earl of March, Edmund, Earl of Rutland, George, Duke of Clarence, Richard, Duke of Gloucester, his sons
> A son that has killed his father and a father that has killed his son
> *Richard III*: King Edward IV and Edward, Prince of Wales and Richard, Duke of York, his sons; Duke of Clarence and Young Son of Clarence; Duke of Norfolk and Earl of Surrey, his son
> *Titus Andronicus*: Titus Andronicus and Lucius, Quintus, Martius, Mutius, his sons; Lucius and Young Lucius, his son; Marcus Andronicus and Publius, his son; Aaron, a Moor, and the blackamoor Child, his son
> *The Comedy of Errors*: Aegeon and Antipholus of Ephesus and Antipholus of Syracuse, his twin sons

The Taming of the Shrew: Vincentio and Lucentio, his son

The Two Gentlemen of Verona: Antonio and Proteus, his son

Romeo and Juliet: Montague and Romeo, his son

Richard II: John of Gaunt and Bolingbroke, his son; The Duke of York and Aumerle, his son; The Earl of Northumberland and Henry Percy (Hotspur), his son

King John: King John and Prince Henry, his son; King Philip of France and Lewis, the Dauphin, his son

The Merchant of Venice: Old Gobbo and Lancelot Gobbo, his son

Henry IV Part 1: Henry IV and Prince Hal, and John of Lancaster, his sons; The Earl of Northumberland and Henry Percy (Hotspur), his son

Henry IV Part 2: Henry IV and Prince Hal, Prince John, Prince Humphrey, Prince Thomas, his sons

The Merry Wives of Windsor: George Page and William Page, his son

Henry V: The King of France and the Dauphin, his son

Julius Caesar: *Octavius Caesar was adopted as his son in Julius Caesar's will; Caesar was Octavius Caesar's great-uncle in actual blood-line

Hamlet: The Ghost of Hamlet, Senior, and Hamlet, his son; Polonius and Laertes, his son

Troilus and Cressida: Priam, King of Troy and Hector, Troilus, Paris, Deiphobus and Helenus, his sons; *Margarelon, bastard son to Priam

King Lear: The Earl of Gloucester and Edgar, his son; *Edmund, bastard son to Gloucester

Macbeth: Macduff and Young Macduff, his son; Banquo and Fleance, his son; Siward, the Earl of Northumberland, and Young Siward, his son; Duncan, King of Scotland, and Malcolm and Donalbain, his sons

Coriolanus: Coriolanus and Young Marcus, his son

The Winter's Tale: Leontes, King of Sicilia and Mamillius, his son; Polixenes, King of Bohemia and Florizel, his son; Old Shepherd and Clown, his son

Cymbeline: Cymbeline, King of Britain and Guiderius and Arviragus, his sons

The Tempest: Alonso, King of Naples and Ferdinand, his son

UNCLES AND NEPHEWS

Henry VI Part 1: Humphrey, Duke of Gloucester, uncle to the King; John, Duke of Bedford, uncle to the King; *Thomas Beauford, Duke of Exeter, great-uncle to the King; *Henry Beauford, Bishop of Winchester, great-uncle to the King

Henry VI Part 2: Humphrey, Duke of Gloucester, uncle to the King; *Cardinal Beauford, Bishop of Winchester, great-uncle to the King

Henry VI Part 3: Richard Plantagenet, Duke of York and Sir John Mortimer and Sir Hugh Mortimer, his uncles

Richard III: Richard Duke of Gloucester and Edward, Prince of Wales, Richard Duke of York and young Clarence, his nephews; George, Duke of Clarence, also uncle to Edward and Richard above; Edward IV, uncle to Young Clarence

Romeo and Juliet: Capulet and Tybalt, his nephew; Montague and Benvolio, his nephew

Richard II: John of Gaunt and Richard II and Aumerle, his nephews; The Duke of York and Richard and Bolingbroke, his nephews

King John: King John and Arthur, his nephew

Henry V: King Henry V and the Duke of Exeter, his uncle

Julius Caesar: *Julius Caesar and Octavius Caesar, his great-nephew (also adopted son)

Hamlet: Claudius and Hamlet, his nephew and step-son

The Tempest: Sebastian and Ferdinand, his nephew

MOTHERS AND SONS

Richard III: Elizabeth, Queen to Edward IV and the Marquis of Dorset and Lord Grey, her sons; The Duchess of York and Edward IV, Clarence and Gloucester (Richard) her sons

Titus Andronicus: Tamora and Alarbus, Demitrius and Chiron, her sons

The Comedy of Errors: Aemilia and Antipholus of Ephesus and Antipholus of Syracuse, her twin sons

Romeo and Juliet: Lady Montague and Romeo, her son

Richard II: The Duchess of York and Aumerle, her son

King John: Queen Elinor and King John, her son; Constance and Arthur, her son; Lady Faulconbridge and Robert Faulconbridge, her son

The Merry Wives of Windsor: Mistress Page and William Page, her son

Hamlet: Gertrude and Hamlet, her son

All's Well that Ends Well: The Countess of Rousillon and Bertram, her son

Macbeth: Lady Macduff and young Macduff, her son

Coriolanus: Volumnia and Coriolanus, her son; Virgilia and Marcius, her son

Cymbeline: Queen and Cloten, her son

The Winter's Tale: Hermione and Mamillius, her son

BROTHERS

Henry VI Part 1: Humphrey, Duke of Gloucester and John, Duke of Bedford, his brother; Thomas Beaufort, Duke of Exeter and Henry Beaufort, Bishop of Winchester, his brother

Henry VI Part 2: Sir Humphrey Stafford and William Stafford, his brother

Henry VI Part 3: Edward, Earl of March, Edmund, Earl of Rutland, George, Duke of Clarence, Richard, Duke of Gloucester, all brothers; The Earl of Warwick and the Marquess of Montague, his brother; Sir John Mortimer and Sir Hugh Mortimer, his brother

Richard III: Edward, Prince of Wales and Richard, Duke of York, his brother; King Edward IV, George, Duke of Clarence and Richard, Duke of Gloucester, all brothers; Marquis of Dorset and Lord Grey, his brother

Titus Andronicus: Saturninus and Bassianus, his brother; Titus Andronicus and Marcus Andronicus, his brother; Lucius, Quintus, Martius and Mutius, sons to Titus, all brothers

The Comedy of Errors: *Antipholus of Ephesus and Antipholus of Syracuse, twin brothers; *Dromio of Ephesus and Dromio of Syracuse, twin brothers

Richard II: John of Gaunt and Edmund, Duke of York, his brother

King John: *Robert Faulconbridge and Philip the Bastard, his half-brother

Much Ado About Nothing: *Don Pedro and Don John, his bastard half-brother

Henry V: King Henry V, and Humphrey, John and Thomas, his brothers

As You Like It: Duke Frederick and Duke Senior, his brother; Orlando and Oliver and Jaques, his brothers

Troilus and Cressida: Hector, Troilus, Paris, Deiphobus and Helenus, sons of Priam, all brothers; Agamemnon and Menelaus, his brother

Othello: Brabantio and Gratiano, his brother

King Lear: *Edgar and Edmund, his bastard half-brother

Macbeth: Malcolm and Donalbain, sons to King Duncan, brothers

The Tempest: Alonso and Sebastian, his brother; Prospero and Antonio, his brother

BROTHERS AND SISTERS

Henry VI Part 3: Lady Elizabeth Grey and Lord Rivers, her brother

Richard III: Elizabeth Grey (now Queen to Edward IV) and Lord Rivers, her brother

Henry V: Dauphin of France and Katharine, his sister

Twelfth Night: *Viola and Sebastian, her twin brother

Hamlet: Ophelia and Laertes

Measure for Measure: Claudio and Isabella, his sister

Antony and Cleopatra: Ocatvius Caesar and Octavia, his sister

The Winter's Tale: Perdita and Mamillius, her brother; *Perdita and Clown, her adopted brother

SISTERS

The Comedy of Errors: Adriana and Luciana, her sister

The Taming of the Shrew: Katherine and Bianca, her sister

King Lear: Regan, Goneril, Cordelia, all sisters

HUSBANDS AND WIVES

Henry VI Part 2: Margaret, Queen to King Henry VI, his wife; Simpcox, an imposter, Wife to Simpcox; Gloucester, Dame Eleanor Cobham, Gloucester's wife

Henry VI Part 3: Margaret, Queen to Henry VI, his wife; Lady Elizabeth Grey and Edward IV, her husband

Richard III: Lady Anne and Richard III, her husband; Duchess of York and Duke of York, her husband

Comedy of Errors: Aegeon and Aemilia, his wife; Antipholus of Ephesus and Adriana, his wife

The Taming of the Shrew: Katherine and Petruchio, her husband; Bianca and Lucentio, her newly-wed husband; Hortensio and the Widow

Romeo and Juliet: Capulet and Lady Capulet, his wife; Montague and Lady Montague, his wife; Romeo and Juliet, his wife

Richard II: Richard II and the Queen, his wife; The Duke of York and the Duchess of York, his wife

Henry IV Part 1: Henry Percy (Hotspur) and Lady Percy, his wife; Mortimer and Lady Mortimer, his wife

Henry IV Part 2: The Earl of Northumberland and Lady Northumberland, his wife

The Merry Wives of Windsor: George Page and Mistress Page, his wife; Frank Ford and Mistress Ford, his wife

Henry V: Charles, King of France and Isabelle, his wife

Julius Caesar: Caesar and Calphurnia, his wife; Brutus and Portia, his wife

Hamlet: Claudius and Gertrude, his wife

Troilus and Cressida: Hector and Andromache, his wife; *Paris and Menelaus contending for Helen as wife

Othello: Othello and Desdemona, his wife; Iago and Emilia, his wife

King Lear: Regan and Cornwall, her husband; Goneril and Albany, her husband; Cordelia and the King of France, her husband

Macbeth: Macbeth and Lady Macbeth, his wife; Macduff and Lady Macduff, his wife

Antony and Cleopatra: Antony and Octavia, his wife

Coriolanus: Coriolanus and Virgilia, his wife

Pericles: Pericles and Thaisa, his wife; Cleon and Dionyza, his wife

Cymbeline: Cymbeline and Queen, his wife; Imogen and Posthumus Leonatus, her husband

The Winter's Tale: Leontes and Hermione, his wife; Antigonus and Paulina, his wife

Henry VIII: Henry VIII and Katharine of Aragon, his wife

FATHERS AND DAUGHTERS

Henry VI Part 1: An old shepherd and Joan la Pucelle, his daughter; Reignier, Duke of Anjou, and Margaret, his daughter

Richard III: Clarence and Young daughter to Clarence

Titus Andronicus: Titus Andronicus and Lavinia, his daughter

The Taming of the Shrew: Baptista and Katherine and Bianca, his daughters

The Two Gentlemen of Verona: The Duke of Milan and Silvia, his daughter

Love's Labours Lost: *The Princess of France, the King of France, her father

Romeo and Juliet: Capulet and Juliet, his daughter

A Midsummer Night's Dream: Egeus and Hermia, his daughter

The Merchant of Venice: Shylock and Jessica, his daughter

Henry IV Part 1: Owen Glendower and Lady Mortimer, his daughter

The Merry Wives of Windsor: George Page and Anne Page, his daughter

Much Ado About Nothing: Leonato and Hero, his daughter

Henry V: Charles VI, King of France, and Katherine, his daughter

As You Like It: Duke Frederick and Celia, his daughter; Duke Senior and Rosalind, his daughter

Hamlet: Polonius and Ophelia, his daughter

Troilus and Cressida: Priam and Cassandra, his daughter; Calchas and Cressida, his daughter

All's Well That Ends Well: Lafeu and Diana, his daughter

Othello: Brabantio and Desdemona, his daughter

King Lear: King Lear and Goneril, Regan and Cordelia, his daughters

Pericles: Simonides and Thaisa, his daughter; Pericles and Marina, his daughter; Antiochus and Daughter to Antiochus

Cymbeline: Cymbeline and Imogen, his daughter
The Winter's Tale: Leontes and Perdita, his daughter; *Old Shepherd and Perdita, his foundling daughter
The Tempest: Prospero and Miranda, his daughter

MOTHERS AND DAUGHTERS

Romeo and Juliet: Lady Capulet and Juliet, her daughter
The Merry Wives of Windsor: Mistress Page and Anne Page, her daughter
Henry V: The Queen of France and Katherine, her daughter
All's Well That Ends Well: The Widow of Florence and Diana, her daughter
Cymbeline: *The Queen and Imogen, her step-daughter
The Winter's Tale: Hermione and Perdita, her daughter
Pericles: Thaisa and Marina, her daughter

AUNTS AND NEPHEWS

Romeo and Juliet: Lady Capulet and Tybalt, her nephew
Richard III: The Duchess of York and Bolingbroke, her nephew

UNCLES AND NIECES

King John: King John and Blanche of Spain, his niece
Much Ado About Nothing: Antonio and Hero and Beatrice, his nieces; Leonato and Beatrice, his niece
Troilus and Cressida: Pandarus and Cressida, his niece
The Tempest: Antonio and Miranda, his niece

COUSINS

Romeo and Juliet: Romeo and Benvolio, his cousin
Richard II: Richard II and Bolingbroke, his cousin; Richard II and Aumerle, his cousin; Bolingbroke and Aumerle, his cousin
Much Ado About Nothing: Hero and Beatrice, her cousin
Henry V: Henry V and the Duke of York (formerly Aumerle), his cousin
As You Like It: Rosalind and Celia, her cousin
Troilus and Cressida: Achilles and Petroclus, his cousin

IN-LAWS

The Comedy of Errors: Aegeon and Aemilia, parents-in-law to Adriana
The Taming of the Shrew: Baptista and Petruchio and Lucentio, his sons-in-law

Romeo and Juliet: Lord and Lady Capulet, parents-in-law to Romeo; Montague, father-in-law to Juliet

Henry IV Part 2: Lady Percy and the Earl of Northumberland, her father-in-law

Othello: Brabantio and Othello, his father-in-law

King Lear: King Lear and Cornwall and Albany, father-in-law

Coriolanus: Volumnia and Virgillia, her daughter-in-law

Appendix B: Stratford: Plays and Players

In researching my earlier book, *Shakespeare's Friends*, I became curious as to whether Shakespeare's family and friends in Stratford ever had the chance to see his plays or see him perform in his hometown. When I asked at the Shakespeare Birthplace Trust Records Office for a list of all acting companies that had played in Stratford between 1569 (the year Shakespeare's father as bailiff had first approved play performances there) and William Shakespeare's death in 1616, I was told no convenient list exists.

While in the Records Office, I was further intrigued to overhear a request to see the declaration by the Stratford Corporation in 1602 not to allow further performances of plays in the Guild Hall and the declaration's confirmation nine years later (1611). The ban on plays and players reflected the increasing Puritanism of the town's Corporation membership, which resulted in a surprising entry in the Stratford records of 1622 concerning the King's Men (addressed at the end of this article).

Knowledge of the ban on Guild Hall performances enabled me to limit my search for plays and players in Stratford during Shakespeare's lifetime to the years between 1569 and 1602.

As revealed in the Minutes and Accounts of the Chamber of Stratford-Upon-Avon, two chamberlains (in effect city treasurers) were elected from and by the aldermen each year, thus keeping a check on the town finances. At the first meeting in January (usually) the senior chamberlain presented the accounts, or what we would call the treasurer's report, to the Corporation council. The accounts consist first of the town revenues, then the town expenditures for the prior year. Revenues include rents for city-owned properties and often long lists, in time of plague or other illness, of names for whom the funeral bell had been rung (often paying for the ringing of the bell brought a good bit of money to the town coffers). Expenditures regularly include such items as the salary of the vicar and the schoolmaster, reimbursable expenses incurred by aldermen, payments for cleaning the streets and public buildings, the repair of bridges and other city property, and fees for the Guild Hall performances of touring acting companies.

In Shakespeare's day a playing company would enter a town and the leaders would go to the mayor or bailiff to request permission to give a public performance. This official, if willing, would ask for a performance in the Guild Hall in front of the aldermen, burgesses, and their families so that the council could judge the value (or at least the harmlessness) of the production. The town paid a fee for these Guild Hall presentations from city funds. If the play met with the approval of the city fathers the company would then be welcome to perform in one of the inns in town. For these later performances the company charged admission and from them most of the company's money was made.

The first Stratford Corporation payment for a Guild Hall performance noted below dates from the tenure of John Shakespeare as high bailiff, when his son William Shakespeare was five years old.

PLAYERS IN STRATFORD, 1569–1602

From the *Minutes and Accounts of the Corporation of Stratford-Upon-Avon and Other Records*
1553–1620
As transcribed by Richard Savage and Edgar I. Fripp, published in 1924

27 Jan. 1569/70	Item payd to the Quenes Pleyers	ix *s*
	[the payment was nine—the roman numeral— shillings – the *s*]	
	Item to the Erle of Worcesters Pleers	xij *d*
	[the payment 12 pence]	
1570/1	[no players listed]	
1571/2	[no players listed]	
1572/3	[no players listed]	
1573/4	pd to mr. bayly for the earle of lecesters pleyers	v *s* viij *d*
1574/5	[no players listed]	
14 Mar. 1575/6	geven my lord of Warwick players	xvij *s*
	[This might tie to the Queen's visit at this time to Warwick and Kenilworth.]	
	pd to the earle of Worcester players	v *s* viii *d*
29 Jan. 1577/8	Paid to my Lord of Leyster players [Leicester]	xv *s*
	Paid to my Lord of Wosters players	iij *s* iiij *d*
1578/9	[no players listed]	
1579/80	Paid to my lord Straunge men the xjth day of February at the commandment of Mr. Bailiffe	v *s*

	Paid at the commandement of Mr. bailliffe	
	to the countys of Essex plears	xiii *s* vj *d*
1580/81	[no players]	
31 Jan. 1581/2	Paid to the Earle of Worcester his players	iij *s* iiij *d*
	Paid to the L:Bartlett his players	iij *s* ij *d*
	[Berkeley]	
11 Jan. 1582/83	Payed to Henry Russell for the Earle of	
	Worcesters players	v *s*

[The 18 year old William Shakespeare
would in all likelihood have seen the 16
year old Edward Alleyn performing
in this company. This was the year of
Shakespeare's marriage.]

1583/4   Payd to Mr. Alderman that he layd downe to
ye lord Bartllite his players and to a preacher   v *s*

[The reimbursement to an alderman for
advancing the fee is interesting in view of
fines later assessed against such officials
paying for performances following the
council's action banning plays in 1602.
Tying a fee to players with a fee to a
preacher indicates that to some extent plays
were thought to be of strong moral persuasion;
this belief was hotly contested by many Puritans.
But as Fripp notes, "Puritan antagonism to the
drama was far from general in 1583."[1]]

Payd to Davi Jones and his companye for his
pastyme at Whitsontyde   xiiij *s* iiij *d*

[Davi Jones was a Stratford man, married
to Frances Hathaway, a cousin of
Shakespeare's wife[2]; this is the only entry
found relating to a locally produced
theatrical event.]

1584/5	geven to my lord of oxfords pleers	iij *s* iiij *d*
	geven to the earle of worceter pleers	iij *s* iiij *d*
1585/6	[no players listed]	
1586/7	paide to Mr. Tiler for the pleyers	v *s*

[Mr. Tiler, the bailiff, was the father of
Shakespeare's friend, Richard Tyler.[3]]

1587/8	It. gyven to the Quenes players	xx *s*
	It. gyven to my Lo: of Essex players	v *s*
	It. gyven to therle of Lycester his players	x s
	It. gyven to another Companye	iij *s* iiij *d*
	It. gyven to my Lo: Staffordes men	iij *s* iiij *d*

[This is the famous year when five troupes
played in Stratford. The Queen's Men

were missing an actor: one of their
players, William Knell, had been killed
in a fight. Leicester's Men were also
missing some company members who were
traveling in Denmark and Saxony. Leicester's
Men included at this time: James Burbage,
Will Kempe, George Bryan, and Thomas Pope
(actors with whom Shakespeare would later work).
These facts fuel speculation that Shakespeare
joined one of these companies in this year
and went with them to London.[4]]

1588/9	[no players listed]	
1589/90	[no players listed]	
1590/1	[no players listed]	
1591/2	[no players listed]	

[Beginning with 1593, we come to volume
V of the transcribed records, which now
have a new editor, Levi Fox. Savage and Fripp
used slashes to indicate that the records that
were submitted early in any given year covered
expenses of the previous year. The subsequent
volume gives only the year covered by the
expense report, not the year the report was
submitted.]

1593	paid to the queenes players	xx *s*
1594	paid to the Queenes players	xx *s*
1595	[no players listed]	
1596	[no players listed]	
1597	[no players listed]	
1598	payd to him for foure companies of players	xix *s* iiij *d*
	[The "him" is difficult to identify as antecedent names are unclear.]	
12 Jan. 1599	[no players listed]	
11 Jan. 1600	[no players listed.]	
9 Jan. 1601	[no players listed]	
8 Jan. 1602	[no players listed]	

Observations on the above data:

Two peculiarities in the English dating system make these early records hard
to interpret accurately. At this time, the fiscal year for the Corporation went
from September 25 (Michaelmas) of one year to the following September 25.
Therefore, though the first entry on the above list was in the accounts presented
to the Corporation on January 27, these accounts covered the time from September 25, 1568 to September 25, 1569. Furthermore, according to the old calendar the
English waited to change the year until March. Therefore when Fripp and Savage

show a submission in January 1569/70, it helps to understand that at that time January for them was still 1569 when we would have already changed the year to 1570. To further confuse the issue, in the 1590s (and surely by the time covered in volume V of the Stratford minutes and accounts edited by Fox) the accounting year changed from beginning in September (Michaelmas to Michaelmas) to beginning in December (Christmas to Christmas). The above accounts need to be interpreted with these dating inconsistencies in mind.

It becomes readily apparent that there was no precise standard either of spelling or of bookkeeping style, and much of the pleasure in reading the transcriptions of the original records is the variety in entry style and orthography. Each chamberlain was a businessman in his own right and the city records probably indicate how each kept his own books. (The keeping and presenting of these town financial records is an argument for the literacy of Shakespeare's father, John, as he was twice elected chamberlain as well as serving as high bailiff.)

There was an extremely wide divergence in monies paid by the town to the different companies. The most paid was to the Queen's Men—nine shillings for the first performance of any company in Stratford (1569) but twenty shillings each time they performed thereafter. By contrast, an entry five years after the Queen's Men's last appearance (1594) shows nineteen shillings four pence divided among four different companies. Some companies received as little as three shillings four pence. Davi Jones received fourteen shillings four pence to produce his community Whitsuntide performance.

The list reveals that presentation of plays in Stratford was irregular. A small and not greatly prosperous town, Stratford-Upon-Avon was normally bypassed as a destination on the circuit of touring companies. They would have stopped only when Stratford was on the route to or from Warwick, Coventry, Gloucester, Bath, or other large towns nearby.

As can be seen by the Corporation accounts, neither the Lord Chamberlain's Men nor the King's Men (Shakespeare's companies) played in the Stratford Guild Hall during his lifetime.

Shakespeare's friends such as Thomas Greene and Richard Quiney, both of whom frequently traveled to London and wrote numerous letters home, did not mention seeing his plays or seeing Shakespeare perform. However, Thomas Greene was a law student at the Middle Temple in 1601–1602, and during the Christmas season that year Shakespeare's *Twelfth Night* was performed there at the Great Hall. It seems more than likely that Greene would have seen that performance.[5] Shakespeare had two brothers who followed him to London: Gilbert, a haberdasher, who helped settle some of William Shakespeare's business at home when it wasn't easy for the latter to get back to Stratford[6]; and Edmond, the youngest brother, who became an actor. Edmond died in 1607 at the age of 27, and the records for ringing the bell at his funeral in Southwark Cathedral show that the service took place in the morning—this was unusual, but such timing would allow actors in attendance to play their afternoon performance. Edmond and Gilbert surely saw William Shakespeare perform, but it's possible few if any other family members did.

THE CORPORATION BAN ON PLAYERS
IN STRATFORD-UPON-AVON

In December 1602 the Stratford Corporation council passed the following resolution:

> 45 Elizabeth (17 Nov. 1602—24 Mar. 1603)
>   At this Halle yt ys ordered that there shalbe no plays or enterlewdes played in
> the Chamber, the Guild Halle, nor in any parte of the House or Courte from hens-
> forward, upon payne that whosoever of the Baylief Aldermen and Burgisses of this
> boroughe shall gyve leave or licence thereunto shall forfeyt for everie offence 10 s.
> 17 Dec. 45 Eliz B. 95

Edgar Fripp in the *Minutes and Accounts of the Corporation, Volume ii*, speculates that it was not just that the council had become more puritanical in denying
the right of companies to play in the Guild Hall, but a change in the kinds of plays
offered. He quotes from Robert Willis's memoirs of 1639, recollecting a play he
had seen as a boy:

"'This sight took such an Impression in me that when I came towards man's
estate it was as fresh in my memory as if I had seen it newly acted. From whence
I observe that out of my own experience, what great care should be had in the
education of children to keep them from seeing of spectacles of ill examples
and hearing of lascivious or scurrilous words, for that their young memories
are like fair writing-tablets wherein if the fair sentences or lessons of grace be
written, they may by God's blessing keep them from many vicious blots of life,
where withal they may otherwise be painted, especially considering the general
corruption of our nature, whose very memories are apter to receive evil than
good, and that the well seasoning of the cask at the first keeps it the better and
sweeter ever after, and withal we may observe how far unlike the plays and
harmless morals of former times are to those which have succeeded many of
which, by report of others, may be termed school masters of vice and provocations
to corruption, which our depraved nature is too prone unto, nature and grace being
contraries.'

The old Puritan squire's last observation will sufficiently explain why Stratford
and many other boroughs which encouraged players in 1569 and for a generation
afterwards at a later date, when the drama had lost, for the most part, its didactic
aim and religious earnestness, refused to allow them to perform and even paid
them to go away."[7]

This ban held until 1611, the year Shakespeare moved back to Stratford. One
wonders if the reiteration of the ban (quoted below) and the twenty-fold increase
in the fine bear a relationship to the knowledge on the part of the Corporation
council that one of the preeminent theatre professionals of the day was about to
come home to live in their city. When one speculates on why Shakespeare took
so little part in civic life, part of the answer may lie in the nature revealed below
of the men he would have had to work with. One suspects William's father, who

so loved civic life, and who encouraged the first players to perform in Stratford, would not have sympathized with the majority of this group either.

> 9 James (1611)
> The inconvenience of plaies being verie seriouslie considered of, with the unlawfulness and howe contrairie the sufferance of them is againste the orders heartofore made and against the examples of other well governed cities and burrowes, the Companie heare are contented and thaie conclude that the penaltie of 10 *s* imposed in Mr. Bakers yeare for breakinge the order shall from henceforth be £10 upon breakers of that order; and this to holde until the nexte common councell, and from thenceforth forever, excepted that be then finally revoked and made voide,
> 7. Feb. 1611, 9 James I B.220[8]

Curiously, despite these two resolutions, the chamberlain's accounts of 1618 show payments to "a company that came with a shew to the town" and to another anonymous "company of players"[9] the same year.

STRATFORD AND THE KING'S MEN

The only time Shakespeare's company came to play in Stratford was in 1622. Shakespeare had died in 1616 and Richard Burbage, his close friend and the leading actor of the troupe, in 1619. However, the company was led by his closest friends still living, John Heminges and Henry Condell. In 1622 these two men were at work preparing the First Folio of Shakespeare's work that would be published the following year. We have no way of knowing if they had ever been in Stratford before. But it appears the company was in the vicinity and they felt the need to stop in their friend Shakespeare's town—the town he loved so dearly.

A short entry that reverberates through this whole story is on an as yet untranscribed page in the Stratford chamberlain's records for 1622. Hidden among so many other records of miscellaneous town expenditures is the one line:

> X   payd to the kings players for not playing in the hall   vi *s*

Though other towns are known to have paid an acting company not to perform, this is the only time we see Stratford choosing this option.[10] If the bans of 1602 and 1611 show that the puritanical element had feared Shakespeare's return to Stratford might bring along theatrical riffraff, the eventuality never materialized. After 1611 there were no plays for seven years, none until two years after Shakespeare's death when, as noted above, a more liberal group of town fathers suddenly paid for "shews" from two companies (1618). But four years later the pendulum had swung and the council this time did not choose to see even the King's Men.

As often as Shakespeare's father, his cousin Thomas Greene, his son-in-law John Hall, and his friend Richard Quiney went to London, there is every likelihood they might have seen Shakespeare's plays and performances. Furthermore, Coventry, where the King's Men played from time to time, was not an impossible distance from Stratford, so that anyone really wanting to see a performance of Shakespeare's plays might have so. But lacking evidence that major companies performed in Stratford without the approval of the council, it seems all too likely that most of Shakespeare's family and friends never saw him perform or saw any of his plays there. And the actions of the council make it abundantly clear that from his youthful days when he left Stratford to join the theatre until the end of his life, William Shakespeare and his family lived with the stress of tension between his chosen London work and his home in Stratford-upon-Avon.

Appendix C: Katherine and Petruchio, Journey to a Happy Marriage

JUNG AND *THE SHREW*

Transcendence and Redemption in *The Taming of the Shrew*

Nowadays readers, producers, audience members, literary theorists, and particularly feminists worry over *The Taming of the Shrew* more than Shakespeare or his contemporaries would have thought rational. In fact, of Shakespeare's plays, only *The Merchant of Venice*, burdened with indications of Shakespearean anti-Semitism, provokes more anguish in the contemporary sensibility. Producing, playing in, or (heaven forbid!) enjoying *The Taming of the Shrew* are considered by many articulate modern-day critics to be reprehensible. After all, does its content not affirm the need for powerful men to dominate, control, and silence emotional women who must acknowledge male supremacy? The modern mind is challenged to give reasons for *The Taming of the Shrew*'s holding stubbornly to its place as one of the most popular and most often produced of the Shakespeare comedies. If *The Taming of the Shrew* shows women abused and demeaned by dominating males, why do modern audiences buy tickets to it? Why do they laugh at it? Why is it still performed? To understand just how this early comedy of Shakespeare's transcends the stereotypical expectations created by its title, we must analyze the play's deep structure and decode the archetypes hidden within the text.

Shakespeare knew that the tale of a man dealing with an ungovernable woman was popular with audiences and readers alike and in it he saw a subject to which he could give a new treatment. He adapted it quickly. Unusual for him, he started with a play-within-a-play structure established by an opening scene called The

Induction. Here, a hunting party led by a young lord discovers one Christopher Sly, a drunken tinker, asleep at the doorway to an inn. To play a joke on the hapless tramp, the lord and his followers take Sly into the inn to dress him as a lord; and when Sly awakes from his drunken sleep, all treat him as a wealthy aristocrat. Sly's disbelief and his adjustment to his new status amuse the lord and his party. At last a troupe of players come to the inn and a play (that happens to be *The Taming of the Shrew*) is offered for Sly's amusement.

Shakespeare's youthful haste and inexperience betray him, however, for he lets this structure, so brilliantly established in The Induction, fade as the play proceeds. He does not return to it to end the play, nor does he go back and excise it. To the frustration of subsequent producers and stage directors, he simply lets it drop. For even as he wrote, Shakespeare found the metaphor of life-as-play (that he had created with Christopher Sly and The Induction) taken over by a new symbol, one which could be fully expressed in the main story of *The Taming of the Shrew*. Beginning with Kate and Petruchio's initial encounter, life-as-game replaces life-as-play to become the *Shrew*'s controlling metaphor; and the story itself becomes all about how one plays. With this new structure, Shakespeare realized that the resolution of the Kate and Petruchio story made anticlimactic a return to Sly and the practical joke of a now-forgotten young lord.

Developing his new and preferred metaphor, Shakespeare shows that the game of life is experienced and enjoyed most fully by those who know and accept rules—rules that are necessary because (as he reveals) a happy life is not about demanding personal expression but about achieving successful relationships. For as long as individuals expend energy both fighting against restraint as Katherine does . . .

> *Baptista*
> Katherina, you may stay,
> I have more to commune with Bianca.
> *Katherine*
> Why, and I trust I may go too, may I not? What,
> shall I be appointed hours, as though belike, I knew not what to
> take and what to leave? Ha! (I, 1, 102–105)

or claiming that rules don't apply to them (what the psychologist Carl Jung would cite as the anima out of control), they create their own lonely hell. This situation is Katherine's in her early scenes.

But *The Taming of the Shrew* tells a tale of two superior but imperfect human beings in need of redemption. Notice the "two." The woman and the man are both trapped. Katherine's flaw is her uncontrollable temper. She "acts out" because of neglect: her mother, as far as one can tell, is dead; her sister is favored by a father who doesn't know how to value his older daughter; in fact, no one in the little town of Padua has any way of understanding, valuing, or validating Katherine. She rages out of hurt and frustration.

But Petruchio swaggers into town emotionally closed and thus also damaged. He scorns women and the values they represent. He gives no room for expressions of sympathy from his best friend for the loss of his father:

> *Petruchio*
> Signor Hortensio, thus it stands with me:
> Antonio, my father, is deceas'd,
> And I have thrust myself into this maze
> Haply too wive and thrive as best I may.
> Crowns in my purse have I, and goods at home,
> And so am come abroad to see the world. (I, 2, 52–57)

He has "come to wive it wealthily in Padua"; he is going to marry for money, and money alone. If there is dowry enough, he does not care who comes with it:

> ... wealth is burden of my wooing dance—
> Be she a foul as was Florentius' love,
> As old as Sibyl, and as curst and shrewd
> As Socrates' Zanthippe, or a worse,
> She moves me not, or not removes at least
> Affection's edge in me. (I, 2, 65–71)

When Katharine and Petruchio meet for the first time, an immediate and electric connection flashes between them. He expects an ugly, shrewish harridan, a woman to conquer, ignore, or endure; enter a young, beautiful, vibrant woman. She expects an unattractive old gold digger, as witless as all the other men in Padua; instead, she is stunned by a brilliant, vital, determined young man. In shock, they challenge each other and immediately discover their minds are equal.

> *Petruchio*
> Good morrow, Kate, for that's your name I hear.
> *Katherine*
> Well have you heard, but something hard of hearing.
> They call me Katherine that do speak of me.
> *Petruchio*
> You lie, in faith, for you are call'd plain Kate,
> And bonny Kate, and sometimes Kate the curst,
> But Kate, the prettiest Kate in Christendom ... (II, 1, 182–187)

Neither has ever met anyone like this before: another human being of one's own level. And Shakespeare finds his new and improved metaphor established when the wooing scene becomes a spirited game, as exciting as a good tennis match or sword fight where each unexpected thrust is met by an expert parry.

> *Petruchio*
> Myself am mov'd to woo thee for my wife.
> *Katherine*
> Moved in good time. Let him that mov'd you hither
> Remove you hence. I knew you at the first
> You were a movable.

> *Petruchio*
> Why, what's a movable?
> *Katherine*

A joint stool.

> *Petruchio*
> Thou hast hit it. Come, sit on me.
> *Katherine*

Asses are made to bear, and so are you.

> *Petruchio*

Women are made to bear, and so are you. (II, 1, 194–200)

The sharp pick-up of the half-lines indicates the quickness of wit on either side; and audiences become as exhilarated by their encounter as the players themselves, thrilled by the brilliance of mind, the sharpness of retort, the equality of opposites in a game played by masters. Katherine and Petruchio equal each other, both physically (she is the one who hits him; he is the one who kisses her) and verbally. As the game plays out, the two fall in love—though the feeling is so strange that neither knows quite what to do with it. Neither can yet let go of old behavioral patterns; but for them and everyone (audience and characters alike) fascination and tension build: who will win? who will change? how will things will work out in the contest between these extraordinarily vibrant creatures? Their game becomes the deep structure of the play.

That Katherine loves Petruchio there can be no doubt: on the wedding day she eagerly awaits him in front of the church. Had she been determined not to marry Petruchio, she would have refused, screamed, locked herself in her room, lashed out physically at her ineffectual father. He has never been able to control her, and so one can only assume she has come to her wedding not because he demands it but because she wants to. But her first effort to play a life-game (the wedding game with herself playing the bride) seems doomed to failure. Petruchio is late. When she protests "I must forsooth be forc'd / To give my hand, oppos'd against my heart / Unto a madbrained rudesby, full of spleen" (III, 2, 8–10), it is her disappointment crying out. Her father had said before he would not make her marry against her will; when Petruchio says he will take her, Baptista answers:

> Ay, when the special thing is well obtain'd,
> That is her love; for that is all in all. (II, 1, 129–130)

Petruchio has gained her love but now fails her. She is anxious, disappointed (and therefore infuriated) when he is late to their wedding.

> *Katherine*
> I told you, I, he was a frantic fool
> Hiding his bitter jests in blunt behavior.
> And to be noted for a merry man
> He'll woo a thousand, 'point the day of marriage,
> Make feast, invite friends, and proclaim the banns,
> Yet never means to wed where he hath woo'd.

Now must the world point at poor Katherine,
And say, "Lo, there is mad Petruchio's wife,
If it would please him come and marry her." (III, 2, 12–20)

Surely the audience sympathizes with her betrayed vulnerability when witnessing his outrageous behavior before and after the wedding ceremony.

When he takes Katherine to his home, Petruchio continues to confound her expectations. Displaying behavior deliberately chosen to reflect her own in Padua, he demonstrates uncontrollable and inexplicable anger toward his servants, pushed to the point where Katherine finds herself empathizing with them. "Patience, I pray you," she cries out in defense of one who spilled water: "t'was a fault unwilling" (IV, 1, 143). Next, Petruchio will not let Katherine eat; later he tells the audience he plans not to let her sleep. Note, however, he also takes no food, and he will find himself as deprived of sleep as she. Lest anyone misunderstand this treatment, Petruchio conflates gaming and hunting images as he reveals that he intends to train Katherine as he trains a hawk:

Petruchio
My falcon now is sharp and passing empty,
And till she stoop she must not be full-gorg'd,
For then she never looks upon her lure.
Another way I have to man my haggard,
To make her come and now her keeper's call
That is, to watch her, as we watch these kites
That bate and beat and will not be obedient. (IV, 1, 177–183)

As the notes in the Arden edition of *The Taming of the Shrew* explain, "All hawks generally are manned after one manner, that is to say, by watching and keeping them from sleep, by a continual carrying of them upon your fist, *and by a most familiar stroking and playing with them, . . . and by often gazing and looking of them in the face, with a loving and gentle countenance, and so making them acquainted with the man*"[11] (the italics are mine). Elizabethans would have known that successful training results not from cruelty but from deprivation coupled with affection. Also noteworthy is the fact that in the scenes at Petruchio's house, he never strikes Katherine (though wife-beating was condoned by many in Elizabethan society) and he never forces himself on her sexually (though as her husband he could have claimed that right). These restraints in his character enable audiences, even in the twenty-first century, to go along with the story.

In fact, the audience has witnessed something astonishing happen to Petruchio. From the time he meets Katherine, he has become deeply involved with another human being, a capability he lacked and one that crippled his spirit at the beginning of the story. He admires her. He thinks (and tells her) she's beautiful. He loves her. And she will see all his love expressed when she shows she has learned to play the relationship game by the rules—which means that she has learned to control herself. Carl Jung would say that Katherine must learn to find the balance in herself between the anima and the animus, the feminine principle and the masculine. Audiences do not need to be either psychologists or psychoanalysts to intuit these truths; they know instinctively that Shakespeare's retelling of the story goes far beyond advocating husbands' beating of wives or men breaking the spirit of women.

The Taming of the Shrew demonstrates that at both its deepest and its most superficial level, life is a game to play; in each situation one asks: What game are we playing and what are the rules here? Maturity gives one the power to respond by rational choice, not uncontrolled emotion, in reference to these precepts.

Now, accommodating one another out of love is one of the rules of a happy relationship. In the fourth act of the play, Katherine, Petruchio, and Hortensio are on the road back to Padua and, at Hortensio's request and in sympathy with his exhaustion, Katherine at last chooses to accommodate Petruchio. She lets him say, according to his mood, whether the sun or the moon shines in the sky.

> *Petruchio*
> I say it is the moon that shines so bright.
> *Katherine*
> I know it is the sun that shines so bright.
> *Petruchio*
> Now by my mother's son, and that's myself,
> It shall be moon, or star, or what I list
> O'er ere I journey to your father's house. . . .
> *Hortensio*
> Say as he says, or we shall never go.
> *Katherine*
> Forward, I pray, since we have some so far,
> And be it moon, or sun, or what you please.
> And if you please to call it a rush candle
> Henceforth I vow it shall be so for me. (IV, 5, 4–15)

For the first time she cedes to a primary rule of the game of life and love: concern for another is sometimes more important than having one's own way.

Of course, if the relationship between those playing the game of life together is to be equal and enduring, love must be the response for such accommodation as Katherine's. And, indeed, Petruchio shows his pleasure with her; she becomes "Sweet Kate" (IV, 5, 28) as the next scene begins and he starts the next game.

Does this mean her spirit is broken? Shakespeare indicates the contrary. She is as spirited as ever, but her actions now find a productive channel. As she continues to play the games Petruchio sets for her, she begins to test her skill. Her ability to exceed whatever he asks of her, to best him at his own game, will be her vindication and the full expression of her quick spirit.

When Vincentio enters, Katherine goes far beyond what Petruchio asks of her in recognizing and praising him, an old man, as a beautiful young girl; then instantly she reverses herself when Petruchio indicates that the opposite is wanted. He raises the bar, she easily vaults over it; and Petruchio, reveling in her brilliance, starts to show her how deeply he admires her.

As an important mark of his full and total acceptance of her, Petruchio wants the world to see (and for her to know he wants the world to see) how much he loves her; so he asks for a kiss in the street. This request tests her; she is embarrassed to kiss him in public. But when, at her hesitation, he threatens to leave, she pleads: "Pray thee, love, stay" (V, I, 136). She then shyly grants him the kiss and he responds warmly: "Is not this well?" (V, 1, 137). Again she is "my sweet Kate" (V, I 137). And he at last has become "husband" (V, I, 130).

Petruchio and Katherine go to the dinner celebrating her sister Bianca's wedding filled with the exhilaration of newly found and newly expressed love. Knowing Petruchio loves her, Katherine would now do anything for him. Knowing Katherine loves him, Petruchio believes she can now be his full partner in playing both their own game and society's. Sharing this secret, they long for a forum to demonstrate their mastery of the game of life to each other and to everyone else. So when, as part of a public wager, Petruchio calls for her, she comes—she can hardly wait to come.

No one has ever loved Katherine before, and gratitude spills out of her in her long speech. From their first meeting, Katherine has surprised Petruchio with her beauty, her temper, her high wit, her mind, her vitality, her integrity. She has always offered more than he expected. And so it is with this last speech. He asks her to scold the other women. As she does so she becomes much more eloquent than he could have imagined.

In writing for the stage, Shakespeare mastered the art of revealing characters' progressive self-discovery as they work through a dilemma while speaking aloud. Katherine's speech at the end of *The Taming of the Shrew* is an early and brilliant example of this technique. As she speaks the words that she starts to say only at Petruchio's request and only to play the game, she discovers that she means them. The audience watches their game-playing become real life as Katherine's speech turns into an outpouring of her love for Petruchio.

She means it when she says to the wives "Thy husband is thy lord, thy life, thy keeper, / Thy head, thy sovereign; one who cares for thee..." (V, 2, 147–148). Katharine never had anyone to claim this before: never anyone who wanted to be her lord, her husband, her life, her keeper. She had known only inadequate men who feared and scorned her and a father who was eager to be rid of her. What must it feel like to her when she says these words, filled with the knowledge that Petruchio loves her.

But she still has the wit to tease him: imagine the glint in her eye, and his reaction to the other men, when she says expectantly:

> And for thy maintenance commits his body
> To painful labour both by sea and land,
> To watch the night in storms, the day in cold,

(And even more teasingly alludes to what she plans to do):

> While thou liest warm at home, secure and safe. (V, 2, 149–152)

And all a husband asks of his wife for these sacrifices is "love, fair looks, and true obedience" (V, 2, 154): *true* obedience—to him but more important to the rule of life that says in loving one another, partners must sacrifice for one another, give over to one another. This reciprocity is the only way to true and lasting love. In this speech, far from diminishing women, Shakespeare uses the power of Katherine's eloquence to demonstrate a heightened human capacity to love; and Katherine's challenge to Petruchio concerning what men have to do to earn the love and obedience of their wives quoted above is evidence that her quick mind has not been lost nor her voice silenced in her new-found ability to comply with rules.

Often the most telling moments of a Shakespeare play come not *in* the lines, but *between* them. At the end of *Measure for Measure,* for instance, the Duke asks Isabella to marry him; but Shakespeare fails to tell us in the text whether she accepts him—or not (V,1, 489–490). Similarly, a most important moment of *The Taming of the Shrew* is at the end of the play when Katherine offers to put her hand under her husband's foot as a mark of her duty and submission (V, 2, 178–179). Petruchio could allow her to do so. He could rejoice over her in a superior way with the other men. But everything leading up to this moment—Katherine's relationship with Vincentio, the old man; the kiss in the street; her request to Petruchio, "Pray thee love, stay"; his heart-felt "Is not this well?"; his calling her "Sweet Kate"; her calling him "husband"; Katherine's eagerness to come when called—all suggest the opposite. At this moment when she is willing to do anything for him, Petruchio shows he does not want an overly submissive wife; he shows Katherine the kind of partner he does want. He stops her self-abnegation and praises her, saying, "Why, there's a wench!" (V, 2, 181) then expresses all his love for her with "Come on and kiss me, Kate" (V, 2, 181). They have redeemed each other, and there is more hope for happiness in their marriage than for any of the other couples in the play—in fact, more for them than for most of the couples in Shakespeare's other plays.

Some readers and some audience members will always find *The Taming of the Shrew* hard to accept because, in the end, the play cannot escape its origins in an earlier time of Western thought and human development. It is often seen, with many cogent examples aduced, as a simplistic demonstration of male dominance and female submission. So much depends on the eye of the beholder, and enough language in this play expresses outmoded gender roles to make the text problematic to the modern mind.

Still, *The Taming of the Shrew* remains one of the most popular of Shakespeare's plays for audiences to watch, companies to produce, and actors to perform. Surely, then, it must speak subliminally to a powerful need in the human psyche.

And the fact is that here Jungian truths are at work. Each human being carries internally the potential for discipline, focus, exclusivity, energy, and pride—which are, in Jung's view, "masculine" qualities. Each also carries within the emotion, warmth, inspiration, inclusiveness, and creativity that Jung called the "feminine" qualities. When these opposite qualities spiral out of control, the feminine ones turn hysterical and the masculine ones militaristic. On either side the victim longs to be back in balance. When, internally, the discipline of the "masculine" is able to restrain the hysteria of the "feminine," the individual feels in control of life, feels safe. When this control has been achieved through sacrificial love, human beings feel transcendent, redeemed.

Petruchio and Katherine represent not only two different characters, but also different and opposing parts of every individual. Through the ritual of this play, a psychic balance is attained by the characters and felt by the audience: an internal equilibrium achieved by the successful exercise of discipline over uncontrollable emotion; and Shakespeare has his characters negotiate this achievement with brilliance, humor, and affection. For in his *The Taming of the Shrew*, Shakespeare has transformed the old tale of male dominance and female submission into a story of two remarkable but flawed human beings redeeming each other through love.

All human beings yearn to feel some form of transcendence. People, consciously or unconsciously, seek out rituals that affirm this ultimate human experience. The redemption by love experienced by Katherine and Petruchio gives everyone who shares their story a thrilling vision of human possibility. And that is why—despite the critics, the theorists, the analysts, and the feminist protesters—producers and directors and actors and audiences will continue to enjoy this remarkable play.

Notes

PREFACE AND INTRODUCTION

1. Ackroyd, 449.
2. Jones, xix.
3. Chartier, 5.
4. Margaret Wood, 393.
5. Ibid.
6. Ibid.
7. Markham, xxvi.
8. Abbott, 50.
9. Ibid., 54.
10. Riggs, 9.
11. Such a death is described by Mistress Quickly in Shakespeare's *Henry V* (act 2, scene 3) when she tells of the death of Falstaff.
12. Abbott, 29.
13. Chartier, 9.

1: SHAKESPEARE'S GRANDFATHERS

1. Halliday, *A Shakespeare Companion*, 26; Schoenbaum, *William Shakespeare, A Compact Documentary Life*, 19.
2. Eccles, 14. According to Eccles, a Roberte Ardern (sic) was listed as the bailiff of the Earl of Warwick's manor in Snitterfield in 1438–1439.
3. Elton, 113. Charles Isaac Elton, in his unfinished *William Shakespeare His Family and Friends*, describes the character of an English yeoman farmer as follows: "Sir Thomas Overbury drew an excellent picture of an English yeoman of his time, who 'says not to his servants, "Go to the field," but "Let us go"; and with his own eye doth both fatten his flock and set forward all manner of husbandry.... He never sits up late but when he

hunts the badger, the vowed foe of his lambs; nor uses any cruelty but when he hunts the hare; nor subtilty but when he setteth snares for the snipe or pitfalls for the blackbird; nor oppression but when, in the month of July, he goes to the next river and shears his sheep. He allows of honest pastime, and thinks not the bones of the dead anything bruised or the worse for it though the country lasses dance in the churchyard after evensong. Rock Monday, and the wake in summer, shrovings, the wakeful catches on Christmas Eve, the hockey or seed-cake, these he yearly keeps, yet holds them no relics of popery. He is not so inquisitive after news derived from the privy closet, when the finding an eyry of hawks in his own ground, or the foaling of a colt come of a good strain, are tidings more pleasant, more profitable . . . lastly, to end him, he cares not when his end comes, he needs not fear his audit, for his quietus is in heaven.'" In this quote, we can see suggested the men of Shakespeare's heritage, and hear in the writing the voice of characters like Old Adam and Corin the shepherd (*As You Like It*).

4. Eccles, 16. Eccles reports that "Robert bought a second freehold there from the daughters of William Harvey and their husbands, part from Richard and Agnes Rushby in 1519 and part from John and Elizabeth Palmer in 1529."

5. Ibid., 16. This continues a long tradition as Eccles notes that an earlier Robert Ardene and his wife joined the Stratford Guild in 1440–1441 (14).

6. Bearman, ed., *The History of an English Borough*, 62–79. Christine Carpenter, in Chapter 5, "Town and 'Country': the Stratford Guild and Political Networks of Fifteenth-century Warwickshire," discusses in detail the history, membership, activities, and purpose of the Guild of the Holy Cross in Stratford.

7. Eccles, 16.

8. Fripp, *Shakespeare, Man and Artist*, 30.

9. If Robert was buying land of his own in 1519, and had joined the Guild two years before, he must have been born by 1495.

10. Gray, 261. Gray reprints the entire will from which these selections were taken.

11. Stopes, *Shakespeare's Family*, 43. Mrs. Stopes makes a valiant attempt to clarify Mary's share in the Snitterfield property, detailing how she possibly came into fractions of the land as two of her sisters died.

12. Gray, 261. "Apone this condysione that shall (she) sofer my dowghter Ales quyetlye to ynyoye halfe my copye-houlde in Wyllmecote dwryng the tyme of her yddowewhoodde and if she will nott soffer my sowghter Ales quyetlye to ocupye halfe wth her then I will that my wife shall have butt iij. li. vj. s. viij. d. three pounds six shillings fourpence and her ginture in Snyterfylde."

13. Fripp, *Shakespeare, Man and Artist*, 31.

14. Eccles, 8. Eccles cites the testimony of Adam Palmer in 1582 for this information.

15. Halliday, *A Shakespeare Companion*, 441. Halliday notes that the Hales owned the property from 1546–1599.

16. I am grateful to Robert Bearman for the following explanation: "Freeholders within a manor could owe suit of court or be fined for neglect of regulations as well as lease holders. The Ardens held their land freely of the College, so Richard's involvement with the College manor might just have been because he was Arden's tenant."

17. Ibid., 440.

18. Eccles, 7.

19. Honan, 28.

20. Fripp, *Shakespeare's Haunts near Stratford*, 88.

21. Schoenbaum, *William Shakespeare, A Compact Documentary Life*, 15.

22. Fripp, *Shakespeare, Man and Artist*, 35.

23. Stopes, *Shakespeare's Family*, 50.

24. Eccles, 8.

25. Ibid., 99.

26. Schoenbaum, *William Shakespeare, A Compact Documentary Life,* 15; B. Roland Lewis writes the amount as xxxviiijli, xvijs, claiming that Lee (35 pounds, 17 shillings), Fripp (38 pounds, 7 shillings), and Adams (38 pounds, 17 shillings) had each computed it wrong.

27. Gray, 259.

2: SHAKESPEARE'S FATHER

1. Rowse, *Shakespeare, The Man*, 12.

2. Abbott, 163. No record of John Shakespeare's birth exists as he was born more than eight years before Henry VIII sent out his directive of 1538 that all baptisms, marriages and deaths were henceforth to be registered weekly in the parish churches.

3. Payne, 4, 5.

4. Adams, 63.

5. Wood, Michael, 39.

6. Honan, 12, 13.

7. Adams, 23.

8. Rowse, *Shakespeare the Man*, 12.

9. Fripp, *Minutes and Accounts*, vol. I, xxv.

10. Adams, 25.

11. Riggs, 20.

12. Ibid., 19.

13. Chute, 6.

14. Ibid., 6.

15. I am grateful to Robert Bearman for this point of view.

16. Eccles, 26.

17. Chute, 10.

18. Ibid., 10, 11.

19. Ibid., 11.

20. Adams, 46.

21. Ibid.

22. Ibid., 23.

23. Ibid.

24. Halliday, *A Shakespeare Companion*, 441.

25. Stopes, *Shakespeare's Family*, p 61.

26. Honan, 43.

27. Ibid., 51.

28. Riggs, 15.

29. In the eighteenth century a document was discovered hidden in the rafters of the Henley Street house attic, a Catholic testament with each page purportedly signed by John Shakespeare. Found and commented upon by scholars of the time, the document was then lost. Though scholars continue to debate the issue, Robert Bearman in his article "John Shakespeare's 'Spiritual Testament': A Reapraisal," *Shakespeare Survey* 56 (2003), demonstrates that this particular document is without doubt a hoax. The loss of this "evidence" does not mean the Shakespeares held no Catholic beliefs. We are simply

reminded that in a day when religion was such a (literally) burning issue for the country, when its citizens had gone through repeated dogmatic changes forced upon them by the state, the Shakespeares and others could have held Catholic beliefs despite their outward conformity. There is simply no way to know.

30. Adams, 24.
31. Ibid., 27.
32. Wood, Michael, 39.
33. Adams, 27.
34. Eccles, 27.
35. Edwards, 69.
36. Fripp, *Master Richard Quyny*, 44.
37. Cook, 265.
38. Chute, 97, 98.
39. Wilson, 210.
40. Adams, 20, 21.
41. Ibid., 21.
42. Chute, 6.
43. Rowse, *Shakespeare The Man,* 17.

3: SHAKESPEARE'S UNCLE

1. Eccles, 9.
2. It is unknown how this property relates to the land Henry's father had leased from the Hales and Henry himself had farmed as a boy; one assumes it could well be the same.
3. Lewis, 22.
4. Stopes, *Shakespeare's Family*, 56.
5. Henry is sometimes referred to as impoverished, but both the tithe suits and his will show him to have been, in spite of his debts, a successful and rather wealthy farmer.
6. Lewis, 23.
7. Ibid., 24.
8. Eccles, 10.
9. Lewis, 24.
10. Ibid., 27.
11. Ibid., 25.
12. Eccles, 10.
13. Lewis, 22.
14. Eccles, 10.
15. Halliday, *A Shakespeare Companion*, 441.
16. Schoenbaum, *A Documentary Life*, 14.
17. Eccles, 10.
18. Greenblatt, 214–220.

4: SHAKESPEARE'S MOTHER

1. Gray, 261. "I give and bequethe to my youngste dowghter Marye all my lande in Willmecote, cawlide Asbyes and the crop apone the grounde sowne and tyllide as hitt is and vj. li. xiiij.*s.* iiij*d.* of money to be payde ore ere my goodes be devydide.... Also I

ordene and constitute and make my ffull exceqtores Ales & Marye my dowghteres: of this my last will and testament: And they to have no more for ther peynes taking now as afore geven them."

2. C.C. Stopes, the indefatigable Shakespeare researcher of the early twentieth century and author of the only other book entitled *Shakespeare's Family*, claims Robert Arden had only seven daughters (p. 36). She finds no evidence confirming Elizabeth as one of them. Most other scholars, however, include Elizabeth and count the number as eight.

3. Eccles, 17.

4. Ibid., 18.

5. Cook, 265.

6. Wilson, 34, 35.

7. In *Shakespeare, the Man*, 15, A. L. Rowse writes, "This is where William Shakespeare got his emphasis on gentility from and, in fact, the characteristics of it in his behavior, which marked him off from all the other theatre-folk, many of whom were decidedly ungentlemanly in their behavior. Nor is it superfluous to point out that some social disparity between parents has an effect in sharpening the social awareness and sensibilities of a clever, observant child."

8. In a curious coincidence, both Mary Arden who married John Shakespeare, and Anne Hathaway who married their son William Shakespeare, had lost their mothers early in life and their fathers shortly before marrying. Their inheritances had come to them from the wills of their fathers, they were of age, and therefore they were free to choose the man they wanted to marry. Upper class marriages in the sixteenth century were most often arranged by families for practical dynastic and monetary reasons. When great inheritances were not important, personal affection could carry more weight, but the complete freedom of Mary Arden and Anne Hathaway to make their own choices was unusual. Anne's choice was complicated, certainly, by the fact that the man of her choice was only eighteen, still a minor, and could not marry without his parents' permission.

9. McDonald, 247.

10. Ibid., 166.

11. Abbott, 189. Mirroring the publications of the La Leche league encouraging women of the present day to breastfeed, in 1628 Elizabeth Clinton, Countess of Lincoln wrote a pamphlet advocating breastfeeding called "The Countess of Lincolne's Nursery." Noting how unusual it was for an aristocratic lady to breastfeed, Mary Abbott quotes from the countess's work: "Therefore, be no longer at the trouble and at the care to hire others to do your own work. Be not so unnatural as to thrust away your own children. Be not so hardy as to venture a tender babe to a less tender heart. Be not accessory to that disorder of causing a poorer woman to banish her own infant for the entertainment of a richer woman's child, as it were, bidding her unlove her own to love yours. We have followed Eve in transgression, let us follow her in obedience. When God laid the sorrows of conception, of breeding, of bringing forth, and of bringing up her children upon her, and so upon us in her loins, did she reply any word against? Not a word. So I pray you all mine own daughters and others that are still child-bearing, reply not against the duty of suckling them when God hath sent you them." The woman wrote from experience. She had (and evidently nursed) eighteen children.

12. Ibid., 247, 248.

13. Bearman, "John Shakespeare: A Papist or Just Penniless?" *Shakespeare Quarterly* (Winter 2005). This is the most detailed and cogently argued analysis of John Shakespeare's financial difficulties.

14. Ibid., 419.

15. Chambers, *The Elizabethan Stage*, vol. 1, 309:

> And so, tentatively up to 1584, and thereafter with a security which received final confirmation in 1597, the actor's occupation began to take its place as a regular profession, in which money might with reasonable safety be invested, to which a man might look for the career of a lifetime, and in which he might venture to bring up his children. As early as 1574 the patent to Leicester's men refers to playing as an "arte and facultye." In 1581 the Privy Council calls it a "trade"; in 1582 a "profession"; in 1593 a "qualitie."
>
> The player of the seventeenth century is in fact as necessary a member of the polity as the minstrel of the twelfth or the fourteenth.

16. Eccles, 33.

17. Lewis, 93.

18. Abbott, 39. Some bodies were loosely shrouded, some wound tightly in a winding sheet like a newborn baby was swaddled. "Indeed there is some evidence that strips of swaddling clothes were saved to tie grave clothes. The Cambridgeshire yeoman Richard Goodyear (died 1522) left his daughter Mary 'a christening sheet and a towel and all the other childbed linen which was her mother's but one sheet' for his burial; his will does not explain the thinking or emotions which lay behind his instruction, but the strength of the link between being born and dying is clear."

5: SHAKESPEARE'S BROTHERS

1. Fripp, *Shakespeare's Stratford*, 65.

2. Eccles, 56, 57.

3. Maguire, 166. Laurie Maguire has much to say about family life and relationships as reflected in Shakespeare's plays in this insightful self-help via Shakespeare book.

4. Spurgeon, 99.

5. Ibid., 106.

6. Ibid., 110.

7. Schoenbaum, *A Compact Documentary Life*, 74. Here Schoenbaum is quoting E.I. Fripp, *Shakespeare: Man and Artist* (1938), i. 79–90.

8. Eccles, 108. Halliday, in *A Shakespeare Companion*, p 442, identifies Sampson as a cloak maker, however Eccles indicates the original spelling as "clookmaker" and identifies him as Sampson the Clocksmithe in Stratford to whom the parish of St. Nicholas in Warwick sent their clock to be mended.

9. Palmer, 219.

10. Halliday, *A Shakespeare Companion*, 442.

11. See the discussion above in "Shakespeare's Brothers," Chapter Five, concerning Richard Shakespeare's unmarried status.

12. Fripp, *Master Richard Quyny*, 27.

13. Palmer, 221.

14. Riggs, 75.

15. I refer here to the subject of the sonnets, a man I believe, as many others do, to be the Earl of Southampton.

16. Shapiro, 72.

17. Ibid., 72.

18. Fripp, *Master Richard Quyny*, 148.

19. Baldwin, 419.

20. Yet another name for what is now Southwark Cathedral. In the Middle Ages the church was part of the Priory of St. Mary Overie, run by Augustinians. After the dissolution of the monasteries by Henry VIII the church became the parish church of St. Saviour. In 1905 St. Saviours's became the Cathedral for the new diocese of Southwark. This information comes from "Southwark, A History of Bankside, Bermondsey and 'The Borough'" by Robert J. Godley, 1996.

21. When Baldwin refers to a "line" he means a character type that an actor was assigned to according to his physical type and talents. Here it refers to the female part of Rhodope in *The Seven Deadly Sins* for which Baldwin discovered a cast list helping him with his speculations on which actors played which parts in other plays, and similar parts a young actor suitable for Rhodope might play.

22. Which company Shakespeare was affiliated with at this moment is unclear. Likely it was Lord Strange's Men, as this was the company to which went several of the actors of the Earl of Leicester's Men when the Earl died in 1588 (Ian Wilson, 489). F. E. Halliday, in *A Shakespeare Companion* (133) details the development and membership of Derby's (Lord Strange's) Men.

23. Baldwin.

6: SHAKESPEARE'S SISTERS

1. Eccles, 142.

2. Gray, 268. "My Sister Johane Harte . . . xx li and all my wearing Apparrell . . . And . . . the house with thapurtenances in Stratford wherein she dwelleth for her naturall life under the yearlie Rent of xii.*d.*"

3. Three versions of the complete Joan Hart genealogy traced from Joan Hart's great-grandfather through to all the family members to the present time are available for purchase at a modest price from the Public Record Office, Stratford-uponAvon.

7: SHAKESPEARE'S WIFE

1. Hole, 38.

2. Halliday, *A Shakespeare Companion*, 224.

3. Palmer, 108.

4. The assumption that Richard had a second wife, and how the children were apportioned between the wives comes from the references to his wife and children in Richard's will. For instance in referring to his wife Joan he does not identify Joan as the mother of his son Bartholomew. For more details, see Gray, 31.

5. The name of Richard Hathaway's first wife is unknown; however, as it was common at that time to name a first child after a parent, the first daughter Anne indicates that the mother's name in all likelihood was Anne also. The fact that Anne Hathaway listed Temple Grafton as her home village in her request for a marriage license indicates, also, that this was likely her mother's home. The name of his oldest daughter is written "Agnes" in Richard Hathaway's will; however, Agnes and Anne were common alternative spellings for the same name in this period.

6. Anne's story can only be cobbled together by analyzing sparse documentation and making reasonable surmises. Her birth date, for instance is not registered in any extant

documents, but is deduced from her death in 1623, when her age was noted on her tombstone as sixty-seven.

7. Richard Hathaway first had two baby boys—both named Richard—who died, while John Shakespeare first had two baby girls who died, before each father had children who thrived.

8. Lewis, 157.

9. Gray, 6.

10. Lewis, 174. Mr. Lewis argues powerfully that the necessity for the marriage rested in the desire of the families to become part of the gentry. "Yeomen in 1582 were ambitious to achieve the status of landed gentry. For establishing their family in the landed gentry via an oldest son, a 'handfast' or pre-contract marriage, though valid, was inadequate because it would not clearly legitimize their children."

11. Gray, 10.

12. Halliday, 210.

13. Gray, 2, 3.

14. Ibid., 24. I would like to suggest another possibility. As Anne's father had died the year before, leaving Anne, an adult woman, living in the house of her stepmother, is it not possible that Anne might have gone to live in Temple Grafton, at least temporarily, with her mother's relatives? She could therefore have claimed both Temple Grafton and Stratford (the parish for Shottery) as her residence at this confusing time.

15. Ibid., 11.

16. Samuel Schoenbaum includes a delightful story about Luddington, a village three miles west of Stratford, sometimes suggested as the site for the Shakespeare wedding: "In Victorian times S.W. Fullom visited Luddington in quest of information, and in his *History of William Shakespeare* of 1862 he has a curious tale to tell: 'The [old parsonage] house is occupied by a family named Dyke, respected for miles round, and here the report of the marriage can be traced back directly for a hundred and fifty years. Mrs. Dyke received it from Martha Casebrooke, who died at the age of ninety, after residing her whole life in the village, and not only declared that she was told in her childhood that the marriage was solemnized at Luddington, but had seen the ancient tome in which it was registered. This, indeed, we found, on visiting the neighbouring cottages, was remembered by persons still living, when it was in the possession of a Mrs. Pickering, who had been housekeeper to Mr. Coles, the last curate, and one cold day burnt the register to boil her kettle!' Fullom, 202." Quoted in a note on p. 87 of Schoenbaum, *A Compact Documentary Life*.

17. Peter Ackroyd, in *Shakespeare: The Biography*, imagines William and Anne's wedding ceremony having a Catholic basis because of the proclivities of the priest at Temple Grafton. He describes it as follows: "The favored day was Sunday. It began at the church porch, where the banns were recited three times. Anne Hathaway's dower, of £6 13s 4d, was then displayed and exchanged. She was no doubt 'given' by Fulke Sandells or John Richardson who had stood surety in Worcester. The woman stood on the left side of the groom, in token of Eve's miraculous delivery from Adam's left rib; they held hands as a symbol of their betrothal. In the church porch the priest blessed the ring with holy water; the bridegroom then took the ring and placed it in turn on the thumb and first three fingers of the Bride's left hand with the words '*In nomine Patris, in nomine Filii, in nomine Spiritus Sancti, Amen.*' He left it on this fourth finger, since the vein in that finger was supposed to run directly to the heart. The couple were then invited into the church, where they knelt together in order to partake in the nuptial Mass and blessing; they wore linen cloths or 'care

cloths' upon their heads to protect them from demons. It was also customary for the bride to carry a knife or dagger suspended from her girdle, the reasons for which are uncertain. (Juliet possesses a dagger, with which she stabs herself.) The bride's hair was unbraided, hanging loose about her shoulders. After the Mass it was customary for a festive procession to return from the church to the house where a wedding feast, or 'bridle-ale,' was prepared. The newly joined couple might then receive gifts of silver, or money, or food. The guests were in turn often given presents of gloves—since Shakespeare's father was a glove-maker, there was no great difficulty in procurement. So we leave them on this apparently auspicious day" (93).

18. Ibid., 16.

19. Recent findings now show that the back wing to the house, with a separate entrance, kitchen, living, and sleeping quarters where the young married couple was once thought to have taken up residence, was in fact a later addition. In *The Shakespeare Houses* (8) Roger Pringle says, "The back wing was probably added to the main building shortly after the death of Shakespeare's father in 1601, when part of the house became an inn."

20. Pogue, 132. For an extended description of Shakespeare's friendships with the wives of his colleagues, see *Shakespeare's Friends.*

21. Shakespeare, *The Sonnets*, Introduction by W.H. Auden, lv.

22. Three sonnets seeming to express personally experienced anguish may be particularly cited. Shakespeare's complicity in a shameful act committed by the one to whom he was so attracted is expressed in Sonnet 35:

> No more be grieved at that which thou hast done:
> Roses have thorns, and silver fountains mud,
> Clouds and eclipses stain both moon and sun,
> And loathsome canker lives in sweetest bud.
> All men make faults, and even I in this,
> Authorising thy trespass with compare,
> My self corrupting salving thy amiss,
> Excusing thy sins more than their sins are;
> For to thy sensual fault I bring in sense—
> Thy adverse party is thy advocate—
> And 'gainst myself a lawful plea commence:
> Such civil war is in my love and hate
> > That I an accessory needs must be
> > To that sweet thief which sourly robs from me.

His struggle to separate himself from his enslavement is the subject of Sonnet 36:

> Let me confess that we two must be twain,
> Although our undivided loves are one.
> So shall those blots that do withy me remain
> Without thy help, by me be borne alone. . . .
> I may not evermore acknowledge thee,
> Lest my bewailed guilt should do thee shame;
> Nor thou with public kindness honor me,
> Unless thou take that honor from thy name.
> > But do not so; I love thee in such sort
> > As, thou being mine, mine is thy good report.

And his disgust with sex fills Sonnet 129:

> Th' expense of spirit in a waste of shame
> Is lust in action: and, till action, lust
> Is perjured, murd'rous, blood, full of blame
> Savage, extreme, rude, cruel, not to trust;
> Enjoyed no sooner but despised straight,
> Past reason hunted, and no sooner had,
> Past reason hated as a swallowed bait
> On purpose laid to make the taker mad;
> Mad in pursuit, and in possession so;
> Had, having, and in quest to have, extreme;
> A bliss in proof, and proved, a very woe,
> Before, a joy proposed; behind, a dream.
>> All this the world well knows, yet none knows well
>> To shun the heaven that leads men to this hell.

Many others of his sonnets show the same strength of personal feeling.

23. Chute, 183. While Marchette Chute assumes that Shakespeare was traveling with his company at this time, Ian Wilson, in *Shakespeare, the Evidence*, points out that the theatres were closed that summer because of an outbreak of plague in London, and suggests that it might have been plague that killed Hamnet, and that Shakespeare might have gone home rather than touring, and thus been there when his son died (Ian Wilson, 208).

24. Halliday, *A Shakespeare Companion*, 210.

25. Gray, 29.

26. Ibid., 168.

27. McDonald, 268.

28. The pun is more inescapable when it is realized that the "th" sound in Hathaway was often pronounced as a 't' (for example, the puns on "death" and "debt" in *Henry IV*, when Henry tells Falstaff he owes God a "death").

29. Stopes, *Shakespeare's Family*, 90. Mrs. Stopes suggests that Susanna wrote the tribute, and her husband, John Hall, translated it into the Latin version on her tombstone.

8: SHAKESPEARE'S CHILDREN

1. Palmer, 103.

2. Stopes, *Shakespeare's Family*, 90.

> Mother, to me thou gavest thy breast and milk and life,
> Woe is me! For such great gifts I give a tomb!
> I would far rather that the good angel should
> From its mouth the stone remove
> That like Christ's body thy image might come forth.
> But vain our wishes. May'st thou come quickly Christ!
> And then my mother, though entombed, shall rise again
> And seek the stars.

3. Palmer, 213.

4. For a discussion of the Shakespeare testament, see Bearman, "John Shakespeare's 'Spiritual Testament': A Reappraisal."

5. Palmer, 102.

6. Ibid., 231.

7. Eccles, 16. The Palmer farmhouse had once been mistaken for the Arden's, and can be seen by visitors to Wilmcote as the building next to the one now correctly identified as Mary Arden's home.

8. Halliday, 111.

9. Chute, 320.

10. Sonnet 71.

11. See quoted in note 2 and at the end of the chapter on Anne Hathaway.

12. Though the house called Nash's House is next door to New Place, but Thomas Nash does not seem to have lived there, and no one knows where the young couple lived before the death of Elizabeth's father John Hall in 1635 when they moved into New Place. Thomas Nash left the house to Elizabeth when he died in 1647. Pringle, "The Shakespeare Houses," 12.

13. Halliday, 332.

14. Ibid., 446.

15. Ibid., 214.

16. Stopes, *Shakespeare's Family*, 91.

17. Shoenbaum, *A Compact Documentary Life*, 292.

18. Halliday, *A Shakespeare Companion*, 401.

19. Palmer, 199.

20. Schoenbaum, *A Compact Documentary Life*, 295.

21. Stopes, *Shakespeare's Family*, 92.

22. Halliday, *A Shakespeare Companion*, 400.

23. Stopes, *Shakespeare's Family*, 92.

24. Halliday, *A Shakespeare Companion*, 520. Ward provides biographers with some of the earliest information on Shakespeare. One of his books has the note, "This booke was begunne Feb. 14, 1661/2, and finished April the 25 1663, att Mr. Brooks his house in Stratford-uppon-Avon," and contains the following entries:

"Shakespar had but 2 daughters, one whereof M. Hall, ye physitian, married, and by her had one daughter, to wit, ye Lady Bernard of Abbingdon.

"I have heard ye Mr. Shakespeare was a natural wit, without any art at all; hee frequented ye plays all his younger time, but in his elder days lived at Stratford: and supplied ye stage with 2 plays every year, and for yt had an allowance so large, y thee spent att ye Rate of a 1,000 pounds a year, as I have heard.

"Remember to peruse Shakespears plays, and bee versd inn them, yt I many not bee ignorant in yt matter.

"Shakespear, Drayton, and Ben Jhonson, had a merry meeting, and itt seems drank too hard, for Shakespear died of a feavour there contracted."

25. Shoenbaum, *A Compact Documentary Life*, 94.

26. Wilson, 208.

27. Chute, 183.

28. Hugh Maclean, 8.

9: SHAKESPEARE'S SONS-IN-LAW

1. Honan, 355. Park Honan gives us this charming description of an Elizabethan wedding ceremony:

"To judge from his plays, Shakespeare viewed the role of a father at a wedding as of deep sacramental importance. In *Lear, Othello*, or *Romeo and Juliet*, it suggests tragic consequences to come if a father flouts his sacred role, either by 'giving away' his child without her consent, or by withholding it when she marries. And as at Holy Trinity, a country wedding's symbolism would have been important to him. Boys wore sprigs of rosemary tied to their sleeves as symbols of fidelity; bridesmaids carried cakes or garlands of gilded wheat to symbolize fertility. The father accompanied the bride to the altar.

"'Who giveth this woman to be married unto this man' the priest would call out. The father then relinquished the bride, and after that his role in his daughter's life had ended. He watched as the couple plighted troths, and as the groom placed the ring on the bride's finger with these words: 'With this ring I thee wed, with my body I thee worship, and with all my worldly good I thee endow.'"

2. Eccles, 112.

3. B. Roland Lewis prints the will of William Hall in its entirety in *The Shakespeare Documents*, Chapter CX, 587.

4. Scholars disagree on whether John Hall attended Oxford or Cambridge. Samuel Schoenbaum (*William Shakespeare: A Compact Documentary Life*, 287), Mark Eccles (*Shakespeare in Warwickshire*, 111), and Park Honan (*Shakespeare A Life*, 355) all claim his degrees were from Queen's College, Cambridge. Eccles says (112) John was described in records at Cambridge as born in Bedfordshire; he further notes that Sara Hall, a sister to John and Dive, married William Shepherd, M.D. and fellow of King's College, Cambridge, who later became a physician at Leicester. However, B. Roland Lewis (*The Shakespeare Documents*, Vol. II, 589) quotes directly from the Oxford records as follows: "In The Registers of the University of Oxford (1887,1888, Vol. II, Part II, p. 187, and Vol. II, Part III, p. 190) are the following entries: "[1591, Matriculations] 4 Feb. Ball[iol] Haule [Hall], John; Worc[ester] gen[erosi] f[ilius] 16 [years of age]." There follows: "[1595, entries for degrees conferred] Balliol, Halle (Haule), John; adm[itted] B.A. (Ball.) 28 Feb. 1594/5, det[erminen—performed the final exercises for the B.A. degree] 1594/5; lic[ensed] M.A. (St. Edm. H.) [St. Edmund Hall] 11 Nov. 1597, inc[eption or incepted=completed the final exercises for a Master's or a Doctor's degree], 1598." Lewis further observes: "Fripp and Ransford both accepted this record as applying to our John Hall. . . . " 589. Marchette Chute (*Shakespeare in London*, 295) also accepts this evidence for an Oxford degree. All agree that John Hall had a university education but did not receive a medical degree.

5. Cook, Judith. *Dr. Simon Forman*.

6. Honan, 357.

7. Stopes, *Shakespeare's Warwickshire Contemporaries*, 183.

8. Ibid., 183.

9. Eccles, 115.

10. Ibid., 112.

11. Stopes, 176.

12. Eccles, 113.

13. Stopes, *Shakespeare's Industry*, 596.

14. Lewis, 588. The will is at Somerset House, London, the Prerogative Court of Canterbury.

15. Eccles, 115.

16. Ibid., 86.

17. Ibid., 45.

18. Ibid., 26.

19. Act 4, scene 4, 158–159.

20. Act 4, scene 4, 133–135.

21. The Quineys had nine children when Richard died in 1602. Mark Eccles lists them as Elizabeth, Adrian, Richard, Thomas, Anne, William Mary, John, and George (Eccles, 99). However, Edgar Fripp in the exhaustive *Master Richard Quyny* includes two who died in infancy: Elizabeth, baptized Nov. 27, 1582 (p. 34); Adrian, 1584 (died in infancy), Adrian, 1586; Richard, 1587 (pp. 46–47); Thomas, baptized Feb. 26, 1589; William, 1590, died 1592 (p. 53); Anne, baptized January 5, 1592; William ii, 1593; Mary, 1594; John, 1597 (p. 54), and George, 1600 (p. 166).

22. Eccles, 99; Fripp, *Master Richard Quyny*, 195.

23. Ibid., 132.

24. Ibid., 203.

25. Fripp, *Master Richard Quyny*, 204.

26. Ibid., 205.

27. Ibid., 206–207. According to Fripp the French motto as Thomas wrote it reads: "Bien heureux est celui qui pour devenir sage / Qui pour le mal d'autrui fait son apprentissage." The original, from a medieval romance called Saint Galias, on the other hand reads: "Heureux celui qui pour devenir sage, / Du mal d'autrui fait son apprentissage." This means: "Happy is he who to become wise, serves his apprenticeship from other men's troubles."

28. Palmer, 199.

29. Fripp, *Master Richard Quiney,* 207.

30. Eccles, 140–141.

10: SHAKESPEARE'S GRANDCHILDREN

1. Lewis, 597. "Observation XXXVI Elizabeth Hall my onely Daughter was vexed with Tortura Oris or the Convulsion of the mouth, and was happily cured as followeth. First I exhibit these pils Rx pil, Coch, et Aurean, ana zl.f, pik 10. She took five the first day. . . . For an Opthalmia of which se laboured, I used our opthalmick water, dropping two or three drops into her eye. . . . "

2. Fripp, *Master Richard Quyny*, 152. Fripp notes that in a letter to Richard Quiney from his father, "George Badger's wife meaneth to be at London the next week." Anne Digges Shaw, who was a London widow subsequently married to one of Shakespeare's Stratford neighbors, must have made the journey; it is possible Shakespeare's mother accompanied her husband to London for a court appearance and that Susanna Shakespeare Hall might have accompanied her husband to prove her father's will in 1616. It is evident, then, that women did travel, but not as extensively as men.

3. Lane, 67. Ms. Lane suggests that the reason for Elizabeth's trip to London was to participate in the coronation celebrations for Charles II. Those, however, took place in 1625 whereas the date of the journey in Dr. John Hall's casebook indicates the spring of 1624.

4. Leiws, 583.

5. Pringle, 12.

6. Wells, *Shakespeare for All Time*, 38.

7. The action is detailed in C.C. Stopes' *Shakespeare's Family*, pp. 100–103.

8. Halliday, *A Shakespeare Companion, 1564–1964*, 214.

9. Lane, 69.

10. These epitaphs are quoted in their entirety in this book in the chapters on "Shakespeare's Wife: Anne Hathaway" and "Shakespeare's Daughters: Susanna Shakespeare."

11. Stopes, *Shakespeare's Family*, 106.

12. Lewis, 609.

13. Ibid., 584. Roland Lewis traces the Nash family back to Master Thomas Nash, an agent of the Earl of Leicester's steward.

14. Ibid., 584.

15. Stopes, *Shakespeare's Family*, 102.

16. Ibid., 101.

17. Ibid., 102.

18. Schoenbaum, *Shakespeare, A Documentary Life*, 261.

19. Lane, 69.

11: SHAKESPEARE'S AUNTS

1. Robert Arden left his daughters a complicated inheritance that is explored in detail by Mrs. C. C. Stopes in her books *Shakespeare's Environment* (in the chapter entitled "Shakespeare's Aunts and the Snitterfield Property") and *Shakespeare's Family* (chapter 6, "The Ardens of Wilmcote").

2. Stopes, *Shakespeare's Family*, 41.

3. Ibid., 36.

4. Ibid., 40.

5. Eccles, 19.

6. Stopes, *Shakespeare's Environment*, 38, 39.

7. Ibid., 43.

8. Fripp, Records and Accounts Vol. III, xliii. Edgar Fripp theorizes here that the eagerness of the Lamberts to hold onto Asbies could be attributed in part to Joan's feeling that the property had been unjustly inherited by the youngest daughter, Mary Arden Shakespeare.

9. Stopes, *Shakespeare's Environment*, 45.

10. In *Shakespeare's Environment*, 21, Mrs. Stopes writes, "On 16th October 18 Eliz. (1576), Thomas Stringer of Stockton, co. Salop, and his sons John and Arden Stringer, bargained and sold to Edward Cornwell and Margaret his wife all the reversion which was the inheritance of Agnes, late wife of Thomas Stringer, and daughter of Robert Arden, deceased. A curious complexity comes in here, for they also sell, as if they had bought it, 'the residue of the said tenements which late were the inheritance of Thomas Edkyne and Katharine his wife, in the right of the said Katharine.' The Stringers sell this double share for £68, to be paid beforehand, and they agree that at Christmas term next they shall sue out a fine of the parcel of the premises of the said Thomas Edkins and his wife Katharine, 'if the said Katharine do so long live.' They have full power to sell all, except the life interest of Agnes Arden. They set their hands and seals to this in the presence of the same witnesses as last deed." I quote this to indicate how technical and complex the ultimate dispersal of Robert Arden's inheritance was, and how difficult for the modern historian to make it comprehensible, much less interesting, to the contemporary reader.

11. Fripp, *Shakespeare, Man and Artist*, Vol. 1, 31. "Palmer's farm extended to that of the Skarlett's on the one side and that of the Edkinses on the other, and again 'to the closes of John Shakespeare on the west' and a close of the Skaarletts on the north—the closes of John Shakespeare in 1561 being land of his wife, Mary Arden's inheritance of 'Asbies.'"

12. Eccles, 20.

13. Stopes, *Shakespeare's Family*, Chapter 6, "The Ardens of Wilmecote," 35–49.

14. See chapter in this book on "Shakespeare's Cousins."

15. Ibid., 36 n. Mrs Stopes says Elizabeth Arden married Skarlet ("Halliwell Phillipps mentions Elizabeth Skerlett as an eighth, surely in error"). All subsequent historians agree with Halliwell-Phillips, perhaps because as Eccles says, on March 18, 1581/2, "John Skarlett of Newnham in the parish of Aston Cantlow, husbandman, son and heir of Elizabeth Skarlett, daughter and coheir of Robert Arden, sold his share of land in Snitterfield to Robert Webbe." Eccles, 20.

16. Eccles, 20.

17. Ibid., 20.

18. Fripp, *Shakespeare, Man and Artist*, Vol. 1, 30.

19. Stopes, *Shakespeare's Family,* 38.

20. Stopes, *Shakespeare's Environment*, 36.

12: SHAKESPEARE'S COUSINS

1. Eccles, 19–23 *passim.*

2. Ibid., 19.

3. Ibid., 29.

4. Schoenbaum, *A Compact Documentary Life*, 40.

5. Eccles, 29.

6. Ibid., 21, 22.

7. Fripp, *Shakespeare's Stratford*, 58. Mrs. Stopes, *Shakespeare's Family*, 116, notes that "A 'Thomas Green, *alias* Shakespeare,' was buried in Stratford-on-Avon, March 6, 1590." She goes on to assert: "He was probably the father of Thomas Green . . . " When a man's name carries with it an "alias" it means he claims relationship with the family named. But the Thomas Greene that is the subject of this chapter identified Thomas Greene of Warwick as his father in the pedigree he submitted at the Gloucestershire visitation in 1623. County visitations were carried out by the Heralds from time to time to ensure that those claiming gentry status and bearing arms had the right to do so. Many of these have been printed by the Harleian Society, including the one for Gloucestershire (vol. 21, 1885). (I am indebted to Robert Bearman of the Shakespeare Birthplace Trust for this information). However, the burial in Stratford of a Thomas Green *alias* Shakespeare would indicate that our Thomas Greene's claim to be Shakespeare's cousin perhaps had some blood-relation basis.

8. Stopes, *Shakespeare's Family*, 116.

9. Fripp, *Shakespeare's Stratford*, 58.

10. Palmer, 96.

11. Eccles, 138.

12. Fripp, *Shakespeare's Stratford*, 45.

13. Halliday, *A Shakespeare Companion*, 196.

14. Chute, 298, 299.

15. Stopes, *Shakespeare's Environment*, 82–83. As Mrs. Stopes' book is hard to find, here is what she says about the tithes: "On 7th September, 1544, Anthony Barker, steward of the dissolved College of Stratford-on-Avon, granted to William Barker, gent, certain messuages, lands, and tithes of Stratford, hitherto belonging to the College, for a period of ninety-two years. This may or may not have been legal, but the transfer has never been questioned. In time this grant was inherited by John Barker, who in 22 Eliz. sold the bulk of his estate to Sir John Huband, *reserving to himself a yearly rent of 27 pounds 13s. 4d., with the condition that if any part of that rent were left unpaid for forty days, he could enter and retake possession of all until the end of his term* (emphasis mine)" (i.e. Mrs. Stopes).

The charter granted by Edward VI to the Corporation of Stratford-on-Avon settled on it the tithes for the support of the refounded school and almshouses, and I have not at present time to discuss the complex relations between the town and Barker's lease. Dr. Ingleby is entirely wrong in his account of the tithes, which were not owned only by Shakespeare and Greene. They were sold by Sir John Huband in 1605, either directly or indirectly, to a large number of holders, among whom was Shakespeare, who was said to hold a "moietie"; but this by no means represented a half, as we might be inclined to read it, even of the tithes, and the "property" consisted, beyond the tithes, of houses, cottages, and fields. It may help the consideration of the question to note the chief holders.

Richard Lane had a proportion worth £80 a year in the tithes of Old Stratford; Shakespeare's share was worth £60 a year; Thomas Greene's, £3, and 20 marks in the tithes of Drayton; Sir Edward Greville's 40s.; Sir Edward Conway's, £30; Mary Combe, widow, an estate for six years to come, worth £10; John Lane, £8; Anthony Nash and William Combe, £5; Daniel Baker, £20; John Smith, £8; Francis Smith, £12; William Walford, 40s.; William Court, £3; John Brown, £4; Thomas Jakeman, £10; Richard Kempson and Stephen Burman, £15; Thomas Burman, £3; 'Thomas Hohrneby, an estate of the messuage in which he now dwelleth, of the yearely value of £3'; and eighteen others had similar shares, most of the smaller holdings being in land or houses, and the larger in tithes.

Shortly after the poet's purchase, he discovered that, though he was careful to pay his share of Barker's reserved rent of £27 13s. 4d. to Henry Barker, then lessee, many of the other tenants were not paying theirs, and he ran the risk of losing his property through the fault of others. So he co-operated with Richard Lane and his lawyer cousin Thomas Greene to file a complaint in Chancery against those other tenants who did not pay their due share of the reserved rent. The complainants acknowledged that some of the tenants were willing to pay, but refused for fear of the others; some made light of the claim; and the complainants, for the preservation of their estates from forfeiture, have had much loss and trouble. They prayed that subpoenas be sent to the chief defaulters to appear and make answer. The case was entered as 'Lane, Greene, Shakespeasre, and others, con. W. Combe and others.' See Misc. Doc., ii, 2. The suit appears to have been successful, or at least some settlement was come to, for the possession of the tithes was not lost by Shakespeare or his family."

16. Ibid., 84. All the next quotes from Thomas Greene's diaries are from Mrs. Stopes' *Shakespeare's Environment*, pp. 84–91 *passim*.

17. Robert Bearman notes that "[s]ome people transcribe this as 'W. Shakespeare telling J. Greene that J. was not able . . . ' which makes better sense." E-mail Sept. 17, 2007.

18. Ibid., 86.

19. In answer to observations that Thomas Greene does not make mention of his cousin's death in his diary, Robert Bearman points out that the manuscript at issue is not really a diary, but simply a record of the enclosure dispute. E-mail Sept. 17, 2007.

20. Fripp, *Shakespeare's Stratford*, 59.
21. Halliday, *A Shakespeare Companion*, 197.
22. Ibid.

13: SHAKESPEARE'S HATHAWAY IN-LAWS

1. Schoenbaum, *A Compact Documentary Life*, 82.
2. Shapiro, 258.
3. Lewis, vol. 1, 158, 159.
4. Mark Eccles (67) identifies a yardland (also called a virgate) as a piece of land that varied in size from twenty to forty-six acres. This land was copyheld, not owned, by the Hathaways.
5. Eccles, 68.
6. Lewis, vol. 1, 159.
7. Eccles, 69.
8. Ibid., 68.
9. Ibid., 67.
10. Palmer, 109.
11. Lewis, 159.
12. Palmer, 108.

14: SHAKESPEARE'S HART NEPHEWS AND NIECE

1. Honan, 400, 401.
2. Halliday, *A Shakespeare Companion*, 208.
3. Eccles, 143.
4. Ibid.
5. The Shakespeare Birthplace Trust Record Office keeps copies (for public purchase) of three different genealogies or pedigrees of the Hart family, tracing it from Joan Shakespeare Hart to the descendants of the twenty-first century, most of whom live in Australia.

15: CONCLUSION

1. Bobrick, 202.
2. Stopes, *Shakespeare's Environment*, 44.
3. I am grateful to Robert Bearman for this information.
4. See my book *Shakespeare's Friends* for details on these men.

16: FAMILY RELATIONSHIPS IN SHAKESPEARE'S PLAYS

1. The thirty-six plays in the First Folio of 1623, plus *Pericles*.
2. The reader is referred to any Complete Works for the play texts, synopses of plots, and lists of characters. For the purposes of this section of the book, knowledge of the plots and characters of the plays of Shakespeare is necessarily presupposed as there is here neither the time nor the space to summarize each play referred to.

3. See the appendix for a complete listing of relationships. When tabulating these relationships every separate relationship was valued. In *The Taming of the Shrew*, for example, Baptista, as the father of both Katherine and Bianca counted as having two father-daughter relationships.

4. Two references to motherhood are found, one each in *Macbeth* and *All's Well that Ends Well*. Technically Lady Macbeth is not a mother at present, though she claims to have been once, and she represents a horrifying picture in her image of taking a baby from her breast and dashing its brains out had she sworn to do so as Macbeth had sworn to kill the king (*Macbeth*, act 1, scene 7). In *All's Well That Ends Well* (act 1, scene 3), the Countess Rousillon tells Helena to view her as a mother, which Helena would be happy to do did she not prefer to hope for the Countess as a mother-in-law.

5. Wilson, John Dover, 718.

6. To see this interpretation of the play detailed, turn to Appendix C at the end of this book.

7. In addition to the uncle/nephew relationship, Gaunt with Bolingbroke and York with Aumerle are also excellent examples of the father/son relationship.

8. A reprint of the first page of text from the Quarto of 1600 is reprinted on page lxxiii of the Signet Classic *Much Ado about Nothing*, 1998.

9. Quoted in *Smithsonian Magazine*, July 2007, p. 58.

APPENDICES

1. *Minutes and Accounts of the Chamber of Stratford-Upon-Avon*, Savage and Fripp, ed. V. II, 136, n. 13.

2. Honan, *Shakespeare, A Life*, 88.

3. Fripp, *Shakespeare's Stratford*, 39.

4. Halliday, *A Shakespeare Companion*, 275.

5. I am indebted to Stanley Wells' *Shakespeare for All Time* for this insight. 66.

6. SBTRO ER 27/9. Commentary by Miss Anne Wheeler.

7. Fripp, *Minutes and Accounts of the Corporation of Stratford-upon-Avon, 1553-1620*, vol. ii, xxxvi. *The Minutes and Accounts of the Chamber of Stratford-Upon-Avon with Other Papers 1553–1620*, transcribed by Richard Savage and Edgar I Fripp (London: Oxford University Press, 1924). The Chamberlains' accounts from 1569 to 1576 are found in the above *Minutes and Accounts Volume ii*; from 1577 to 1584 in *Volume iii*, from 1585 to 1592 in *Volume iv*, and from 1593 to 1598 in *Volume v* (where Levi Fox appears as the new editor). Edgar I. Fripp's introductory material to the *Minutes and Accounts* and his internal comments present some of the most interesting and perceptive Shakespeare commentary I've read as they consistently interpret the adjacent records.

8. Halliwell, ed., "The Stratford Records, A Descriptive Calendar," 95.

9. Bearman, 103.

10. Eccles, 81. Mark Eccles points out that "Players of the Earls of Oxford, Worcester, and Essex came to Stratford during 1583–1584. Worcester's men, who included Robert Browne and the seventeen-year-old Edward Alleyn, were forbidden to act at Leicester on March 6, 1583/4, but they 'went with their drums and trumppytts throrwe the towne, in contempt of Mr. Mayor,' and were finallky allowed to play that night at their inn."

E. K. Chambers notes that in 1603 the Admiral's men were refused the right to play at Canturbery "in regard that our late Queen was then either very sick or dead as they supposed."

"Several cases are recorded at Norwich, in which companies played contrary to orders, and were punished by committal to prison, or by threats that their lord should be certified of their contempt, and that they should never more have reward of the city." Chambers, Vol. 1, pp. 339–340.

11. Markham, Gervase, *Country Contentments* (1615) (4th ed., London, 1631, 36–37): quoted in The Arden Shakespeare, *The Taming of the Shrew*, Brian Morris, ed. 1981, n. 250.

Selected Bibliography

ORIGINAL DOCUMENTS

Folger MS V.a. 340 Shakespeare, John Warwickshire. A roll of jurors listed by Hundreds, begun in 1592. Mention of a John Shakespeare on f.29v.

Folger MS z. c. 36 (110–111) Shakespeare, William 1564–1616 [Deed 1602] Great Britain. Court of Common Pleas. Final concord. Mich. 1502. William Shakespeare v. Hercules Underhill, gent. Messuage in Stratfsord [New Place].

Folger MS z. c. 22 (45) Shakespeare, William 1564–1616 [Deed March 10, 1613] Walker, Henry d. 1615 Bargain and sale. To William Shakespeare of Stratford upon Avon, gent. And to his trustees, William Johnson, Vintner of London, John Jackson and John Hemmyng of London, gentlemen. Dwelling house within the precinct of the late Blackfriars, London. Consideration: 140 pounds.

Folger MS z. c. 22 (44) Shakespeare, William [Deed 1618] Jackson, John ca. 1596–1625 Bargain and sale, Feb. 10, 1618. To John Greene of Clements Inn and Matthew Morryes of Stratford upon Avon, gent., trustees for the heirs of Wm. Shakes. Dwelling house within the precinct of the late Blackfriars, London.

SBTRO (The Shakespeare Birthplace Trust Record Office).

The Minutes and Accounts of the Chamber of Stratford-upon-Avon with Other Papers 1553–1620, transcribed by Richard Savage and Edgar I Fripp. London: Oxford University Press, 1924.

The Chamberlains' accounts from 1569 to 1576 are found in the above *Minutes and Accounts Volume ii*; from 1577 to 1584 in *Volume iii*, from 1585 to 1592 in *Volume iv*, and from 1593 to 1598 in *Volume v* (where Levi Fox appears as the new editor). Edgar I. Fripp's introductory material to the *Minutes and Accounts* and his internal comments present some of the most interesting and perceptive Shakespeare commentary I've read as they consistently interpret the adjacent records.

SBTRO BRU 4/2 Chamberlain's Account Records Beginning 1622/3.

SBTRO Class P. 29.64, Acc. No. 83411062. Alcock, N.W. and R.A. Meeson. *Mary Arden's House, Wilmcote, Warwickshire*, Stratford: The Birthplace Trust, 30 April, 2000.

SBTRO Class 29.64, Acc. No. 38 173 83381732. Meeson, Bob. *Glebe Farm, Wilmcote, Warwickshire*, an architectural analysis, Stratford: The Birthplace Trust, January, 2000.

SBTRO ER 27/9. Document with signature of Gilbert Shakespeare. Commentary by Miss Anne Wheeler.

SBTRO ER 3. Catalogue of Deeds, etc. Volume II #1923. From the Halliwell-Phillips papers. 17 June 1550: Grant from Robert Arden of Wilmcote in the parish of Aston Cantlow, husbandman.

The Stratford Records: A descriptive calendar of the ancient manuscripts and records in the possession of The Corporation of Stratford-upon-Avon, including notices of Shakespeare and his family and of several persons connected with the Poet, edited by James O. Halliwell, Esq. FRS, London: James Evan Adlard, 1863.

Abbott, Mary. *Life Cycles in England 1560–1720*. London: Routledge, 1996.

Ackroyd, Peter. *Shakespeare the Biography*. New York: Anchor Books, 2006.

Adams, Joseph Quincy. *A Life of Shakespeare*. Boston, MA: Houghton Mifflin Company, 1925.

Asimov, Isaac. *Asimov's Guide to Shakespeare*. New York: Avenel Books, 1978.

Aughterson, Kate. *Renaissance Woman: A Sourcebook*. London: Routledge, 1995.

Bainton, Roland H. *The Reformation of the Sixteenth Century*. Boston, MA: The Beacon Press, 1952.

Baldwin, Thomas Whitfield. *The Organization and Personnel of the Shakespearean Company*. Princeton, NJ: Princeton University Press, 1927.

Bearman, Robert, ed. *The History of an English Borough Stratford-upon-Avon 1196–1996*. Thrupp: Sutton Publishing The Shakespeare Birthplace Trust, 1997.

———. "John Shakespeare: A Papist or Just Penniless." *The Shakespeare Quarterly* 56 (Winter 2005): 411–433.

———. "John Shakespeare's 'Spiritual Testament': A Reappraisal." *Shakespeare Survey* 56 (2003): 181–202.

———. "Was William Shakespeare William Shakeshafte." *Shakespeare Quarterly* 53, no. 1 (2002): 83–94.

Bentley, Gerald Eades. *The Profession of Player in Shakespeare's Time 1590–1642*. Princeton, NJ: Princeton University Press, 1984.

Bevington, David. *Shakespeare*. Malden, MA: Blackwell Publishing, 2002.

Bobrick, Benson. *Wide as the Waters, The Story of the English Bible and the Revolution It Inspired*. New York: Simon and Schuster, 2001.

Boyce, Charles. *The Wordsworth Dictionary of Shakespeare*. New York: Wordsworth Reference, 1990.

Brinkworth, E.R.C. *Shakespeare and the Bawdy Court of Stratford*. London: Phjllimore, 1972.

Chambers, E.K. *The Elizabethan Stage*. Oxford: Clarendon Press, 1923.

———. *William Shakespeare, A Study of Facts and Problems*. 2 vols. Oxford: Clarendon Press, 1930.

Chartier, Roger, ed. *A History of Private Life Vol. III Passions of the Renaissance*. Cambridge, MA: The Belknap Press of the Harvard University Press, 1989.

Chute, Marchette. *Shakespeare of London*. New York: E.P. Dutton, 1949.

Cook, Ann Jennalie. *Making a Match Courtship in Shakespeare and His Society*. Princeton, NJ: Princeton University Press, 1991.

Cook, Judith. *Dr. Simon Forman, A Most Notorious Physician*. London: Vintage, 2002.

Coryat, Thomas. *Coryat's Crudities*. Glasgow: James MacLehose and Sons, 1905.

De Lisle, Leanda. *After Elizabeth: The Rise of James of Scotland and the Struggle for the Throne of England*. New York: Ballantine Books, 2005.

Douglas, Audrey, and Peter Greenfield, eds. *Records of Early English Drama, Cumberland Westmorland Gloucestershire*. Toronto: University of Toronto Press, 1986.

Duncan-Jones, Katherine. *Ungentle Shakespeare*. London: Arden Shakespeare, 2001.

Eccles, Mark. *Shakespeare in Warwickshire*. Madison, WI: The University of Wisconsin Press, 1963.

Edwards, Anne-Marie. *Walking with William Shakespeare*. Madison, WI: Jones Books, 2005.

Elton, Charles Isaac. *William Shakespeare, His Family and Friends*. London: J. Murray, Albermarle Street, 1904.

Foakes, R.A., and R.T. Rickert. *Henslowe's Diary*. Cambridge: Cambridge University Press, 1961.

Fripp, Edgar I. *Master Richard Quyny*. Oxford: The University Press, 1924.

———. *Shakespeare, Man and Artist*. London: Oxford University Press, 1938.

———. *Shakespeare's Haunts near Stratford*. Oxford: The University Press, 1929.

———. *Shakespeare's Stratford*. Oxford: The University Press, 1928.

Godley, Robert J. *Southwark, A History of Bankside, Bermondsey and "The Borough."* London: Planart (Reproduction) Ltd., 1997.

Granville-Barker, Harley, and G.B. Harrison, eds. *A Companion to Shakespeare Studies*. Cambridge: Cambridge University Press, 1934.

Gray, Joseph William. *Shakespeare's Marriage*. London: Chapman and Hall, 1905.

Greg, Walter W., ed. *Henslowe's Diary*. London: A.H. Bullen, 1908.

Halliday, F.E. *A Shakespeare Companion 1564–1964*. Baltimore, MD: Penguin Books, 1964.

———. *Shakespeare*. New York: Thames and Hudson Inc., 1998.

Halliwell-Phillips, J.O. *Outlines of the Life of Shakespeare, The Sixth Edition*. London: Longman, Green and Co., 1886.

Hey, David. *The Oxford Companion to Local and Family History*. Oxford: Oxford University Press, 1996.

Hole, Christina. *The English Housewife in the Seventeenth Century*. London: Chatto & Windus, 1953.

Honan, Park. *Shakespeare, A Life*. Oxford: The University Press, 1998.

Hull, Suzanne W. *Chaste, Silent & Obedient English Books for Women 1475–1640*. San Marino, CA: The Huntington Library, 1982.

Jones, Jeanne. *Family Life in Shakespeare's England Stratford-upon-Avon 1570–1630*. Stroud: Sutton Publishing The Shakespeare Birthplace Trust, 1996.

Kelly, Alison. *The Book of English Fireplaces*. Feltham, Middlesex: Country Life Books, 1968.

Klein, Joan Larsen, ed. *Daughters, Wives, and Widows*. Urbana, IL: University of Illinois Press, 1992.

Lane, Joan. *John Hall and His Patients, The Medical Practice of Shakespeare's Son-In-Law*. Stratford-upon-Avon: The Shakespeare Birthplace Trust, 1996.

Laslet, Peter. *The World We Have Lost*, 2nd ed. New York: Charles Scribner's Sons, 1971.

Lee, Christopher. *1603: The Death of Queen Elizabeth, the Return of the Black Plague, the Rise of Shakespeare, Piracy, Witchcraft, and the Birth of the Stuart Era*. New York: St. Martin's Press, 2003.

Lewis, B. Roland. *The Shakespeare Documents, Vol. 1*. Stanford University, CA: Stanford University Press, 1940.

Macfarlane, Alan. *Marriage and Love in England 1300–1840*. New York: Basil Blackwell, 1986.

Maclean, Hugh, ed. *Ben Jonson and the Cavalier Poets*. New York: W.W. Norton & Company, 1974.

Maclean, Ian. *The Renaissance Notion of Woman*. Cambridge: Cambridge University Press, 1980.

Maguire, Laurie. *Where There's a Will There's a Way*. London: A Perigee Book, Penguin, 2006.

Markham, Gervase. *The English Housewife* (1615, first edition). Michael R. Best, ed. Buffalo: McGill-Queen's University Press, Reprint 1986.

McDonald, Russ. *The Bedford Companion to Shakespeare, An Introduction with Documents*. Boston, MA: Bedford Books, 1996.

Neilson, Willilam Allan, and Ashley Horace Thorndike. *The Facts about Shakespeare*. New York: The MacMillan Company, 1918.

Palmer, Alan and Veronica. *Who's Who in Shakespeare's England*. New York: St. Martin's Press, 1999.

Partridge, Eric. *Shakespeare's Bawdy*. London: Routledge and Kegan Paul, 1968.

Payne, Robert. *By Me, William Shakespeare*. New York: Everest House, 1980.

Pogue, Kate Emery. *Shakespeare's Friends*. Westport, CT: Praeger, 2006.

Pounds, Norman J.G. *Hearth & Home: A History of Material Culture*. Bloomington, IN: Indiana University Press, 1989.

Pringle, Roger. *The Shakespeare Houses, The Official Guide*. Norwich: Jarrod Publishing, in association with the Shakespeare Birthplace Trust, Stratford-upon-Avon, no date.

Riggs, David. *The World of Christopher Marlowe*. New York: Henry Holt and Company, 2004.

Rowse, A.L. *Shakespeare, The Man*. New York: St. Martin's Press, 1988.

———. *Simon Forman Sex and Society in Shakespeare's Age*. London: Weidenfeld and Nicolson, 1974.

———. *William Shakespeare, a Biography*. New York: Harper and Row, 1953.

Schoenbaum, S. *William Shakespeare, A Compact Documentary Life*. New York: Oxford University Press, 1987.

———. *William Shakespeare, A Documentary Life*. New York: Oxford University Press, 1975

———. *William Shakespeare Records and Images*. New York: Oxford University Press, 1981.

Seaver, Paul S. *Wallington's World A Puritan Artisan in Seventeenth-Century London*. Stanford, CA: Stanford University Press, 1985.

Shakespeare, William. *The Complete Works of William Shakespeare*. The Cambridge text established by John Dover Wilson for the Cambridge University Press. London: Octopus Books Limited, 1980.

————. *The Sonnets*, Introduction by W.H. Auden. Harmondsworth, Middlesex: The Signet Classic Shakespeare, Penguin Books Ltd., 1999.

Shapiro, James. *1599 A Year in the Life of William Shakespeare*. London: Faber and Faber, 2005.

Spurgeon, Caroline. *Shakespeare's Imagery*. Cambridge, UK: Cambridge University Press, 1966.

Stopes, C.C. *Shakespeare's Environment*. London: G. Bell and Sons Ltd., 1914.

————. *Shakespeare's Family*. London: Elliot Stock, 1901.

————. *Shakespeare's Industry*, London: G. Bell and Sons, Ltd., 1916.

————. *Shakespeare's Warwickshire Contemporaries*. Stratford-upon-Avon: Shakespeare Head Press, 1907.

Thomas, David. *Shakespeare in the Public Records*. London: Her Majesty's Stationary Office, 1985.

Travitsky, Betty S., and Adele F. Seeff, eds. *Attending to Women in Early Modern England*. Newark, DE: University of Delaware Press, 1994.

Vendler, Helen. *The Art of Shakespeare's Sonnets*. Cambridge, MA: Belknap Press of Harvard University Press, 1997.

Wells, Stanley. *Dictionary of Shakespeare*. Oxford: Oxford University Press, 1998.

————. *Shakespeare for All Time*. Oxford: Oxford University Press, 2003.

Wilson, Ian. *Shakespeare, the Evidence*. New York: St Martin's Press, 1993.

Wilson, John Dover, ed. *The Complete Works of William Shakespeare*. London: Octopus Books Limited, 1981.

Wood, Margaret. *The English Mediaeval House*. London: Studio Editions, Random House, 1994.

Wood, Michael. *Shakespeare*. New York: Basic Books, 2003.

Index

About the Author

KATE EMERY POGUE is Adjunct Professor in the Department of Drama, University of Houston—Downtown. She is a playwright, Shakespearean actress, teacher, producer, and director. For ten years she was the Artistic Director of the Shakespeare-by-the-Book Festival. In addition to the fourteen productions she directed for that company, she has directed for the Houston Shakespeare Festival, Summer Shakespeare at Notre Dame, Bucknell University, Houston Community College, and the University of Houston—Downtown. She founded and for twenty years was head of the Drama Department at Houston Community College Central College, and, on a grant from the National Endowment for the Humanities, she was one of eighteen teachers selected nationwide to participate in the Folger Shakespeare Library's Teaching Shakespeare through Performance project. She is the author of *Shakespeare's Friends* (Praeger, 2006).